Out & About Campus

Out & About Campus

Personal Accounts by Lesbian, Gay,
Bisexual, & Transgendered
College Students

Edited by Kim Howard and Annie Stevens

alyson books
los angeles | new york

MANUFACTURED IN THE UNITED STATES OF AMERICA.
COVER DESIGN BY B. ZINDA.

THIS TRADE PAPERBACK ORIGINAL IS PUBLISHED BY
ALYSON PUBLICATIONS,
P.O. BOX 4371, LOS ANGELES, CA 90078-4371.
DISTRIBUTION IN THE UNITED KINGDOM BY
TURNAROUND PUBLISHER SERVICES LTD.,
UNIT 3 OLYMPIA TRADING ESTATE, COBURG ROAD, WOOD GREEN,
LONDON N22 6TZ ENGLAND.

FIRST EDITION: APRIL 2000

02 03 04 a 10 9 8 7 6 5 4 3

ISBN 1-55583-480-9

LIBRARY OF CONGRESS CATALOGING-IN-PUBLICATION DATA
OUT & ABOUT CAMPUS : PERSONAL ACCOUNTS BY GAY, LESBIAN, AND
TRANSGENDERED COLLEGE STUDENTS / EDITED BY KIM HOWARD AND
ANNIE STEVENS.—1ST ED.
    ISBN 1-55583-480-9
    1. GAY COLLEGE STUDENTS—UNITED STATES—BIOGRAPHY. 2. LESBIAN
COLLEGE STUDENTS—UNITED STATES—BIOGRAPHY. 3. BISEXUAL COLLEGE
STUDENTS—UNITED STATES—BIOGRAPHY. 4. TRANSSEXUALISM—UNITED
STATES—CASE STUDIES. 5. HOMOSEXUALITY AND EDUCATION—UNITED
STATES—CASE STUDIES. I. TITLE. II. HOWARD, KIM. III. STEVENS, ANNIE.
LC2574.6.O87 2000
378.1'9826'64—DC21   99-059703

CREDITS
COVER PHOTOGRAPH BY PHOTODISC.

For everyone who has walked onto a college
campus and wondered if they belonged

Contents

* Contributors' names with asterisks indicate pseudonyms. Though they may
not be indicated as such, many names of characters in the stories, as well as
names of fraternities and sororities, have been changed. All college/university
names are the actual institutions at which a contributor studied; if no institution is listed, the contributor requested it not be named.

Acknowledgments

We owe an enormous debt to many individuals who helped us throughout the five years it took to complete this project.

First, we must acknowledge the "bookends," those at the very beginning and at the very end of the process. Our thanks to David Schoem (editor) and the contributors to *Inside Separate Worlds: Life Stories of Young Blacks, Jews, and Latinos* (University of Michigan, 1991) whose stories inspired this collection. Our colleagues at Alyson Publications—Angela Brown, Dan Cullinane, and Bruce Zinda—get all of the credit and our sincere appreciation for turning a big box of paper into something you can pick up at the bookstore.

Thanks also to Bernard Ohanian (one of Kim's writing instructors) and the other members of Kim's writing group in Washington, D.C., who enthusiastically supported this book when it was little more than a draft letter to a publisher. Bob Witeck and Wes Combs taught us everything we know about marketing gay-themed book titles, knowledge without which we wouldn't have had the confidence to pursue the project. Robin Bernstein and Shane Windmeyer generously shared with us their experiences editing anthologies of first-person accounts, which made us believe it is indeed possible to see such a large task through to the end. We also are grateful for the gay newspapers that published our call for submissions and for the many student affairs professionals and students who spread word through E-mail and let us know how important they think the project is.

During our time in Takoma Park, Md. (the early years), Sharon Grimm, Stacey Horn, Lisa Kiely, and Elizabeth ("Wiff") Olson folded, stuffed, sealed, and stamped hundreds of letters to solicit contributors. In addition to these faithful friends, Zina Evans, Heidi Jones, and Hugh Morris read drafts of query letters and proposals and listened as we talked incessantly about "the book," encouraging us to keep going when we weren't sure we had it in us. Susan Komives and Marylu McEwen provided professional advice and support. Joanna Palmer, in addition to giving us timely kicks in the butt, spent hours on research, managing our initial database of student contacts and doing a plethora of other critical tasks.

In Burlington, Vt. (the later years—for some it takes a village; for others, it takes two cities), a number of friends, mostly undergraduate and graduate students at the University of Vermont, graciously read stories and provided editorial comments. Their enthusiasm for the project also provided much-needed motivation. Thank you to Kellie Arbor, C. Chad Argotsinger, Pat Buckley, Anne Claxton, Jennifer Ellis, Kirsten Freeman, Deanna Garrett, Anastasia Goff, Jennifer Helvik, Jill Hoppenjans, Leah Howell, Ann Kirzl, Chris McGrath, Paul McLoughlin II, Mollie Monahan, Laurie Mossler, Erika Nestor, Jennifer Smith, and Amy White. In particular, Jill Hoppenjans and Laurie Mossler spent more than one Saturday night helping with the final editing, for which we are eternally grateful. Jennifer Pigza gets special kudos for jump-starting the introduction when our brains were just plain empty.

If paper weren't so expensive, Ann Kirzl would get her own page of thanks for helping us with all of the above, for being our cheerleader, as well as for spending hours upon hours on the Library of Congress Web page helping to ensure the accuracy of the resources section.

To our family and friends, thank you for forgiving us when so much of our time went toward completing this project.

Finally, we wholeheartedly thank the contributors, those whose stories we published and those whose stories we couldn't, for making the time and for having the courage to put their life experiences on paper.

Introduction

So, how do you know?

If there is one thread that binds the stories in this collection, it is the question of "How do you know...?" "How do you know you're gay?" "How do you know who's safe to come out to?" "How do you know how to respond to hate?" "How do you know how to create change on campus?" These questions and a variety of others asked and answered in the following stories are the same questions many lesbian, gay, bisexual, transgender (LGBT), and questioning college students across the country ask.

Though the issues raised in these stories clearly speak to the experiences of LGBT students, they also speak to the questions asked by many student allies and college faculty, staff, and administrators: "How do you know how to be an ally?" "How do you know if your campus is safe?" "How do you know what to do when hate happens?" "How do you know what efforts will make a difference?"

While many excellent research studies and books discuss issues facing LGBT college students, when we began this project we found no major publications that allowed students simply to give voice to their experiences. Indeed, over the time that we solicited contributions to this collection, more than 500 students wrote us to say they wished they had a book like this. We hope *Out & About Campus* will fill part of this need.

There is no question that for many people, college is a time of intensive personal exploration. College students questioning their sexuality or gender identity and students coming out or transitioning gender identities face an added dimension in their identity exploration. Many students who question their sexuality or gender identity do so for the first time in college. But even for those who know going into college that they are LGB or

T, those years may be the first time they have had the chance to meet others like them or search out meaningful resources.

In the last decade there has been an explosive growth of lesbian, gay, bisexual, transgender, questioning, and ally resources on college campuses. More than 800 LGBT college campus student groups exist across the nation; approximately five dozen colleges and universities (and the numbers are increasing rapidly) have opened resource centers or hired professionals to specifically address the needs of LGBT and questioning students; and lesbian, gay, bisexual, and transgender courses are becoming more common. Increasingly, many of us on college campuses—both students and professionals—are asking, "Who and where are all of these students?"

As we began to receive contributions, the answer to that question, and our vision for the anthology, became clear. We wanted:

- A collection of stories that represents voices from colleges and universities from regions across the United States.
- A collection that speaks to student issues at a diversity of campus environments, including public and private, secular and religious, urban and rural, technical and liberal arts, historically black and predominantly white, co-ed and single-sex, two-year and four-year.
- A collection of stories that features perspectives from and about different segments of campus life, including academic coursework, residence halls, athletic teams, sororities, fraternities, student organizations, orientation, health centers, counseling centers, Reserve Officer Training Corps, study abroad, and interactions with roommates, classmates, faculty, and administrators.
- A collection that gives voice to students with different personal backgrounds and perspectives, including class, race, gender, sexuality, religion, geography, ability, nationality, HIV status, and age.

In short, we wanted to do it all. We soon realized, of course, that "doing it all" is not only difficult but also impossible. You will note (we hope) the imbalances. For example, though the narratives that follow represent campuses in 18 states and the District of Columbia, about 20% represent campuses in California. Also, though there is a fairly even split between public and private colleges, all stories but one focus on four-year institutions. Despite the imbalance in institutional representation, we are pleased to include stories that share the special challenges and joys of "nontraditional" campus environments. For example, in "An Unfailing Sufficiency," Owen Garcia* shares his experiences at the Mormon institution of Brigham Young University; Ruth Wielgosz gives us a glimpse into an all-women's campus in "Competitive College"; Cory Liebmann explores life at a Bible college; and in "The Iconoclast," Sapphrodykie* speaks candidly about coming out to herself at Howard University, an historically black institution.

We also are pleased that nearly every segment of campus life we had hoped to include is represented in this book. Among others, Stephanie Stillman talks about coming out as lesbian in a sorority in "Sisterhood"; Rick Andreoli takes us to the student health center in "And Then They Came..."; Susie Bullington addresses the conflicts she faced as a member of Inter-Varsity Christian Fellowship; and Ian Fried talks about his freedom to explore a transgendered identity while studying abroad in Holland.

These stories represent only a snapshot of LGBT American college life. There are approximately 13.5 million college students at more than 3,000 colleges and universities in the United States, and this book includes just 28 accounts! We hope the voices that are missing will provoke as much reflection and discussion as the voices that are included. The following stories represent the experiences of 28 individuals at 28 institutions. Just as the experiences of each of these individuals vary from each other, the experiences of any two students on any given campus also may vary considerably. Please also note that no one story reflects that institution as a whole, nor does any one story reflect everyone's experiences at that institution.

Even though we know we can't "do it all" with one book, we do have a clear set of hopes for this anthology:

- For students who are questioning, in the closet, coming out, or starting to transition, we hope this book will provide comfort, strength, and inspiration. We hope you will see yourselves in these pages and know that you are not alone.
- For students who are out and active, we hope this book will motivate you to raise visibility of LGBT issues on your campus. We also hope it

will remind you that each individual has her or his own method and timeline in coming out or in transitioning and that no one place or way is better than another.

- For allies, whether you are students, faculty, staff, or administrators, we hope these accounts will lend insight into the day-to-day experiences of lesbian, gay, bisexual, and transgender students on your campuses.

- For faculty, staff, and administrators, we hope this book will demonstrate that the campus gay student organization (if there is one on your campus) does not and cannot meet everyone's needs. We need to challenge ourselves to diversify our outreach, educational, and research efforts.

Though some of the contributors to this volume are writers by trade, most are not. Some of the accounts made us laugh out loud, and some made us tear up. Some of the accounts angered us, and some left a hollowness in our hearts. But we felt fortunate to have read each one. We hope these writers' stories will move you too and that, as you read them, you will search for your own answers to the question, "How do you know...?"

—Kim Howard and Annie Stevens
January 2000

Preface: How We Compiled *Out & About Campus*

Over the three years that we distributed calls for submissions, we found that traditional methods for reaching lesbian, gay, bisexual, and transgender college students target only a thin slice of the population. We solicited stories by:

- Distributing fliers to more than 500 LGBT college and university student groups and to all LGBT college student centers in existence at that time.
- Sending fliers to every racial-ethnic, bisexual, transgender, disability, or youth organization listed in the *Gayellow Pages*.
- Sending fliers to bookstores and community centers in parts of the country for which we had no student group listings.
- Sending our call for submission to every LGBT-identified American newspaper, magazine, and radio program of which we were aware.
- Creating a Web page and sending calls for submissions over E-mail listservs for college-student and professional organizations.

Despite our seemingly diverse methods for soliciting contributions, however, we realized many of these methods targeted only people affiliated with a campus or community group or living where they might have access to a gay media outlet (and would be comfortable accessing it). Other methods required that students have access to computers (and, for some, access where they'd feel comfortable with whomever else was around). Unfortunately, many college students do not have access to these resources and, as a result, did not have the opportunity to contribute their perspectives. For others who attempt to reach this student population in the future for organizing, research, and other purposes, we hope these limitations can be considered and addressed.

Coming In

by Frankie M. Morris

University of California, Berkeley

Freshman Year: Second Semester

March

I glanced across the room, careful not to make it obvious. She was lying on her bed reading an organic chemistry book. Her thick hair was relaxed, flowing in soft, loose curls to the center of her back. It wasn't at all as it had been one month before, when we were still friends. She had worn her hair naturally, in thick and fluffy brown clouds. I had spent hours twisting it into long, thin braids that fell around her neck. Rebecca was beautiful to me once, and I had loved her. That's why our friendship had to end.

Freshman Year: First Semester

August

College was heaven and hell for me. On one hand I was free—free to do and be whatever it was I had struggled to do or be in high school. I also had more expendable cash than I'd ever had before or since. And, most of all, I was alone. I no longer had to parent my dependent mother or tolerate my abusive father. I was free to be me.

But that was the problem.

I had no idea who I was. As I searched for an answer, I realized I'd spent my entire life trying to please everyone else. I had no idea how to please myself. I felt completely alone.

My hometown, Vallejo, while only 25 miles away in the valleys of the San Francisco Bay area, seemed a world away. My two roommates were from Southern California. Rebecca's family lived in Garden Grove, and Misty was from Newport Beach. The blond-haired, blue-eyed daughter of a successful doctor, Misty was a "Valley Girl" whose love of hair spray I blame for single-handedly depleting the ozone layer. She was my bunk-mate, while Rebecca had the single bed on the other side of our 18-foot by 18-foot room. Misty and I couldn't have been more different.

Misty was always accompanied by the overwhelming smell of Tea Rose perfume. She placed her boom box on the corner of her dresser, just above my pillow. "Loud music helps me study," she'd replied when I asked why she played her music late at night. She went on wild spending sprees and drank until she was incapable of walking.

Rebecca was not quite as alien to me. She described herself as white, black, and Seminole Indian, but people assumed she was Puerto Rican. Her caramel-colored face was fat and oblong, with bushy hair standing up at every angle. Her body was stout but well-proportioned, with large round breasts. Rebecca had come from a predominantly white world in which she felt herself and her brother never completely fit. It was the "outsider" in her that initially attracted my attention.

College proved to be not much more academically challenging than high school. But just as in high school, I had no social life. The shyness I had always known made me feel isolated and paralyzed. Fellow freshmen seemed more adept at meeting one another. The only thriving relation-ship I had was with Rebecca. She and I became fast friends, spending most of our time together. Misty socialized only with her numerous friends from high school, which left little time for us to build a relation-ship strong enough to nullify our obvious differences and which made it easy for us to remain strangers. For the first three weeks of school, Rebecca and I ate, did laundry, and socialized only with each other. We had four-hour conversations about everything from evolution to extra-terrestrials. We shared our life stories, hopes, dreams, and fears. I thought we were inseparable.

September

I started to notice other people in the residence halls broadening their social horizons. Only two women, roommates, on our floor kept to them-selves. I walked by their room one day and saw their beds pushed togeth-er. For a fleeting instant, the thought of them being lovers flashed through my mind, but immediately I assumed they were just close friends. *That's the kind of relationship I want with Rebecca,* I thought.

My greatest fear was that Rebecca would be stolen from me, engulfed by someone else's social circle. At night I prayed my friendship with Rebecca would stay the same, with no outside intrusion. I had grown to need her for support and companionship. I felt I needed her to survive.

Early October

"Rebecca, are you going to lunch?" I asked as I did almost every day. She had been eating with other people for a few days, and I missed her. I had practically stopped using the dining commons because I felt pathetic sitting alone.

"I'm eating with someone else," she replied. Then, in a rehearsed manner, like in soap operas, she quickly added, "I think we should spend time with other people."

"OK," I chirped, pretending I wasn't hurt, even though I thought my heart would be digested from sinking into the pit of my stomach.

After she left the room, I cried for hours. I couldn't make the tears stop. I looked at the clock every 15 minutes, but tried to convince myself that I didn't care when she came home. By midnight I'd decided I hated Rebecca and would never again speak to her. As I fell asleep, I heard the door open. My anger and pain suddenly turned to concern and made me sit up in bed.

"Rebecca, where have you been?" I asked in a loud whisper. Her quizzical expression made me feel stupid.

"Why?"

"Why? Because I was worried about you. I thought you had been raped and were lying dead in the eucalyptus grove. You could have called."

Rebecca became hostile, and I instantly regretted my words.

"Frankie, what's wrong with you?" She took a deep breath, and so did I. "I went to the movies with a friend, OK? You don't have to worry about me. You are not my mother." Her voice grew louder. Misty's tremendous snoring thinned into a light rumble. I didn't want to involve her, so I decided to end the conversation.

"Fine. I won't bother you anymore." I slunk under my blankets and turned toward the wall. I listened to the sound of Rebecca undressing.

Late October

I had a dream that surprised and alarmed me. In the dream Rebecca and I were lying in her bed, as we had done so many times, peering at her

5-inch black-and-white television. But this time I was lying close behind her, our bodies touching. I wrapped my arm around her waist as she snuggled her head into my breasts. It was so vivid. I could smell the Ivory soap and Nivea lotion she used. I felt Rebecca's round, soft body next to mine, noticing the dark brown of my hand as it gently caressed and massaged her full, tanned breasts.

The next day I felt rejuvenated, like I was on a mission. I finally knew what I wanted. I had to get things back to normal, the way they were before Rebecca decided she needed other friends. To do that I had to let Rebecca know I had a life without her. I didn't need her; I just wanted her.

That day I tried to act casual. I went to class and later took myself out to dinner. I walked among the trees and shadows after midnight in the most secluded parts of campus, wearing my shortest skirts. I'd heard so many stories of campus rapes and murders, and without telling myself, I'd decided I wanted to be hurt so I would have a good excuse to leave school. But no one ever bothered me, which made me feel even more undesirable.

When I came back to the dorm, Rebecca was waiting for me. "Hi. You were out late."

"Yeah," I said indifferently, pretending that staying out late was the most normal thing in the world. "I was out with a friend." Rebecca looked impressed. My plan was working.

November

Rebecca had decided she was in love with a guy in Freeborn Hall, the dorm next door. Most of our conversations centered on how she planned to capture his heart. At the same time, my mother's calls, updating me on the latest horrors and abuse in the family, became more frequent and graphic. I still had no social life, and I couldn't understand what was wrong with me. I wanted to move on, give up Rebecca, and make new friends. But the thought of putting effort into meeting people made me feel tired and more depressed. I longed to be part of something comfortable and natural. I believed my relationship with Rebecca was the answer. The fact that she wasn't interested blared in my face every day as she spoke of her love and passion for a guy who didn't even know her last name. It was more than I could bear.

The emotional strain began to wear on me physically. I was constantly sick and couldn't sleep at night. Instead, I slept all day, at least 14 hours. I missed classes, stopped eating, and cried at every little thing.

One morning I stood alone crying in the dorm room. Rebecca's bed was empty and messy. Misty's former bed was bare. After only nine weeks she had requested a room change, telling us she didn't have enough space. Rebecca and I knew her move was racially motivated. A few weeks before, we had found a letter on her desk that spoke of how she didn't like black people but had to live with "two of them." She talked about our "greasy" hair, how we smelled "funny," and how we spoke, dressed, and socialized. Misty had also written that she suspected "something is going on between them." Rebecca looked at me accusingly as we read that part.

As I stared out the seventh-floor window, remembering the day we read the letter, the hard pavement looked so far below me. I saw myself floating to the ground and landing dead—but intact. It was a peaceful thought. My mind wandered to thoughts of Rebecca. How would she react if she came home and found me splattered on the ground outside our window? It dawned on me that the impact might be greater if she were to discover me in bed, overdosed on sleeping pills. I liked that idea a lot, too much.

I'd been fascinated with suicide since my older sister's attempt when I was 10, but I'd never felt as comfortable with the idea as I did that day. I knew I couldn't handle it anymore. I would kill myself unless I found support. I had thought about seeking therapy but wasn't prepared to share my problems with anyone. I was too afraid I would be mocked and shamed for having such strong feelings for someone who couldn't care less. On that day, however, I knew my only two options were life or death.

I trudged up the hill to Cowell Hospital, the campus medical center. I'd been there several times in the past few weeks, seeking cures for my stress-related illnesses: headaches, chest and body pains, colds, sore throat, and dizziness.

The receptionist who always greeted me looked like a formidable monster that day. I considered leaving, but the thought of dying made me stay.

"Hi," I spoke quickly. "I need to see a counselor."

"Excuse me?" she asked, smiling.

"I need to see a…therapist," I managed.

"Psychological services are in the basement. Go to the end of the hall and take the elevator to the basement. You can't miss it." Her smile seemed genuine, but I wanted nothing more than to never see her again.

When I reached the basement, I found a seat away from the others in the waiting room. I started to cry as I filled out the information sheets and waited. I was completely exposed. If anyone from the dorm or my classes happened to walk by and see me sitting in a room clearly marked PSYCHI-ATRIC DEPARTMENT, I would be ruined. Not that I had a reputation to uphold. No one, except Rebecca, knew anything about me. I was "the quiet, shy one who lives with Rebecca." Finally, my name was called, and I was led to a small counseling room.

Meeting with the short middle-aged balding intake counselor made me feel very adult. He looked kind, like Bill Cosby. I knew I'd done the right thing by coming to see him. But I didn't know what to say. In fact, I had no idea why I was there or what he could do for me. He encouraged me with questions, and I responded with rivers of tears. With his help I was able to talk about my family problems and the loneliness I felt. But I stayed clear of discussing Rebecca. At that moment she seemed unimportant. Then I mentioned my fantasy of sailing out the window of my seventh-floor dorm room.

"Have you tried to hurt yourself before?" He looked concerned.

"No," I laughed.

"If you think you might hurt yourself I'll need to hospitalize you for the weekend."

Needless to say, I was horrified. I had midterms coming up and wanted to go home for the weekend. I quickly retracted my statement, ensuring him I would be fine. He took my word but gave me his phone number and a referral to Kathy Walker, a counselor I began to see the following week.

Kathy's hair was a mass of tiny, tight curls. She looked like Rebecca but thinner, older, and prettier. I looked forward to my weekly trips to Cowell Hospital. For two weeks I spoke of nothing but my family, especially my mother. I told Kathy about the domestic violence, poverty, and isolation that had been part of my life since I could remember. Hearing myself ver-bally express my anger, disappointment, and regret helped me begin to heal. But, again, I never spoke of Rebecca.

Each week I felt a little more stable, though every day was a different roller coaster. Sometimes I'd feel so overwhelmed with life that I couldn't get out of bed. My body ached; I felt incapable of walking the two blocks to campus. When I felt better I'd go on eating binges until I felt sick again. I gained 40 pounds my freshman year.

One night near the end of our first semester, Rebecca was lying on her bed studying. I sat at my desk, which faced her bed. I had told Rebecca a few weeks earlier that I was seeing a therapist, but we hadn't discussed it in detail.

"Oh, yeah. It's Thursday, huh? You went to see your therapist today," Rebecca said.

"Yeah, I did," I responded, still reading.

"Well, how did it go?" Rebecca could be demanding, which was something I liked about her.

"It was fine."

"What did you talk about?" she asked. Rebecca knew only she could get away with being so nosy. I didn't know what to say. How much was too much to tell? Before I could respond Rebecca spoke again.

"Did you tell her about me?"

I knew we'd been having a deep conflict, but I'd stopped believing my therapy had anything to do with her. It was about me, something I was doing for myself.

"I told her you're my roommate and that we've been arguing a lot. She knows I've been stressed out about it," I said honestly.

Rebecca stared at me from across the room. She looked puzzled or annoyed, like she thought I was hiding a secret.

"Well, did you tell her? Did you tell her I'm straight?"

I was stunned to silence. Rebecca's tone had accused me of being other than straight. Unbelievably, I'd never thought of my feelings for her as sexual. I had dreamed, many times, of kissing, holding, and touching her but hadn't equated those acts to lesbianism. It just seemed like a logical development in our already intimate relationship, especially with Misty out of the way. We could be like the other two women down the hall. They seemed so happy together.

I was a naive virgin holding onto prudish, childlike concepts of sex. I almost considered myself asexual.

"Rebecca, I'm not gay," I said flatly. "You're just my friend."

She smiled smugly and said nothing. Deciding not to argue with me, Rebecca went back to reading. I sat at my desk for a while, not able to see the words in my book. I went to bed hearing Rebecca's words repeat themselves all night. I felt betrayed that she had apparently spent time thinking about my sexual identity and that my behavior demonstrated a sexual attraction toward her.

I scrutinized myself, every action and thought. I had to know if Rebecca was right. Of course, I knew she wasn't. As a young girl I'd told my younger sister that I'd be a lesbian when I grew up, but that was child's play. How could Rebecca know my sexual orientation before I did?

I decided that being in a room full of lesbians would help me decide if I was one or not. Colorful fliers around campus advertised various student groups. Two of them always caught my attention: the Multicultural Bisexual, Lesbian, Gay Alliance's Women's Rap Group and a support group run by the Women's Resource Center called Sistah Sistah. Both groups were for lesbian, bisexual, and questioning women.

It was hard to get myself to either meeting. I knew that MBLGA's Women's Rap Group consisted of mostly white women because I'd seen them leaving the student union one night. I decided I would go to that group first because it was a larger group than Sistah Sistah. It would be less likely that I would have to speak. Also, I feared the sometimes brutal honesty that people of color can dish out, and Sistah Sistah was just for women of color.

MBLGA's Women's Rap could have been a sorority or church youth group and I would not have felt more uncomfortable. I definitely stood out among the clean-cut white lesbians. My hair was short and curly and in no particular style. I wore a short skirt, footless tights, and platform shoes. Almost everyone else was dressed in jeans, shorts, T-shirts, and flannel. I didn't speak, except to say my name. I listened to the discussion, which had something to do with sex. When the women laughed, I had no idea a dirty joke had been told. I didn't know what lesbian sex was and definitely didn't know how to do it.

After that meeting I ran back to the dorm and did something I'd never done. I called an old friend from high school who still lived in Vallejo. We had never been particularly close and hadn't spoken since high school, but I felt compelled to tell someone about my experience with "the lesbians," and thought she was unimportant enough in my life to be safe. I didn't fear losing her friendship and knew she didn't know any of my family or friends at home.

Ginger and I chatted for more than an hour. She was attending a local community college, still living at home, and was dating the same guy she'd been seeing since she was 14. My life seemed exciting in comparison. At the end of the conversation, I told Ginger I had a secret to tell her. I hadn't mentioned "the lesbians" at all and was dying to tell her, but the words wouldn't come out. She told me to write it down in a letter. It took me a few days, but I did.

I continued to attend Women's Rap and to see my therapist, without telling her about my exploration. I spoke of it with no one except Ginger. She became intimately interested in every detail of my life. We talked on the phone every night for at least two hours, which meant I was spending no time with Rebecca. Ginger wanted to know if I had decided I was a lesbian. I still wasn't sure. But I knew I wasn't a lesbian like the women in the MBLGA group. If I were going to be a lesbian, I would have to be a different kind, one who wore dresses and makeup and dated other women of color.

Throughout all of this I'd managed to make one friend other than Rebecca—Shantay—and only because of her persistence in calling and visiting me. We spent time together at her apartment near campus, mostly watching television and trying to study. She had a boyfriend who made it obvious that I was unwelcome. He constantly asked Shantay and I if we were lovers, which I ignored because it seemed completely random.

Shantay and her friends put extensions and perms in each other's hair, went to clubs, and discussed their problems with men. They were like a family of sisters, and I was a distant cousin. I wasn't interested in joining any of their activities but found comfort in being with them because they were young black women. They helped me realize my desire to belong to a similar circle of friends, women more like myself.

A few weeks before the end of the semester, I felt ready to attend a Sistah Sistah meeting, expecting it to be like Women's Rap with color. I hoped I would fit in a bit better. My shyness didn't help; I was so afraid to speak that I tried to sit perfectly still so as not to invite questions. I found out that some of the women from my classes were lesbian or bisexual, which surprised me because they didn't meet my stereotypical images of lesbians. Eventually I grew comfortable with the women of Sistah Sistah.

The group was fundamentally different from Women's Rap, which focused on light subjects that wouldn't stir too much controversy. There was a rift in the MBLGA group between the bisexual women who slept with men and the "pure" lesbians. As an effort to appease everyone, the discussions never dealt with variations in sexuality, racism, class differences, or anything political. Sistah Sistah was open to anything. We discussed issues that affected us as women of color who loved other women. Together we celebrated birthdays, holidays, and graduations. Sistah Sistah became my family when I needed one most. In my junior year I became a group co-facilitator.

I decided to call myself bisexual to leave my options open. Bisexuality seemed as neutral as asexuality and easier to explain. Ginger was the first person I told. Rebecca was the second. I developed a love of all things lesbian: literature, art, magazines, and more.

Ginger and I had decided, over the phone, that we should experiment with lesbianism together. To my surprise, as a child she had experienced crushes on girls. Over the holidays we became much closer than we had been in high school.

Rebecca reacted with an "I told you so" attitude. She asked if Ginger was my girlfriend. I told her, "Yes, something like that." From that point on our conversations grew more infrequent.

Freshman Year: Second Semester

January

With the support of my budding relationship with Ginger, I was finally able to speak to my therapist about my sexuality. During one of our sessions, I steered the conversation toward Rebecca.

"I've been having problems with my roommate again," I blurted.

"What kind of problems have you been having?" she asked.

I hesitated.

"Well, Rebecca knows I like her more than as a friend."

"How exactly do you 'like her'?"

"Sexually," I managed to say.

Kathy was supportive and referred me to the groups I'd already been attending. Letting her know about my sexuality had been difficult. She knew more about my life than anyone, all the secrets I'd never told. Telling Kathy about my new bisexual identity was like giving her the key to my deepest self, and I had to know I could trust her that much. It was such a relief that someone could know almost everything about me and not be scared away.

February

Rebecca left the room every time I called Ginger. She "misplaced" my messages and tried to read my letters. She was hurt that I no longer desired her. At one point she stopped speaking to me entirely—for exactly 28 days. She explained it away: "I needed time to think." Our relationship was never the same. It deteriorated slowly, but I could see it fading, along with my desire to hold onto her. After a while I couldn't remember what I ever saw in her, but I knew my experience with her had forever changed me. By the end of our freshman year, we were both glad to move apart. For a while we remained civil. But that turned out to be too much.

We went our separate ways. Rebecca chose her own path, academics and celibacy, as I emerged into my new self. Not only was I coming out, but I was also coming into myself, my own identity. I'd begun my lifelong course of self-discovery and was ready to face the challenge.

Getting Real at ISU: A Campus Transition

by Johnny Rogers

Iowa State University

Whatever you can do, or dream you can, begin it. Boldness has genius, power, and magic in it. —Johann Wolfgang von Goethe

I fought the tide of students pouring through the door as I headed toward the professor who was collecting his overheads and lecture notes.

"Dr. Clark?"

"Yes, Carol," he said, curling his papers under his arm, reaching for his Styrofoam coffee cup, and straightening to full height. I had to look up to make eye contact. The second week of the fall semester was beginning, and this tall English professor, an administrator no less, seemed an imposing fixture of a rigid, conservative establishment, an establishment that might oppose what I was about, what I was doing.

"I was too timid to say anything when you took attendance last week," I stammered, "but I'd like to go by a different name than the one on the class list." God, what would he say? I felt as though I were about to step off a cliff. I wasn't just changing my name; I was taking the first step toward living and moving in the world as a whole person, instead of keeping a chunk of myself buried and covering the remainder with a protective facade. I'd been an out lesbian during my first year on campus, but now, in my second year, I was about to transition to living life as a male.

"Certainly," Dr. Clark responded. "What is it?"

"Johnny."

"No problem, Johnny. I'm glad you said something. The roster is in this bunch of papers here, but I'm sure I can remember to change it later. How do you spell that?"

John had been the name that instantly came to mind when I was first asked if I had chosen a masculine name. As I tried it on, though, by rolling it around in my thoughts and being called John by those closest to me, I realized the name sounded too serious. So I opted for Johnny. My grandfather's family, the Rogerses, came from the South, and though John is the family name Johnny would certainly not be unheard of in Southern states. As I thought more about my Southern family ties, I realized the Confederate soldiers' nickname of "Johnny Reb" was also appropriate: I have often seemed like a rebel, frequently crossing social boundaries in the process of just being myself. Usually the boundaries have been those designed to favor a particular elite group of people, and boundaries, like national borders, can be heavily guarded.

"Where do you think you're going?"

He had just stepped out of the men's room and was blocking the doorway, leaning toward me with his fists on his hips. Down the hall from the Dean of Students office, in the one building on campus where I felt safe, the bearded and bulky staff member wasn't about to let me pass. My stomach churned, my heart raced…and then I got some inspiration: I got mad. Taking another step toward him, I said, "I'm going to use the head." The words came out with authority, quiet but bitten off, as I pointed to the door behind him. I'd assumed an attitude that I'd learned as a sergeant in the army, and the effect was dramatic. The man's sneer became an open mouth, one eyebrow raised, and his hands dropped to his sides. "Rob," I explained, "I'm a guy. I'm transsexual."

"Uh, oh, OK," he stammered, as he slowly moved away from the door looking confused and embarrassed.

Finally in the men's room, I closed the stall door behind me, leaned against it, and exhaled. Would he follow me in when he recovered from his surprise? I braced myself for the possible confrontation and tried to relax enough to relieve myself. Neither event happened. Instead, I gave up on pissing and left. Rob didn't show up again until the following day. He came looking for me in the LGBT student services office, where I worked, to apologize for hassling me. Apparently when I'd been introduced to him as the new work-study office assistant, Rob had assumed I was a butch lesbian. He never expected to meet a transitioning transsexual. It didn't take long for him to make the switch, however, and after a short period of discomfort, awkwardness, and floundering with feminine and masculine pronouns, he accepted me as a guy.

Not everyone I've encountered on campus has been like Rob—initially surprised, then accepting—and some people have yelled "fuckin' dyke!" and "faggot!" as I've walked to class. One day, early in the fall semester and my transition, when I appeared very androgynous, both of these remarks were lobbed at me within two hours. Apparently one person's butch is another person's fairy, and hostility toward both is still candidly displayed at this university.

"Damn it," I vented to my friend Gordon, "out on the sidewalk I'm anybody's guess at queer. In the queer community some lesbians have me pegged as a traitor to all that's female, while gay guys act like I have an infectious disease. I'm taking shit from all directions."

"I can relate," Gordon commiserated in his gravelly voice, "because I've caught a lot of the same stuff for being bisexual. I'm either a fence-sitter or stuck in a phase, according to all sorts of people. It never dawned on me that transgenders would experience the same sort of thing bi's do." After a bit he added, "You know, a lot of people don't come out 'til they go to college...maybe they're trying so hard to be proud of being gay, lesbian, and straight that they can't accept anyone who doesn't seem to be at one end of the scale or the other."

The concept of fluid gender expression or sexuality is frightening to a lot of people, especially in cultures that have maintained rigid gender roles and haven't experienced diversity. This is why it seems ironic to me that I ended up coming out and transitioning in the Midwest. In fact, I never dreamed I would move to a traditionally conservative state such as Iowa.

Several years ago layoffs and unemployment were on the rise in California, so a friend suggested I move to Iowa to find work. If I hated it, she reasoned, I could always go back. So I packed up and moved to the corn belt. After a couple of years, I'd paid off my car, taken care of some other bills, and turned 30. Then I decided to finish the undergraduate degree I'd started working toward years ago. Being in a new place had allowed me to get a fresh perspective on life and to do some growing. This growth process involved a lot of soul searching, reading, talking with friends, working at resolving issues concerning religion and spirituality, deciding who I wanted to be and what I was about, and dealing with painful events from my childhood.

"Mom, I'm a boy," I remembered saying around age 5 or 6.

"Now," my mother had answered firmly, "don't you mean you wish you could do the things that boys do? Girls can do anything they want, you know, just like boys."

I'd already tried to pee standing up, and it had been a messy disappointment, so she obviously didn't understand me. It was also clear from other exchanges like this that there was something wrong with feeling the way I did...there was something wrong with me...and I'd better not mention that I was a boy ever again.

Twenty-some years later, I couldn't keep the truth under wraps any longer. All of my soul-searching, emotional healing, and growth had been like peeling an onion: I was, one layer at a time, getting to the core issues, the center of me. Uncomfortable and nearly overwhelmed with all of this, I contacted the student counseling center for help with sorting things out. Several sessions with a conservative therapist/Ph.D. candidate helped me resolve and let go of some of the traumatic events of my life, but my identity as a male was beginning to crystallize, and I realized I needed to talk with someone who had experience counseling transgendered people, someone who didn't pathologize the trans experience as this guy did. He believed transsexuals are sick, and his idea of "treatment" for my "condition" was for me to wear frilly underwear and put on tons of makeup. I'd already tried to be as femme and woman-identified as possible, and I'd also explored the other end of the spectrum, but riding a motorcycle, welding, and holding my own as a sergeant in the Army hadn't made any difference either. My efforts had only put off the inevitable: dealing with the fact that I was a man who was seen by the world as a woman, and that the configuration of my body—a woman's body—didn't make sense. Late in the summer I was surprised and relieved to find a therapist at the center who had done a lot of work with LGBT people. She was supportive and didn't shy away from asking the difficult questions that helped me sort everything out so I could make some tough decisions.

It seemed to a lot of people that I'd made the decision to transition in a relatively short time. Actually I'd been trying, on one level or another, to resolve my gender dilemma for years. Once I'd faced, or "owned," my male gender identity, I realized I would need to change my body through hormone therapy, go by my masculine name, and live life as a male to maintain my sanity. The sense of incongruity I experienced was acute and overwhelming. It's no wonder people try for as long as they can to avoid dealing with this kind of experience on a conscious level.

If I were going to transition, I would have to do it openly. As a student I certainly didn't have the money to fly to Europe for a discreet instant sex change. I felt it imperative to change my body, to be myself, and to dump the shame I'd felt, that I had to take the risk of "getting real" in front of God and everybody. At least I had some people in my life that I was counting on to be supportive…and most of them didn't let me down.

In a hallway between classes, I ran into one of those people. Andi is a classmate, and though I've interacted with her only on campus, she is an out bisexual who comes off as one of the most fluid unpolarized people I know. She didn't even blink at the beginning of the semester when I told her I was transgendered and had decided to change my name. Now it was early October, one week before I would see an endocrinologist, and I'd just come out to her as transsexual. *Transgendered* can apply to anyone who doesn't identify with the traditional concepts of male, female, gay male, lesbian, or heterosexual (e.g., drag queens, drag kings, people who are intersexed, transsexuals, transvestites and cross-dressers). *Transsexual* specifically applies to those whose anatomical sex does not match their psychological gender, or the way in which their brain was gendered as they developed in the womb. Sexual orientation is separate from gender identity, so a trans person may identify as gay, lesbian, bisexual, or heterosexual (e.g., some drag queens are straight men).

"Cool! I get to see you change and everything!" Andi said as she tilted her head and nervously shifted from foot to foot. The fringe on her black leather jacket made a quiet swooshing noise. "But aren't you afraid of being out? What will you say to people who think you need counseling or that you're fucked-up?" Andi had heard about trans people in the media who were institutionalized, objectified, or pathologized, and she wondered where I was coming from.

"Well, all queers catch the same sort of crap," I said. "I figure stereotypes won't die until more of us live our lives as though being queer is nothing strange, as though we're not ashamed of who we are. I'm writing about transitioning in my creative nonfiction class. I was scared spitless at the beginning, but the prof is supportive and thinks I've got great material. My writing partner had a transgendered friend in high school, and, so far, none of the other students have kicked up a fuss about me."

Looking at me sideways, Andi said, "Huh…" Then, tilting her head the other way, she asked, "What will your transition be like? Will your voice change?"

"Yep. It'll take a while, though. First I'll have to go through menopause symptoms, like hot flashes. Then, the testosterone I'm taking will eventually overtake the estrogen in my body. My voice will get lower, I'll grow whiskers on my face, and the fat in my body will shift to places where men typically carry fat. Because doctors follow a set of rules about how fast a person can transition, I won't be able to have surgery until I've been on hormones and lived as a guy for a year."

"Do you hate your body? I don't get why you'd want to have surgery."

"This is so hard to explain…to put into words. I wouldn't say I hate my body. It's more like my body doesn't feel right to me. It doesn't quite compute that I have a woman's breasts. They shouldn't be there, ya know? And I can almost feel, or sense, a penis that's not there. It's so damn incongruent. That's the best way I can explain what I am experiencing…and it's difficult to live like this. That's why I want to have surgery. I know my body will never function completely like most men's do, but the closer my body is to 'male,' the easier it will be to deal with the incongruence."

"Whoa! Won't that be expensive?"

"I'll be able to afford breast removal, but the genital surgery costs a lot more, and for FTMs (female-to-male transsexuals) it isn't always terribly successful."

"OK," Andi said, waving her arms, "give me a minute to take in all of this." After 30 seconds of silently contemplating her boots, she looked up, shook my hand, and said, "It's nice to meet you, Johnny." We walked into our literary theory class and sat next to each other. My insides had gone to jelly from the coming-out experience, but I felt great, because another friend was making the transition with me.

Do I seem to be having a charmed college transition? There are never any guarantees that people will react positively or professionally to my situation, and not everyone has. The registrar's office practically laughed me out the door when I requested my name be changed on my records according to common law. I ended up having to file papers for a legal name change with a lawyer in student legal aid. More than one student has gotten up from their desk and moved when I've sat next to them. One day as I walked to class, minding my own business, a guy pointed at me and laughed out loud. When I went to student health to get a referral to an endocrinologist and asked for a private consultation with my doctor, I was scared to death to let the nurses know why I was there, because I'd heard so many of the staff were xenophobic. I felt comfortable with my doctor only because I'd already seen him several times about a back injury, and we had a sort of rapport. The stress of continually dealing with these sorts of difficulties, my own issues, and the usual load of course work that students have, caught up with me the end of my second semester of transition. After feeling run down and sick for weeks, I was diagnosed with mononucleosis. My body and soul needed a break.

As I recuperate, reflect on the past year, and look ahead to the fall semester, I realize there are still no guarantees and that my life on campus will probably continue to have its anxious moments. Still, courage I never thought I had seems to materialize when I need it most, and positive events have often followed gutsy moves. I've managed to maintain a 3.5 average, make the Dean's List, and be accepted as a member of the Golden Key National Honor Society. The bottom line, for me, is that shame and embarrassment can't stick in the face of honesty and openness, and that there is magic and power in simply being yourself.

From the Margins

by Stephen Paul Whitaker

Morehead State University, Kentucky

I suppose a "typical" or "normal" sort of student speech for this type of event would involve the definition of success—how we as honors students and you as the people who are responsible for our presence here today can measure our worth by our future achievements.

Uh-oh, I said to myself when I noticed the honors program secretary summoning me from across the parking lot. *Maybe I can pretend I didn't see her.* Three weeks earlier I'd walked out of an honors seminar protesting the instructor's sexist, elitist, and homophobic comments. Although I hadn't dropped the class, I was considering it. In a conversation with the honors program director, I'd been frank about the problems I saw with the class. I figured his secretary, Jo, had heard about my latest episode and was going to offer unsolicited advice about "getting along."

Well, those of you who know me know I don't usually participate in what is considered "typical" or "normal" patterns.

"Shit," I muttered. Out of the corner of my eye, I saw Jo jogging toward me. I stopped, waved, and began a self-lecture about being nice to her. Jo took a maternal interest in and approach to many of the honors program students. I think she was particularly interested in my welfare because she too was a nontraditional-aged student from Eastern Kentucky as well as a university employee. She reminded me of my mother and was among the first people on campus in whom I had confided my sexual orientation. A deeply religious woman, she cried when I came out, but we had remained fairly close despite her belief that I was a "sinner."

"Steve, I need to talk to you," she said, slightly out of breath. I knew the honors program committee had met the day before, and I assumed my latest exploit had been discussed. I also figured I was about to get yet another lecture about "learning to play the game."

I do want to discuss success in the context of responsibility, though. I would like for each of us to consider how we—as people who have been privileged with the opportunity to participate in formal education, who have been privileged with having the opportunity to acquire the skills it takes to surmount educational barriers that keep many other people out—are now obligated to use the success we are celebrating today as an instrument of social change rather than a weapon to maintain or increase our social position at the expense of others.

"The committee met yesterday," Jo said.

I nodded.

"Well, we're putting together the program for the honors convocation, and we selected the speaker."

I nodded again, thinking the committee had probably selected some conservative jerk and Jo was trying to warn me before I threw a public fit.

"They decided they want you to speak," she added.

I dropped my book bag. "What?" I asked. "This is an April Fool's joke, isn't it?" Many of the professors and administrators whom I'd criticized most were members of the committee.

Jo looked at me quizzically. "No. It was unanimous." She paused. "It's quite an honor, you know. But I want you to remember that I'm going to be right there, and you had better not say anything bad."

"Can I wear a dress?" I grinned irreverently, unable to resist teasing her despite my shock.

Jo rolled her eyes and sighed. "Absolutely not! Can I tell the committee you accept?"

"Yeah," I said, picking up my bag and heading toward class a bit stunned.

Each of us has within our power the ability to disrupt and transform some of the barriers we have overcome. But to do so, we each must recognize the privilege of our positions. We must not only fulfill our own potential, but also actively work to foster the potential of our neighbors.

Later that day, I thought back on my arrival at Morehead State University, a small public institution in Appalachian Kentucky. I had walked into the office of the academic honors program at the beginning of my first semester emboldened by the results of my latest ACT scores and asking to be admitted. When classes started the next day, I had trudged into the Honors 101 course with none of my earlier bravado. I was scared to death. I was 29 years old, from a working-class background, gay, and Appalachian. I was nontraditional in nearly every sense of the word. *Why do you do these things to yourself?* an inner voice barked. I knew the students who belonged here, the "normal" or "typical" people, had been recruited.

I entered the classroom that day surreptitiously looking for the danger signs: groups of students talking, whispering, laughing in a corner, a holdover from high school. Keeping my eyes averted, I sought the anonymity of the row closest to the window, taking myself out of the line of fire with the other outcasts. Self-awareness operating at hyper levels, I was sure everyone could tell I was poor and gay, that I was an impostor who did not belong in college, much less in an honors program. Nearly sick with misery, by the time class began I'd convinced myself of complete failure.

We must re-examine our idea of leadership. Activist Mike Clark says that one of the major problems facing Appalachia is that there are too many leaders, that college-educated Appalachians run the risk of "being the people who will attempt to control the lives of Appalachia's poor folks,"[1] those people in this region who are prevented from obtaining the skills necessary to surmount the matrix of obstacles designed to exclude them from success.

My first attempt at college nearly ten years before was a complete failure. I dropped out of school because I didn't see the immediate worth of attending class. People from working-class families, especially those like mine from economically deprived areas like Appalachia, are taught repeatedly that education, "book learnin'," is purely recreational. The only thing that counts is hard, honest labor. The kind that makes others rich. The kind that makes us grow old before our time. The kind that deprives us of our cultural heritage, our identity. The value I placed on education was also marred by the stigma associated with my sexuality. I'd been taunted and physically abused in the public school system for being gay, even though I wasn't out. From those experiences, I'd learned to associate education with oppression. Looking back, I am not surprised that my first attempt at college was unsuccessful. I flunked out of school at 19 and did what was expected of me. I went to work.

Clark cautioned that education in this society often means control, not freedom, a way to enforce the values of the dominant culture on the rest of us, and a way for some of us to fight our way to the top, achieve success, work to control those at the bottom of the hierarchy, and then blame them for being there.

My desire to do "real" work was thwarted about eight years later, however, when I was fired from my job as a reporter for a small-town newspaper. I had become pretty radical on the job as I explored my sexuality and started to come to terms with it. I was no longer acquiescent. In fact, I was angry, so angry that I was fired over an ideological conflict with the newspaper editor.

At various times in my journalism career, I'd attempted to take college classes and planned to "someday" finish my degree. I was intensely interested in education and maintained a fairly good relationship with Dr. Miller, the president of the local community college. I turned to him when I lost my job. "We'll work something out," he said, advising me to make an appointment for the next day with his secretary. Shortly after I arrived the next morning, I found myself sitting across a conference table from Dr. Miller, talking about my media qualifications in newspaper, radio, and television, hoping for the job as public relations coordinator.

"I've worked all over the state," I said, placing emphasis on my television experience because I knew that the person who had worked in the college's video studio had recently retired.

"We've shut down the studio," Dr. Miller said. "And frankly, Steve, there's no way I can hire you for that job without your having a degree. I can find you work here, though, if you'll make me a deal," he added.

I eyed him suspiciously. Refusing to "make a deal" was precisely what had gotten me fired.

"I've reviewed your transcript," he said, his gentle tone belying his words. "You failed English 101 three times. What was going on in your head?"

I looked at him uncomfortably. "I thought it was boring."

"I guess you thought history, psychology, and algebra were boring too? You failed those as well."

"I was working and didn't have time."

Dr. Miller sighed and settled into his chair. After a moment of silence, he said quietly but forcefully, "I cannot begin to tell you how it disgusts me to see people from this region throwing away their potential." His "deal" involved my enrolling in classes in exchange for a job and making a commitment to complete a degree. "I want you to begin classes next semester and get this transcript straightened out," he said.

To attain lasting change in the educational system, we need people from this region who are willing to do as the students here have done: become educated. But those of us who successfully negotiate the educational system must also be willing to return to Appalachia and use our education to promote a voice within and for the region.

Dr. Miller found me a job with student support services, a federally funded TRIO program that provides support for at-risk students. In my hometown that meant working with mainly nontraditional-aged single mothers returning to school. I was hired as a professional tutor and began work almost immediately. Working with these women helped me put my own life into perspective. As my attitudes toward education changed and my self-esteem improved, I became increasingly open in the workplace about my sexuality. But activism centered on sexuality never occurred to me. My geographic and class positions did not include space for the concept of an "out" homosexual or a politics based on homosexuality. I knew there were gay rights groups, but they were in metropolitan areas on the coasts and far from my sphere of reality. I also had no contact with other gays or lesbians, even people who were closeted. Although I was serving as an advocate both within and outside of the institution for my student-clients, and was involved with an environmental group fighting the expansion of the local landfill, when it came to issues of sexuality, I remained silent. I had learned to express myself, but I was still unable to overcome my own homophobia at school, even though the community college system was linked to the University of Kentucky, which had implemented a clause regarding sexual orientation in its nondiscrimination policies a couple of years earlier.

We must also recognize our self-worth and understand that Appalachians have a specialized knowledge and specific methods of resistance. And the people here today who are representative of the educated portion of the Appalachian group, the Appalachian scholars, have a choice to make: We can continue to use the backs and bodies of our brothers and sisters to achieve middle-class "success," or we can use our education to disrupt the status quo.

The emotional progress I'd made at the junior college, however, diminished to a trickle when I transferred to Morehead State University. I hated the city. I hated the school. I constantly felt awkward and out of place. When I had enrolled in the community college, it had been from a position of power. I had the personal interest of the president and a reputation as a journalist and was in familiar territory. My transfer to Morehead forced me to begin again with no influence, no friends, and a lot of bad memories of the educational system despite more recent pleasant ones. I retreated into my shell and remained completely quiet about my sexuality.

In those first few weeks as I scurried around campus lonely and scared, I came to hate my major. Because I was interested in environmental issues and because Kentucky has such a poor environmental protection track record, I had planned to enter MSU's environmental science program with the ultimate goal of completing a law degree. Almost overwhelmingly depressed by the end of that first semester, I started thinking about changing my major. I consulted the coordinator for nontraditional students who suggested I take an interest inventory. After filling in countless bubbles, I turned in the test for scoring. I was shocked to discover I'd scored off the scale in sociology, mainly because I didn't know what it was. My experiences as a reporter were again a valuable asset. I went to the sociology department and asked to talk to a faculty member, where I met Dr. Hardesty, whose areas of expertise were class stratification, racial inequality, and gender constructions. I was intrigued since I'd dealt with all these issues as a reporter.

In our quest for change, we can look at some of the faculty and staff members here who utilize the transformative potential of education rather than its punitive nature. That is, they recognize the influence of the educational institution as a potential instrument of empowerment as well as a historical weapon of enslavement.

For days, I agonized over changing my major. I struggled with the practicality of working and paying for a degree in a field I knew was overpopulated. My background—the barrier created by my experiences with gender, class, and regionality—kept cropping up. How could I major in something without any guarantee of a job? On the other hand, I was definitely attracted to the field. Finally, I called Dr. Hardesty and confessed my reluctance.

"But Steve," she said. "What is more important? Do you want to be happy now or do you plan to keep postponing it?"

Wow! Her words hit home! I was depressed because I wasn't enjoying college, but was reluctant to take steps to change my situation. That day, I changed my major and enrolled in two sociology courses for the spring semester. For the first time since I had arrived at MSU, I was excited about being there.

We can also look to the work of philosopher-activist Angela Davis, who writes that "the process of empowerment cannot be simplistically defined in accordance with our own particular class interests. We must learn to lift as we climb."2

As I sat in Dr. Hardesty's Sociology 101 class, I was entranced. Here was a whole discipline devoted to studying society, and many of that discipline's theories sang out to me, particularly those dealing with societal conflict and inequality. Dr. Hardesty was giving me the means to define my life and the tools to reconstruct it. To say I was enthusiastic would be an understatement. The conversations I'd had with Dr. Hardesty often extended from after class to time in her office. When I came out to her, she treated my revelation with a nonchalance that tested the fabric of my reality. Here was a virtual stranger, a straight woman, who did not care about my sexual orientation! She also talked about some of her gay academic friends at other institutions, and for the first time I realized there were people who had faced similar barriers who had achieved academic success. As we talked that day and in the days that followed, she encouraged me to apply to graduate school. "Your voice needs to be heard," she said. In class, she was relentless about social justice issues, and approached class, racial, and gender inequality with equal fervor. Her attitudes and opinions were beneficial to my personal growth, but so were the attitudes of my classmates. While they were significantly younger than I, for the most part they came to MSU from similar backgrounds. They were the same kinds of students as those I'd attended school with ten years earlier and who had tormented me. And they were talking openly in class about their gay cousins, brothers, aunts, and friends, and their experiences. I discovered I wasn't the only one, that there are plenty of people who don't hate gay men and lesbians—probably the biggest lesson I learned at MSU.

We must recognize that true educators are people who are truly teachers, people who are working not just at their jobs, but ardently at social change, at education as a process of transformation and empowerment.

As I became involved in my new major, I also began taking women's studies classes. Reading about the history of labor protest in my region; learning about women who had, decades before I was born, protested the constraints of gender; and discovering the work of theorists such as Audre Lorde, bell hooks, and Gloria Anzaldúa opened a place in my world for protest. Not only was resistance acceptable, but it was also required, a responsibility.

Of course, there was still a real world outside the sociology classroom. The same semester I declared my sociology major, a woman was assaulted on campus because she was a lesbian. All the anger and fear I held inside since my experiences in high school came boiling to the top. I hesitantly agreed to participate in a meeting to organize a march protesting the administration's decision to treat the matter as incidental and not hate-motivated. At that time I was in a quasi-out stage. That is, I didn't deny my sexuality, but I hadn't been broadcasting it. Fear immobilized me briefly. When I arrived at the meeting after much soul-searching, I met a woman with whom I felt an immediate affinity, Dr. Patti Swartz, an English professor who had successfully battled the administration's decision to exclude a gay and lesbian literature course from the curriculum.

When the day of the march arrived, I was terrified. I'd heard several fraternities planned to counter-protest our "Take Back the Night" march, and we were also expecting wide media coverage. I cannot put into words the fear, sadness, and anger I felt while deciding whether to show up. Would anyone else be there? Would I be assaulted? Would I destroy my future by participating? Dozens of questions and unformed (and sometimes unrealistic) fears ran through my mind. I couldn't let down Dr. Swartz, though, so I went.

When I arrived at our starting place, I was surprised to see about 30 people standing around, including several reporters. Then the crowd grew. And grew. Several hundred people were gathered holding signs by the time we began our march down the main street of campus and around the area where the assault had taken place. I'll never forget it. Even though I had come to terms with my sexuality mostly on my own, the march initiated a period of accelerated emotional growth focused on external, social relationships. During the march I realized I wasn't alone, that being gay wasn't a solitary "burden."

We had organized the march as an anti-violence demonstration. As a result many straight people were involved, as well as many closeted gays and lesbians. But they were all there: Dr. Hardesty, many of my classmates, and activists from other campuses. In addition to the young woman who had been assaulted, several people spoke that night, among them two students from the University of Kentucky's Lambda organization. "I like to have sex with men," one of the Lambda representatives shouted into the microphone as he began his speech. If the fabric of my reality had been tested in sociology classes and by Dr. Hardesty, this display and its response demolished it.

Ultimately, we don't have to tolerate the second-class status of women, people of color, sexual minorities, people who are differently abled, or our own second-class status as Appalachians, in our classrooms, at our institution, or in our communities. We can use our education, our recognized achievement in the area of scholarship, to effect change.

The way that my heritage as an Appalachian from Eastern Kentucky meshes with my socialization in a working-class family is complex. When those issues become even more complicated by gender and sexuality, the effect is stifling. Particularly potent is the added difficulty that accompanies rurality. Ultimately for me, the oppression created by my different cultural positions was surmountable. I realized this during the march.

Riding high on the success of the march, I began working with another student to organize a gay and lesbian group. The campus newspaper interviewed Dr. Swartz and me, and I appeared on a campus television program. Each of my projects required dealing with that old fear, and each time, like the march, I was surprised when nothing bad happened. I worked with both the GLBT group and Students for Social Justice for about a year. Also following the march I began to focus my energy on gender research and present my work at honors conferences across the country. Taking the cue from the young men who spoke at our march, I began my presentations by describing myself as a "white-trash hillbilly faggot." My frankness wasn't always appreciated by the honors program director or the various conference organizers, but I was never silenced.

My campus organizing, combined with my work in social inequality, certainly lit a fire of revolt in me. Rather than remaining reticent about my sexuality, my Appalachian origins, or my class background, I was brutally honest. I unsettled several closeted professors by outing myself in classes, petitioned the Board of Regents to include sexual orientation in MSU's nondiscrimination policies, and frequently complained to the campus affirmative action officer and minority affairs director about instances of hate speech.

One day, for example, I had stopped by the registrar's office to fill out a form. As I waited for my appointment, I noticed three men who were clearly not students talking loudly. They were discussing a sexual harassment incident involving two males.

"A real man wouldn't have put up with that," one said.

"They oughta throw those fags to the sharks," added another.

At first I tried to ignore them, but the longer I listened the more pissed I got. I walked over to them. "Excuse me. Are you gentlemen employees of the university?" I asked. Two of them nodded.

"Well, I'm a gay student at this university, and I don't appreciate your remarks," I said.

They looked at each other, and then one of them looked at me and said, "Isn't that interesting?"

Then I got really pissed. "Not as interesting as you're going to find it in five minutes," I said as I walked out the door and to the affirmative action office where I filed a formal affirmative action complaint. I was later told that all three men, one of whom was a fairly high-ranking administrator, were officially reprimanded.

Now, I was never told not to get an education. I do remember being warned to not ever get above my raisin'. I have to admit I have spent years thinking the prohibition on and the suspicion of formal education expressed by that phrase was a direct attack on learning. I know now it wasn't. I realize now that the people telling me not to get above my raisin' were warning me not to use the backs and bodies of my brothers and sisters to achieve someone else's definition of success.

Dr. Swartz, who is also from a working-class Appalachian background, often talks about the issues of entitlement that have affected us both. "We didn't feel we were entitled to a sexuality any more than we felt we were entitled to an education," she says. For me at least, this is true. As I neared the end of the first semester of my senior year, I began to work on applications for graduate school. I solicited advice from others on the best way to approach the letter of application. Most of them told me to "play the game." So I did. I wrote what I considered to be an "academic" letter.

"You sound like a real prick," Dr. Swartz said after she read my letter.

"What?" I said, taken aback.

"You've taken about 500 words to show off your vocabulary. I think the kind of school that would be excited about this kind of letter is the last kind of school you would want to attend."

Following her advice, I rewrote my letter, discussing the potential for subverting the academic system and launching a critique from the borderlands. I was also explicit about my sexual orientation, my class background, and my activism. Of the six institutions to which I applied, I received offers from four; three included substantial financial aid and tuition waivers.

We must not allow ourselves to be sentenced to doing things the same old way, and we don't have to. We have the ability to make a difference. And the first crucial step is recognizing the privilege of our positions, understanding precisely how our choices can negatively affect those around us. We must understand that lifting others as we climb does not diminish our status or limit our access to resources or tarnish our success.

The honors convocation at MSU represented more than academic achievement for me. As I recognized that gay students possess a viable voice, I came to the culmination of a personal journey. Of course, I was also a nervous wreck. My parents were traveling from my hometown two hours away. And I knew that much of what I had to say directly attacked the institution, both MSU and the education system. I was scared about the reception too. I was placed in line with both the president of the university and the vice president for academic affairs. By the time we reached the stage, I felt completely nauseous. As I was waiting to be introduced, I scanned the audience and located my parents. I walked to the podium with my speech in hand and began: "I suppose a 'typical' or 'normal' sort of student speech for this type of event would involve the definition of success...."

We can manipulate the educational system and use it as a tool to disrupt the status quo and as an instrument of social change. For that to work, we must look for new ways of doing things, and we must all be ready to lift as we climb. Thank you.

I have been deeply moved just a few times in my life. Giving my speech was one of those times. I don't remember hearing the applause as I walked back to my seat. I do remember the president grabbing my arm.

"They're standing for you," he said in a shocked tone. I looked up and saw the faculty standing and applauding. Numbly, I waved and nodded my head. I'm told I was not only the first openly gay student to speak at the honors convocation but that many also thought I was also the first honors student who had anything worthwhile to say. Perhaps my gender, class, and geographical position allowed me to communicate across those boundaries to a fairly homogenous group of people.

My undergraduate experiences represent an enormous struggle: a fight to overcome the label of "white-trash hillbilly faggot" and to reclaim it, as well as resolve my own homophobia. I cannot say that MSU was the optimal environment. The university's upper administration was insensitive and, in some cases, openly hostile to issues of sexuality despite having many gay and lesbian students. Campus activism in marginalized rural areas is further problematized by the lack of understanding from mainstream and urban gay rights groups. I often think that the gay rights movement has remained too urban, white, and middle-class—too homogenous—to deal effectively with the issues most rural gays and lesbians face. As those of us who speak from the margins can attest, we often feel left behind. To us remains the battle of dealing with the isolation, building connections, and carving out lives in areas where difference often results in stigma and sanction. In the words of Audre Lorde, "There's still work to do."[3] And for many of us in rural areas, this work is as basic as the activism that led the drag queens into the streets at Stonewall.

Ultimately, my greatest hurdle was my own homophobia coupled with a dose of class prejudice and personal disdain for Appalachia. I hated those parts of myself that were truly me. Learning how to combat that self-talk was the outstanding, and almost unbelievable, accomplishment of my undergraduate career.

1 Excerpts from Mike Clark's speech "Education and exploitation." In H. Lewis, L. Johnson, and D. Askins, Eds. (1978). *Colonialism in Modern America: The Appalachian Case*. North Carolina: The Appalachian Consortium Press.

2 In Davis, A. (1981). *Women, Race, and Class*. New York: Random House.

3 From "Age, Race, and Class: Women Redefining Difference." (1995). In A. Kesselman, L. McNair, N. Schniedewind, Eds., *Women, Images, and Realities: A Multicultural Anthology*. Mountain View, CA: Mayfield Publishing.

Sisterhood

by Stephanie J. Stillman

Colgate University, New York

Junior Year, Bid Day

As I sat in my room two hours before sorority bids were to be handed out, my heart was racing. More than 200 sophomores and juniors had suffered two weeks of small talk, going from house to house trying to have any conversation with the sisters about topics other than our majors, where we were from, and what we did last summer. *Why the hell am I rushing a sorority?* I thought. Even though I'd visited every house, I wondered if there was a place I could be me and be accepted. I had come out to myself only a year before and shortly afterward had started dating Heather. I remember the two of us walking through the student union one warm fall day.

"Are you still going to rush, Steph?" Heather had asked anxiously.

"I don't know. What does that mean for us? They'd never accept me if they knew who I am. Are you still going to rush?"

"I have to, Steph. Both of my parents were Greeks, and I've always wanted to do it. I don't want to be limited by us. Besides, I'm not sure if I want this to come between us. I know I'm in love with you, but I don't want that to change the other parts of my life."

A few weeks later Heather joined Rho Sigma. We had agreed not to tell anyone about our relationship until we were both more certain about and more comfortable with being gay. We had never been exposed to other students like ourselves, average folks who happened to be gay. As two student leaders, it scared us that our rather high-profile campus lives might be put in jeopardy by coming out. In silence we struggled.

I had spent several nights that year helping Heather get ready for sorority functions. I stood behind her, zipping her short black formal, hoping she wouldn't turn to see the tears in the corners of my eyes. I often watched her walk away on the arm of a young man, wondering why I could not be him. "They aren't ready for a couple like us," Heather had always said. I believed her. And why not, seeing as no other gay couples were heading off to sorority affairs?

After the functions Heather often came back to my dorm room. I'd leave the door unlocked, and she would stumble in late at night and crawl into my arms. I had to swallow the pain as I asked about her night. I wanted to be a part of every aspect of her life.

At 3:30 one morning in the hall bathroom, I stood over Heather in my boxers and T-shirt, holding her head over the toilet as she threw up the numerous drinks she'd consumed. She looked up at me with half-closed eyes and tears on her cheeks. "Steph, I wish you were a Rho Sigma." My heart sank. I could see she also wanted me to be a part of all aspects of her life. But our internalized homophobia and insistence on silence had made it impossible for the time being.

It was now junior year, and Heather was studying in Ecuador for the semester. After the night in the bathroom, I'd decided I was going to rush, even if it meant doing it without Heather. By the time rush arrived, I'd come out to a handful of campus administrators and friends from home. I was feeling nervous and confused about whether to come out to everyone.

After watching many of my friends join Rho Sigma the previous year, and being introduced to the majority of the sisters through Heather, I thought my chances of getting a bid to join were fairly high. If they didn't offer a bid, I would move on without any ties to Greek life. Rho Sigma was the only house I liked out of the four on campus. People seemed real, not your stereotypical blond-hair-and-pearls sorority. Quite a few of the sisters were student leaders, some were athletes, and most seemed genuine and contributed a lot to the Colgate community. Relationships between the members appeared to be based on respect and friendship, and I hoped to be a part of those bonds.

As I sat in my room anticipating the handing out of bids, I wondered if my joining would be good for Heather and me. Would we help each other get dressed for formals only to succumb to our own homophobia and go to dances on the arms of young men? Would we continue trying to fool everyone into believing we weren't seeing each other and fool ourselves that we were OK with hiding our relationship? Only time would tell. The September sun shone into my room, and I collapsed onto the bed. *Is there really a place for me?* I thought. *What am I trying to prove?* I'd have to make a decision soon, but I couldn't shake these hesitations.

I heard a knock on the door, and Amanda, a good friend who was also hoping for a Rho Sigma bid, came in and took a seat at the end of my bed. We tried to make small talk to soothe our butterflies. We talked about how much we disliked the rush process and how we were ready for it to end. My mind kept wandering back to Heather. "You know, I'm still not even sure if this is for me," I said.

"Why not?"

"I don't know. I'm not the sorority type."

"And you think I am?" she smiled.

"It's a lot of money. And is it worth it for only two years?"

She looked at me. "I think it's worth it. Those reasons are sort of small in the grand scheme of things. But you have to decide for yourself. I want you there, though."

The butterflies fluttered even faster. It felt like the right time to tell Amanda the real reason I was so hesitant. "I have to tell you something. I'm not sure because, well..."

"You don't have to tell me."

"I know, but I want to."

"Take all the time you need."

"Guess. No, don't guess," I said. "I think you have an idea anyway. I've never told anyone this."

"It's OK, Steph."

"The reason I'm not sure about joining is because, well, I'm gay."

I felt a sigh of relief. It was out there. I was out there. I had opened up to my first straight friend at Colgate. Whether or not we became sisters, at least she knew the truth.

She hugged me and said, "I'm so glad you felt safe enough to tell me." Then, with a little smile and a laugh, she added, "OK, that might be a valid reason not to pledge."

We had an hour before picking up the bids. Amanda asked a lot of questions about how I knew and about how hard it was to keep it a secret. It felt good to finally be open about my experience and my concerns. I explained that I wasn't sure I could be myself in Rho Sigma and how tired I was of living my life as a lie. The last thing I wanted was another group of people with whom to pretend.

Amanda looked me in the eye. "You have so much to offer the sorority, and they'd be fools not to accept you. You're going to get in. They love you. I think you have to give people the benefit of the doubt."

We met another friend who was also rushing Rho Sigma, and together we walked to the student union. When the big moment finally arrived, the sorority offered all three of us bids. I stood with my rush counselor, and with Amanda's advice in mind I signed my bid card and joined. Give people the benefit of the doubt, I reminded myself. After a year of silence and being bombarded with homophobic comments and heterosexual expectations from family and friends, this simple idea seemed bold.

After the 49 new Rho Sigma sisters signed our bid cards, we gathered at the top of the Willow Path to walk down Broad Street to the house. The rush process was finally complete. Tammy, the president of Rho Sigma, stood on the steps of our small blue house and tried to call some order to the crowd on the lawn. She congratulated us on being selected and expressed how happy the sisters were to have this great new pledge class. She assured us that it would be a fun-filled year. "Now go home and get all your work done for tomorrow," Tammy said. "But be back at the house at 10 tonight dressed in the colors of the pledge group assigned to you." The initial celebration was brief. Pledge period had begun.

Amanda and I walked back to our rooms to finish some last-minute reading for the next day's classes. Along the way she put her arm around my shoulder and said, "I'm happy we're sisters. I want you to know that no matter what happens, I'll always accept you for who you are."

Her words were comforting. But part of me still wondered what the other 113 sisters might think.

Back in my room I called Heather in Ecuador. Our conversation was brief. I told her I had received a bid and that we were finally going to be sisters. She was glad to hear it but said I sounded hesitant. I told her I was but would write more about my thoughts later. "I'm happy for you," she said. "Be careful tonight. And Steph, I love you." Hearing those words felt good.

All of the pledges showed up at the house promptly at 10. We found our leaders and the other eight pledges in our group and headed out for the scavenger hunt, a Rho Sigma tradition. We called ourselves Team Blue and were determined to be the best pledge group in the sorority's history. In each apartment to which we ventured, we found a group of sisters eagerly awaiting our arrival with different tasks for our group. We serenaded some fraternity brothers with a lovely rendition of "You've Lost That Loving Feeling," standing with arms around each others' shoulders in a can-can line; we swooned a young man with our best pick-up line; we did a few pledge push-ups after losing to a group of sisters in a game of *Jeopardy!* where the only category to choose from was Rho Sigma history; and we were "persuaded" by the sisters to share a few beers. In the midst of the madness, we were also trying to learn something about the new friends who were going to be our sisters forever.

In one apartment, six sisters in short black dresses—much like the ones I used to help Heather into before formals—sat across from the eight of us in my group. We got on our knees in two lines in front of the sisters in traditional pledge style. We were all feeling a bit sweaty and tipsy after running from house to house.

Tammy looked at us. "Your tasks are as follows: First, name all of the sisters in front of you; second, give the name of your last hook-up at Colgate."

My heart dropped. Nothing like a little probing of intimate secrets to sober you up quickly. To begin with, I'd never had a one-night stand with anyone at Colgate. The only person I'd ever been intimate with while at school was Heather, and I was fairly sure that wasn't the name the sisters or my group were expecting to hear. My mind raced to come up with a name. It couldn't be a friend who might hear about our supposed "hook-up." It couldn't be anyone someone in the room might know. My stomach churned. Time was running out. It was my turn.

"My name, Stephanie Stillman. My last hook-up, Mike Borderland." My palms were cold with sweat. Some guy named Mike did pursue me freshman year, but the last name was a combination of names from friends of the past. I lied, blatantly, to my new sisters. In uttering a name, I had laid a sledgehammer to the foundations of any supposed honesty and trust among the sisters in that room. As I knelt on the floor, the fun of the night ended for me in one fell swoop. My mood had gone from joyful celebration to bitterness. I had known this would happen eventually. I also knew it wouldn't be the last time I would be asked whom I'd been dating and feel I had to hide the truth.

Each of the six scavenger-hunt teams and all of the sisters crammed back into the Rho Sigma house on Broad Street. Having had a few beers, the pledges and sisters made a lively group. We hugged one another with laughter and joy, thankful we had made it through rush and had become legitimate pledges. But I was still recovering from the line of questioning at the last house.

Megan, the rush chair, made her way through the crowd and onto the couch, and suggested we end the night with a traditional Rho Sigma toast and song. We raised our glasses and recited in unison, "Here's to the men we love, and here's to the men who love us." What had I gotten myself into? We finished the night singing an old Rho Sigma song at the top of our lungs. "Take your man around the corner, when the lights are low. Put your arm around his shoulder and the other down below." I felt myself singing the words, my arm around Amanda on one side and a new pledge sister on the other. I remember smiling until my cheeks hurt and feeling the cage tighten around my heart until that hurt even more. I wasn't in love with any man and had no desire to take one around the corner. I wasn't quietly living a lie; I was shouting it from the mountaintops. Benefit of the doubt. This was going to be a lot harder than I thought.

Commitment Night

I would be lying if I said I never thought about quitting. Thoughts of depledging ran through my head that first night walking home from the house. Between a genuine like for the sisters and a relentless stubbornness to make a place for Heather and me in that environment, I hung on to my commitment to the sisterhood.

When pledge period ended, I took off the pledge pin that had felt like a brand for the last month. There would be no more date parties where I'd have to find some male to drag to the bar on an hour's notice. There would be no more songs sung to fraternity men. There would be no more Rho Sigma history memorization. I was accepted. I was an official Rho Sigma, and that night all 49 pledges celebrated our acceptance with toast after toast at the local bar. I thought pretending might not be as essential now. If they liked me enough to accept me and initiate me, I thought, what difference does it make if I'm gay? It's still the same me.

Retreat Weekend

The entire sisterhood packed into the house for dinner. We were supposed to be in the Adirondacks for a retreat, but 2 feet of snow had fallen throughout the November day, so we were confined to our little hamlet of

Hamilton. It was a Friday evening, and the *Maroon News*, our student paper, was about to land on the doorstep with the latest on a decision to suspend a Colgate fraternity for hazing. When the papers hit the porch steps, a half-dozen sisters ran out to pick them up and bring them to the others eagerly waiting inside. But I wasn't quite as eager. In addition to articles about the decision to suspend the fraternity, the commentary section also featured an article titled "Issues of Diversity Still Need Addressing." The article commented on the need for everyone to take a stand against homophobia because it affects everyone. "Our professors, neighbors, and even our closest friends are increasingly feeling comfortable coming out of the closet," the article read. The article was mine.

With adrenaline pumping through every capillary, I watched my sisters turn to the commentary section and begin reading. I didn't say I was gay in the article, but from the context you'd have been a fool not to figure it out. Not many straight people wrote articles calling for the acceptance of LGBT students. *They will undoubtedly see my article*, I thought. *What will they think? That's it, I'm out. I wonder if anyone already knows? Does anyone already know? How do my friends feel about me now?*

No one said anything right away. The news on the suspension took first priority. We finished our dinner and talked into the late hours of the cold and snowy night.

As the house began to empty, Tammy approached. "I loved your article."

I replied with a rather dumbfounded, "Thanks."

Lauren and Jen, two other house officers, also stopped me before I pulled on my jacket to head out. "Nice article," Jen said.

Lauren added, "I agree with what you said."

I was shocked. Part of me had been hoping they would bypass the article. Another part wanted them to read it and discover I was gay so I wouldn't have to pretend anymore.

Throughout the fall I had come out to more and more individuals across campus and had become fairly active in Advocates and the LGBTA, two student groups. I had attended a semi-annual diversity training weekend for students with a variety of backgrounds and interests, where I came out to 32 students and a handful of faculty members. While Heather and I struggled with our long-distance relationship and our fears about being honest with others, I was growing increasingly comfortable being out to many people on campus.

But Rho Sigma was in many ways the last hurdle to putting the truth into every aspect of my life at Colgate. While I could write an article for the paper, I couldn't tell my sisters the truth face to face.

LGBT Awareness Week

"Are you sure you don't want to sit on the panel?" Dan, a good friend and head of Advocates, asked.

"I can't."

"What's holding you back? Almost everyone on campus knows about you."

"I know, except for some of my sorority sisters, who also happen to work in the women's studies center, where the panel discussion is being held."

I'd been running around campus with an overbooked schedule and an overextended emotional state all week. I'd gone to the coming-out panel discussion the year before and felt frustrated about the representation. Here we were on this small liberal arts campus full of fairly well-to-do young adults with clean haircuts, J. Crew sweaters, and new Pathfinders in the campus parking lot. But the only people who spoke on the panel were the most radical avengers on campus. I couldn't relate to those who spoke. I didn't have tattoos, radical political views, or a horrific story of my parents' rejection of my being gay. What I'd hoped to see was someone in my situation with a personality much like my own.

This year I was offered the opportunity to balance out the representation on the panel. But I didn't feel ready. Instead, I sat in the audience of about 20 and tried to support friends on the panel as they shared their lives with us. After the six students spoke, the meeting opened up for questions. People asked how the LGBT students came to know about their sexuality and what they thought about marriage, children, and religion. The answers were almost routine from the students who'd been asked those same questions many times before. Then one of my sorority sisters, Anne, spoke from the back of the room.

"Do you think there's a place for gays and lesbians in fraternities and sororities?"

I felt every eye in the room turn to me, but I couldn't speak. Maybe I didn't want to reveal myself (even though I'm fairly sure everyone in the room knew I was gay). Maybe I didn't want to give the wrong answer to her question. Maybe I wasn't convinced the answer was yes. I remained silent, and Dan gave words to many of my thoughts we had discussed previously. He explained that there should be a place for gays, lesbians, and bisexual students in sororities and fraternities. Just like any organization, there is no reason why they shouldn't be there. He also spoke of the quiet struggles many gay and lesbian students undergo in the Greek system. "It's the subtle heterosexual assumptions that make it the most difficult for them to survive there," he said.

It was hard to sit with my own vulnerability and fear of exposure, watching my peers take up the slack for me when, unlike me, they didn't have the first-hand experience of being gay in the Greek system. After the question period ended, I nervously approached Anne. "Thanks for your question. It needed to be asked."

"I agree. No one talks about it."

"So true. I mean, well, you know, I'm gay."

"No, really?" she said with a touch of sarcasm.

We both laughed. "Yeah, and it's hard. People assume so many things."

"I know," Anne said. "A group of us were sitting around talking about it the other night and about how painful it used to be to watch you and Heather. We all knew."

"That's what a lot of people have been telling me."

"It really is a compliment to our house. I know it's hard, and because you want to stick through it says a lot about what we stand for and the strength of the friendships in the house. I mean, we encourage diversity and brag that we're the house that holds the most of it. But among us we have a whole gamut of diversity that we don't even recognize, let alone appreciate."

"That's exactly what I think."

"People really are OK with it. And for those who aren't, they need to be. Your sexuality doesn't make a difference. And people need to know that."

I could hardly believe what she was saying. I felt like weeping tears of joy, relieved knowing that a member of the house was so supportive of an issue that I'd been racking my brain about for the last year and a half.

Anne continued, "But people need to hear it from you. I can stand up at our meetings and say something, but it doesn't mean much because people see it as Anne trying to be politically correct again. But from you, it's your life and your experiences, and people will listen."

We talked about things we could do to help educate our Rho Sigma sisters. Unfortunately, Thanksgiving quickly followed, and in the scramble of finals we didn't have the chance to address the issue through LGBT diversity training for the sorority. A week afterward we went to the Rho Sigma winter formal. I took a male friend who knows about my sexuality and kindly served as my date-in-waiting until I was courageous enough to bring my real date. I spent most of the night talking with Anne and others who introduced me to their dates with, "This is Steph. I love this girl!" Not only was it good for the ego, but it also renewed my hope in others' willingness to look past stereotypes and see people for who they are. I spent the entire night telling friends I would bring Heather to our next formal. They all said they couldn't think of anything that would make them happier.

Today

Nearly everyone knows I'm gay. My sisters have adjusted most of their comments to be more inclusive, especially when talking to me. After a year of being in different countries, Heather and I finally attended our first formal together the spring of our junior year. I think our presence in the sorority has made a lot of people look at themselves and their assumptions, along with what we value in our sisterhood. If a sorority is based on the bonds of leadership, trust, service, and friendship, then there is undoubtedly a place for anyone who is either questioning or sure about their homosexuality. In assuming there is no place for gays and lesbians in the Greek system, one not only pins homosexuality as deviant, but also assumes sororities and fraternities are only social clubs for meeting members of the opposite sex. They are so much more than that. But it takes risk to see that. It takes the willingness to be out. It takes the courage to both ask and answer tough questions. And most of all, it takes trust and hope in the good of the human spirit to give those near us the benefit of the doubt.

A Deep, Sad Sorrow

by Carlos Manuel*
Santa Clara University, California

Sitting under my favorite palm tree, I welcome the clear morning and soak myself in the bright sun. It's only 11:30, and the strong sun has warmed the day. Water slowly trickles from the fountains, and the gentle breeze makes the palm trees and bushes steadily rock. It's only the second week of classes, and already I know I've made the right decision to transfer to Santa Clara University from Sacramento State, where I spent my first college year. Instead of 30,000 students, which made me feel lost, there are only 5,000. And the gardens and rose bushes remind me of my home back in Mexico. I feel comfortable here.

I also like my academic department. Today, while the dean conducts the first departmental meeting, I learn there are only 150 students. With those numbers, I know it will be easy to meet everyone and to avoid anyone. After the meeting I mingle with students and teachers.

"Hi, I'm Mike*," someone holding a glass of punch says to me.

"Carlos. Nice meeting you." I shake hands with the handsome guy.

"Everyone seems so nice around here."

A guy wearing bell bottoms and a long-sleeved blouse approaches us. He also has on a few necklaces and rings that reflect the pale lighting of the meeting hall. "Hello, strangers. I'm Richard," he says. His black hair rests on his shoulders, and his platform shoes give him a height that makes me look tiny. He makes me feel uncomfortable, but Mike and I introduce ourselves.

"Nice meeting you," Richard says, extending his hand. "It looks like I'm the only one around here who likes the '70s look." Richard's body language is as fluent as his speech. Every time he speaks, his hands fill the air as if he's trying to draw something.

"Anyone care for punch?" Mike asks.

"Why sure. You'll be kind enough to bring me some, won't you, darling?" Richard flirts with a smile.

"Sure. You want some, Carlos?"

"No, thanks," I say, a little uncomfortable to find myself next to Richard. Mike walks away quickly.

"He's cute, isn't he?" Richard whispers close to my ear.

I'm taken by surprise. "Excuse me?"

"I said he's a handsome guy." He smiles now.

"I...I don't..."

"Oh, come on. You don't have to pretend with me. I can smell my own kind a mile away."

I'm suddenly scared. "I'm sorry. I don't know what you're talking about."

"Sure you do. But if you want to pretend, it's your choice."

"Here's your punch," Mike interrupts.

"Thanks, but I'm allergic to imitation flavors," Richard says, looking at me. "Give it to Carlos. He needs something to drink before passing out." And with that remark, he leaves.

"What was that about?" Mike asks, handing me the punch.

"I don't know." I avoid Mike's look. My hands are shaking, and my legs feel like Jell-O. I take a quick sip of punch and choke. I start to cough as my face turns red. I say good-bye to Mike, leave the meeting, and run to my room. I want to be as far from Richard as possible. I want to be alone. I want to think about what happened, about how Richard has figured it out. I run as fast as I can, open the door to my building, push the elevator button, and wait. I take a long breath. I'm sweating. My stomach hurts; I feel chills. I go to the bathroom and throw up. I go to bed, and in a few minutes I fall into a deep sleep.

✳   ✳   ✳

Until Richard, I have had no confrontations with anyone in college concerning my homosexuality. Until Richard, I'd thought no one could tell I was gay by looking at me. With a height of 5 feet 7 inches, a broad chest and back, strong legs and arms, Latino features, and a background in swimming, weight lifting, running, soccer, and gymnastics, who could possibly think I'm a homosexual? Besides, I'm careful—actually more afraid and ashamed—about expressing my feelings or sharing my ideologies with anyone around me.

The personal agony and the loneliness I felt throughout my first college year were almost unbearable, and such feelings are still with me. Never mind that I had moved to the United States from Mexico during my high school years and couldn't speak English. Never mind that I had to struggle through two years of high school barely understanding what the teachers said or that I had to adjust to a new way of living, of looking at things, and behaving, since cultural and familial customs in the U.S. are quite different from those in Mexico. None of that compares with the emotional and spiritual struggle of accepting that I'm gay.

I learned in Catholic school that homosexuals are not welcome in the kingdom of God. I now ask God why he allows me to feel sexual attraction for other men? My mother expects me to raise a family, but how can I do such a thing if I have a desire to sleep with a man? My feelings are strong, but I don't know how to accept or understand them. I stare at the mirror every day. I cry in the shower at night. And while in bed I hug my pillow because I'm lonely. My painful silence is like a double-edged knife, a knife that slowly rips my heart and soul.

✳ ✳ ✳

Two days after the encounter with Richard, my body trembles at the mere thought of it. I'm not sure how I'm going to feel being around him now that I learned he and I are in our theater department's tap-dance musical, *The Boyfriend*. I can't believe we're going to be working together. I just talked to the dean of students and asked him to remove me from the show. He said it's not possible. "You have to do the show," he said. "There's no alternative for new students, unless you're sick." I wish I could tell him I'm sick emotionally.

✳ ✳ ✳

I'm having a hard time being around Richard. I'm scared of him, afraid he's going to let everyone know about me. I'm afraid I'll be associated with him. Fortunately, I'm befriending a freshman business major, Landon, who's also in the play. We spend a lot of time together during and after rehearsals. We eat lunch together almost every day and help each other with our homework. These are good things, since they keep me busy and away from Richard.

One thing I don't like is that I'm too busy making fun of Richard and his "homo" attitude. Landon is homophobic and likes to make remarks about Richard's mannerisms. I pretend to like making fun of "those fags," as Landon calls them. He enjoys having fun at the expense of others. And I, a coward, pretend to like the way he imitates Richard's walk or high-pitched voice. I'm ashamed of myself; in truth, Landon is making fun of me. I don't have a high-pitched voice, nor do I walk funny. But Landon thinks all homosexuals are like Richard.

By the third week of rehearsal, Landon and I are close friends. He and I spend most of our time together. We go to the gym, study, and eat together whenever possible. But he still doesn't know much about my private life or the emotional struggle I have concerning my homosexuality. I'm careful not to mix my private life with my school life. Richard, on the other hand, is trying to be my friend, but I keep pushing him away since I'm still uncomfortable around him. He's almost become my enemy, and I can't blame him. I'm starting to understand more about my homosexuality. I've spent some time reading about it, and the subject has come up in some of my classes. I've heard people talking about it outside of class too. Surprisingly enough, they seemed to look at homosexuality as something natural and as part of humanity. I need to talk to someone. I wish I could talk to Richard. Unfortunately, since I've been ignoring him, there's too much animosity between us.

❋　❋　❋

After five weeks of rehearsals and 14 performances, the last night of the show arrives and, with it, the cast party. The house is packed with students: cast, crew, friends, and fraternity and sorority members I've never seen before. Landon and I each carry a bottle of champagne. I feel strange having such a "close" relationship with Landon, knowing he doesn't know much about the real me.

"This is my buddy, Carlos," Landon says to a group of people.

My left arm is over and around his shoulder. "And this is my buddy, Landon," I say with the same exciting tone of voice he used.

"Cheers!" someone says.

"Cheers!" someone repeats, raising a glass of champagne that spills all over.

"To my buddy, Carlos. For without him, I would've never learned that tap combination," Landon exclaims.

"And to all of you and our true selves," a familiar but frightening voice says.

Everyone looks around, and there, close to our circle of friends, Richard stands dressed in yet another outrageous outfit.

Landon turns to me and whispers in my ear. "Great! ABBA's faggot child has arrived."

I look at Landon and say nothing. I'm too shocked, too scared, too frightened to even move from where I'm standing.

"Well, do I get a glass of champagne or what?" Richard asks. "Carlos, would you give me some, please?"

I'm speechless. The alcohol is affecting me faster than anticipated. I don't know what to do. "Get your own, fag. This is mine," I say to my surprise as I walk away from everyone. Landon laughs and comes after me. He whispers something in my ear and laughs. I laugh too, even though I didn't understand a word he said.

The DJ music plays loudly in the backyard; people freely dance to its rhythm. I feel like dancing but don't want to ask anyone, so I dance by myself, trying to drown my feelings in the noise. I don't want to think about anything or deal with my emotions here and now. By 1 A.M. I'm so tired I decide to leave the party. I walk back in the house and see Landon talking to some guys. He looks at me angrily; maybe the alcohol has gone to his head. I say good-bye to Landon, but as I hug him I feel a certain coldness. His eyes look distant and his face a bit angry. I feel uneasy. Things are not quite right.

The next day, while the cast and crew take down the set, I try to talk to Landon, but he refuses. I'm not sure what the problem is until someone tells me Landon is angry because he's heard that I'm gay and that I'm his friend only because I'm interested in him. I don't know how to react. I feel like I'm going to faint. Someone else knows I'm gay. The news is shocking. My body trembles, my hands sweat, my face turns red. I feel I'm standing alone, yet the theater is filled with people. I feel like I'm standing in the middle of a silent black hole, yet the whole place is full of loud noises. I feel my legs are about to give up on me; I try to move, but my body does not respond. I look around and feel everyone's eyes upon me, as if I am being accused.

Finally, I'm able to take control of myself. I promise to find the person responsible for the accusation. I want to talk to Landon, but I know this is neither the right time nor place. I decide to wait until later in the day.

That afternoon I knock on his door. At first no one answers; I knock again. Landon opens the door a few seconds after and motions for me to come inside.

"Hi," I say.

"Hey."

"What's going on?"

"Nothing much," he answers, not looking at me.

I can sense his anger and uneasiness. "I called you twice this afternoon."

"I was busy."

"Hey," I try to touch him, "what's going on?"

"Don't!" he shouts, backing away. "Don't touch me, please." His voice has become agitated, and his tone sounds angry and hurt.

"Then tell me what's going on...please."

"You know what it is. You...you lied to me. You pretended to be my friend, and all you are is a manipulator and a liar trying to get me into bed."

My hands shake. I can hardly speak. "That's not true, and you know it."

"Look," this time he looks right at me, "all I know is that you lied, and you're just like Richard. You're a fag, and I don't trust you."

"But..."

"And I don't want to be your friend anymore." With those words he leaves me standing in the middle of his room. I feel numb, and my legs start to give out. I try to gain some strength as I watch my friend walk away.

※　※　※

Two days pass, and I manage to keep myself from everyone. I need time to myself, time to think and come to terms with my own struggle and fear. I need to take control of my life, to be strong and accept myself as I am. I'm pretty sure that by now more people know I'm gay. The idea terrifies me. I don't want to be known as another "faggot" at our university.

✳ ✳ ✳

About one and a half weeks later, Landon calls me wanting to apologize for his behavior.

"How are you?" he asks.

At first I don't know what to say, but calmly I answer, "Fine, and you?"

"OK."

Silence.

"Hey...I'm sorry about the other day."

"So am I," I say.

"I don't know what I was thinking. I was upset because I felt like a fool...I...I..."

"I felt like a fool too, you know," I interrupt. "After all, I was accused of something I didn't do."

Landon says nothing. The awkwardness between us can be felt even through the phone lines.

"Carlos, I think it is a good idea if we talk. What do you think of going out to dinner?" he asks.

"Uh..."

"Afterward, we can play video games with the other guys."

We have not spoken to each other for more than a week, and suddenly he calls to invite me out. I find that odd. I wonder what has made him change his mind. I don't feel good about this whole situation. I know dinner will be awkward. After all, the last words I heard from him before he called were, "I don't want to be your friend anymore." Still, I accept.

I meet Landon and his friends at the cafeteria. At first we hardly say anything to each other. But as time passes, we speak a little more about what we've been doing. I'm not enjoying dinner; all I'm thinking is how to explain myself to Landon and how to let him know I never had a sexual interest in him. But this is not possible since all his friends are sitting with us. Chris, Landon's roommate, sits next to Landon and Juan. Both wear baseball uniforms; they're part of the university's team. Joe and a friend of his sit next to me. It's strange having dinner with this group of people, some of whom I have never met before. No one is saying much. We talk about finals coming up and about whatever event happened the night before. Landon and I say little to each other. Once in a while he looks at me and smiles. But I don't see any sincerity in his eyes. I have a bad feeling in my gut.

I try to excuse myself, but Landon and his friends insist I go up to their rooms and play this new video game. "Just like old times," one of them says. Old times? *I've hardly had any old times with any of you,* I say to myself. Nonetheless, they are persuasive, so I accept. We play for a few hours, and I notice how once in a while Landon and his friends eye each other. I feel a strange sense of discomfort, and my gut feeling still tells me things are not what they appear to be.

I say good-bye to Landon and his friends around 2 in the morning. I walk through the university's gardens, full of rose bushes, vines, and fountains, toward my room on the other side of campus. A lonely soul sits on one of the benches, and a quiet couple slowly strolls through the gardens. With my hands in my pockets, I admire the clear black sky with its multitude of shiny stars. Far away, I hear laughing. Close by, I hear some people running. I'm already halfway through the gardens when someone appears in front of me.

"Do you have a light?"

"Sorry, I don't smoke," I answer, continuing on my way home.

"That's too bad." Suddenly he grabs me by my jacket.

I push him away but don't realize someone else is approaching me from behind. A third person jumps out of nowhere and punches me in the stomach.

"Faggot!" one says.

"So, you like to get it up the ass, eh?" another exclaims.

I kick one of them, but a fourth body appears and punches me in the nose. The blow is so forceful and sudden that I feel dizzy. Immediately after, I feel a third blow on my back; someone has kicked me so hard I feel as if my spine has been broken in two. A fourth blow lands directly on my right eye. The pain is so sharp I know I'm starting to bleed. I'm kicked in the stomach so hard that the air is sucked out of me. Soon I'm on the ground, curled into a fetal position, trying to cover whatever I can of my body.

"Faggot!" someone yells as I'm kicked in the ear.

Another blow to my stomach. "Take this, cocksucker!"

There's not much I can do. Between the kicks and the blows, I hear familiar voices calling me "faggot!" I struggle to see who it is, but it is dark, and the blood has almost made it impossible for me to open my eyes. The voices laugh at me and call me names. I slowly fall unconscious.

＊　＊　＊

When I open my eyes I find myself in an unfamiliar room. My body aches, and my head hurts. Everything around me is blurry. When I'm able to see clearly, I notice my roommate, John. John's girlfriend, Gina; Richard; and my resident adviser, Maggie, are also standing around.

"What's going on?" I mumble.

John looks at me and smiles. Gina simply holds my hand.

"Hey, what's going on?" I ask again.

"Do you recognize this hat?" my RA asks. In her hand, she holds a burgundy hat with the initials SCU in white.

"No."

"It belonged to one of the people who beat you up," John says.

"I'm sorry. I don't remember."

"Do you remember anything at all?" Richard asks.

I don't understand why he's here and why he's asking me questions. I feel dizzy and confused. "I…sorry…what happened? I don't…"

"You were attacked," Gina says. "Don't you remember?"

"I found you in the middle of the garden, next to the big fountain," Richard explains.

A few images rush through my mind. I panic all of the sudden. I feel like screaming, but instead I sigh deeply, and a stream of tears starts to run down my face.

"That's OK, buddy," John says, placing his right hand on my left shoulder. "Good thing Richard found you."

I turn to look at Richard and notice he's sobbing. I'm touched by his reaction.

"Are you sure you don't remember this hat?" my RA asks again.

I shake my head to let her know I don't remember, perhaps to let myself know I don't want to remember.

About an hour later the doctor comes in and asks everyone to give us some time alone. "Feeling better?" he asks.

"I guess."

"What happened to you, Carlos?"

I say nothing.

"You don't have to tell me anything. You don't have to say anything at all. But it sure will help those involved get what they deserve." The doctor's eyes are locked on mine.

"Am I going to be OK?" I ask, not paying attention to his comment.

"You will. It'll take awhile before you can see more clearly. Your right eye is pretty damaged, and you have bruises all over your body. But we'll discuss this later." He looks at his clipboard.

I start crying again. I feel an unexplainable fear.

"Don't worry; you'll be fine. Take it easy. Not a lot of movement and no dancing for a long time."

I feel at ease once I hear what he says. He crosses to the door and lets everyone back in. "Now, if you remember anything at all, let us know. It would help us a lot."

John and Gina help me out to John's truck. We drive in silence. Richard sits next to me crying. I reach out and grab his hand. I guess there is a common understanding and fear between us. I think he feels sorry for me and perhaps lucky he wasn't the one. I wonder if he has any idea who bashed me. As soon as I'm in my room, Richard says good-bye. I lie down and fall asleep listening to John and Gina whisper in the distance.

Three hours later I wake up with a strong headache. The news about the beating has gone around campus, and friends, teachers, and even administrators call all day. Later in the day my RA comes in and asks a few questions. She needs to file an incident/accident report. She shows me the hat once again and asks if I recognize it. I don't.

Landon hasn't called at all, which I find odd; I give him a ring. On the fourth ring I remember the hat. One of his friends playing video games wore it. I remember why the voices sounded familiar. The discovery shocks me and gives me the chills. I hang up the phone right away. My discovery makes me realize the truth: Landon and his friends are responsible for the beating. I feel like the air has been knocked out of me. I can't move. I can't breathe. I start to cry.

A couple of days later, John takes me to the hospital for a check-up.

"You're a lucky guy, Carlos," the doctor says. "Those guys could have caused permanent damage. They broke the bone under your right eyebrow and broke your nose. But your wounds are healing with no problem."

I sigh but say nothing.

"They also gave you two deep cuts: one down and across your right nostril and the other one under your right eye. You're lucky you can even see," he says as he removes my bandages. My body is still in pain, and the bruises are pretty visible. "But don't worry. With time and treatment you won't have any scars on your face. Only the emotional scars will be permanent, if you let them, that is."

* * *

The year goes on with me trying to pick up the pieces of my shattered life. I never admit who has done such an atrocity to my face and body. I guess I'm ashamed, afraid, or feel guilty. I'm not sure what the reason is, but I don't reveal the names of those who hurt me. I never hear from Landon either, but I do find out it was Richard who had told him about my homosexuality the night of the party, with the intention of breaking my friendship with Landon. And even though Richard got in the way of a possibly good friendship, I don't hate him. He has repented and confessed how much he disliked me for being friends with Landon, since he had a crush on him. Richard has also confessed that he feels somehow responsible for what has happened to me. I let him know not to worry. The past is in the past, and now a new life starts. He tells me he knows who beat me up but has said nothing because he knows I'm not saying anything to anyone. He respects my decision, and I grow to respect him.

* * *

By the time my junior year starts, the scars on my face are barely noticeable. I care about how I feel more than how I look, so I become a member of a spiritual group. It isn't a religious organization but a group that focuses on the inner self as the means to improve personal attitude and behaviors. I'm also an indirect member of the Gay and Lesbian Association (GALA) in our school, with the purpose of learning more about homosexual life. And I keep myself occupied as well as motivated to understand my own life. I become more comfortable and more secure with my feelings. I start to understand being sexually attracted toward someone of the same sex is neither immoral nor sinful. It is natural, it is beautiful, and most of all it is something that has happened to many men and women for many years.

I take advantage of any group, organization, or activity that offers workshops in positive personal growth. I'm also thinking of joining a student group led by the associate dean that plans freshman orientations and activity workshops. I'm slowly overcoming the fear and the shame of being known as a homosexual.

By the end of my junior year, most of my friends on campus know about my homosexuality and support my coming out. Still, I feel a strong sense of fear and a deep, sad sorrow inside, something I can't put my hands on.

The summer following my junior year seems to be going well until Miguel, a friend, asks if I am "out of the closet." I answer yes. He also asks if I've come out to my family. I answer no.

"Well," he says, "you're not truly out of the closet and accepting of your homosexuality until your family knows."

Whether or not he is right, his words bring a devastating feeling, since I know I face a stronger challenge: coming out to my family, something I'd ignored until now. At the same time his words help me eliminate the fear and the sorrow I still carry around. I realize I'm afraid and ashamed to tell my family—afraid because I love them too much and don't want them to hate me, ashamed because they look up to me, and I feel they're going to be disappointed. But even with those thoughts, I decide to take the final step.

A month after Miguel and I talk, I gather my mamá, sister, and two brothers at my mamá's house. As I tell them about my homosexual feelings, I'm scared and anxious. At the same time, I feel happy and relieved. There are the usual tears and the usual questions. My younger brother wants to know if I'm sick. My sister asks if someone has emotionally hurt me. My mamá asks if I'm going to dress in women's clothes. My other brother asks how long I've known. Surprisingly enough, no one mentions anything about God, moral issues, or my grandparents. I answer each question as quickly as possible and explain that I'm still the same person; I dress and behave the same; finishing school is still my number one priority; my life goes on as it did before. After a few hours of talking and trying to explain myself as clearly and sincerely as possible, my family gives me their support. And with their support, I gain the confidence and strength I need to become a happier person. Suddenly, after my family's acceptance, I feel liberated and confident to be out wherever I am and to whomever I'm around. I suddenly feel more secure and more comfortable with my sexuality.

＊　＊　＊

My senior year is my best college year. I come out to new students at a social issues presentation during freshman orientation. I participate in panels, conferences, and workshops. I try to help students understand their struggles and feelings by speaking of my experiences as a closeted homosexual. I attend seminars and speak on behalf of gay men and lesbians. I even write in the college paper about sexuality issues. At last, graduation arrives, and I can hardly write how emotional I feel. A knot builds in my throat. I'm proud to be the first openly gay Latino student at this university to graduate with honors.

I am happy. I am proud. I am strong.

* The names in this story have been changed to protect the innocent—and the guilty one.

Competitive College

by Ruth Wielgosz

Bryn Mawr College, Pennsylvania

In my last semester of high school, I took an auto-mechanics-for-guys-who-want-to-mess-around-with-cars class. One day before class I was chatting with one of the guys.

"Where are you going to college?" he asked.

"Bryn Mawr."

"Isn't that a girls' school?"

"Yes," I replied, not wanting to get into the debate over "women's college" terminology.

"What are you, some kind of lesbian?"

He would have taken any answer as a defensive denial, so I ignored the question. Later I thought of the perfect reply: "What are you, some kind of bigot?"

Some people think of Bryn Mawr as a lesbian paradise. That's not why I went there. After six years in a typical suburban public school system outside Washington, D.C., I longed to be in an environment where it was socially acceptable to be excited about learning and to support women's rights. Fondly recalling my all-girls elementary school in London, I had long ago decided to attend a women's college. Near the end of tenth grade, I went to the library to research my options. My other criteria (academically rigorous, liberal arts-based, politically progressive, and not too near or far from home) narrowed my choices considerably. Fortunately, the description of Bryn Mawr in the *Insider's Guide to Colleges* sounded perfect, and my research ended almost as soon as it had begun.

When I arrived at Bryn Mawr in the sticky heat of August, I was shocked to discover it wasn't an intellectual, social, and political utopia.

The other students displayed disconcerting similarities to society at large, even including some (gasp) Republicans and women who had enrolled despite it being a women's college rather than because of it. Still, Bryn Mawr was a huge improvement on my high school. At last I'd found a place where my values were mainstream and I was a social success: "Oh, cool! A freshman who doesn't shave!" was not a reaction I'd experienced before. Students all referred to each other as "women," never as "girls." The vast majority of them were fiercely proud to be liberals, feminists, and intelligent. Furthermore, our freshman orientation included a student-run workshop on sexual orientation issues.

Cross-registration with neighboring Haverford College and having the convenient free Blue Bus running between the campuses meant twice the selection in courses and entertainment and the opportunity to meet men if one desired (not that I particularly wanted to); *I already have a boyfriend*, I thought smugly. Also, under the honor code, professors assumed students were honest—what a refreshing change! Students never discussed grades with each other, maintaining an ethos of "we're all smart women here" egalitarianism, although this sometimes deteriorated into elitism and class prejudice. Academics were tougher than in high school but much more enjoyable, since students were actually interested in learning. I loved my sociology class above all and decided to major in the subject.

In many ways Bryn Mawr exceeded my expectations by introducing me to things I'd never known existed but could never again bear to live without: E-mail, *Dykes to Watch Out For* (which appeared in Bryn Mawr's *College News: A Feminist Newsjournal*), and bra dances. I gained the opportunity to meet people from groups that had been underrepresented in my high school, like Baha'is, pagans, Texans, South Asians, and middle-class black women.

It was probably that year that I learned the term "Big Dyke on Campus," usually abbreviated to BDOC, a take-off on "Big Man on Campus." Both imply someone important, well-known (at their own college), socially powerful, and possibly intimidating. I also learned the standard Bryn Mawr usage of "dyke" to refer to both lesbians and bi women (analogous to "queer").

Halfway through the year many people observing me would probably have had a strong gaydar alert, my satisfaction with my boyfriend notwithstanding. After all, I did not hide my enthusiasm for 1) feminism;

2) refusing to shave for political reasons; 3) queer rights; 4) *Dykes to Watch Out For*; 5) socializing mainly with women; and 6) taking my shirt off at dances. I didn't, however—and still don't—consider any of these inconsistent with heterosexuality.

Nonetheless, I was racking my brain over the question "Am I bisexual?" I knew I definitely liked guys; based on my experiences with my boyfriend, that was not in question. Sure, I had danced with a girl at prom and liked it, but that wasn't enough to go on. I didn't know if I would like sex with a woman, even though I was willing to try it. But did this constitute the basis for an identity? All those "guide to adolescence" pamphlets said you could be straight even if you had homosexual thoughts or experiences. Anyway, I didn't feel queer; I felt like the same person I'd always been. But I needed some proof before I could believe I was bi, and I was certain dykes would expect it before they would accept me. Eventually, though, near the end of the year I decided, "I definitely want to have sex with a woman. Therefore I must be bisexual." There was no need for any more "proof" than the feelings I'd always had, and those pamphlets were full of shit. I broke up with my boyfriend that summer, but it had nothing to do with coming out.

Q. What do you call it when a Bryn Mawr student comes out?
A. Her sophomore year.

This joke haunted me for most of my second year at Bryn Mawr. I knew I was bi now, but I couldn't tell anyone because I still couldn't prove it to them. If I came out now, people would think I was a pathetic stereotype or trying to be trendy. It helped that I started making my first BDOC friend, Deb. She was a freshman, but she had already been out as bi for years. She often wore this totally cool jean jacket with loads of political buttons and always dressed in a sexy, sassy way. She had so much attitude that when she had visited as a prospective student, people had mistaken her for an unattainable upperclasswoman. Although she didn't realize it, Deb was a kind of queerness mentor for me.

She was involved in Bi-Space, a bisexual discussion and support group, which was started that year by a couple of Mawrters in reaction to the insensitivity of a couple of gay Haverford men who were running BGALA (Bisexual, Gay, and Lesbian Alliance, a bi-college organization). The rift was my first inkling that all was not perfect harmony between gay and bi students. Later I heard about a chem major who thought dildos were patriarchal (no doubt she disapproved of sex with live penises too) and a lesbian hallmate who had a policy of not dating bi women. In general, though, the atmosphere was harmonious at Bryn Mawr, not least because more than half the out dykes were bi, so excluding us just wasn't possible. In fact, Bi-Space existed only for a year or two, as if the need for it evaporated when the BGALA heads graduated. But student turnover could easily change the atmosphere again.

Second semester, I had the amazing insight that I would increase my chances of getting together with a woman if people knew I was available. So I started coming out, gradually at first, but it was so easy that it became almost automatic. Near the end of the year, I went home for the weekend to go to the 1993 March on Washington and ended up coming out to my mother (I had forgotten she didn't know what had been going on in my mind). I took the Metro downtown and actually managed to find Deb and the Bi-Space contingent in the crowd. Marching with them and the rest of the massive crowd was exhilarating. Not only did I no longer have any doubt that I felt queer but I also felt as if I belonged in the queer community. I never did join Bi-Space or any other queer organization because my friendships gave me all the social support I needed.

By junior year I was pretty desperate to get laid (it had been over a year!), preferably by a woman. I finally seduced one in February. Despite my beliefs about the nature of sexual identity ("Bisexuality is all about potential, not just who you sleep with" was how Deb put it), I couldn't help feeling I had finally proved myself a dyke. At the end of the year, I felt absolutely no diffidence about signing up to do one of the presentations on sexual orientation for next year's freshwomen.

It was exhilarating to return as a senior. I had gained expertise on getting the best out of campus life and accordingly had chosen to live in a centrally located dorm with most of my friends. I had a kick-ass three-room suite and a roommate, chosen for her air of calm, who soon became a good friend.

One afternoon that spring Deb came into my room to tell me that a senior named Lee had appointed herself Big Dyke on Campus and was going around telling people. We were annoyed—nay, outraged—on both personal and theoretical grounds. Lee was an ex-friend of Deb's, and we considered her uncool behavior at the end of the friendship to be grounds for disqualification. Also, we felt a BDOC shouldn't care what people think of her; she should effortlessly elicit the description just by being herself. Blatant campaigning for the title was exactly the opposite!

I remembered how awed I'd been as a frosh by the BDOCs. No way was Lee as impressive as those tough, sexy, and scary women. (I didn't consider that perhaps my perspective had changed, not the impressiveness of upperclasswomen. Having been out for over a year, I felt I was on an equal social footing with the current BDOCs. Also, knowing what they had been like as freshmen removed a lot of their mystique. Not least, certain BDOC styles—such as Doc Martens, chains, and shaved heads—had come to seem more erotic than terrifying.)

Lee's outrageous arrogance made a juicy piece of gossip, and a couple days later I had to share it with my friend Marina while we waited in line to hear a talk by Susie Bright, a.k.a. Susie Sexpert, of *On Our Backs*.

"Well!" said Marina, "I wouldn't have picked Lee out as BDOC."

"Yeah, well just because she plays rugby, she thinks she's the shit."

"But that's not enough. You have to have something else about you."

"What fucking nerve she has, to tell people..."

As we bitched about Lee, trying to come up with the definitive disqualification for her, a group of dyke friends in line next to us couldn't resist getting in on the discussion.

"Yeah, you have to have short hair."

"No way, man. Femmes can be BDOCs too!"

"Like who?"

"What about Emilie?"

"OK, OK, you're right. But what does make someone BDOC?"

"Hmm...I don't know...I just know it when I see it."

"That's a cop-out! It's gotta be someone that everyone's hot for."

"No, someone who's really political."

"You have to be a big jock."

"It's all in the attitude."

"Well, if it's not Lee, who is it?"

"What about Blaine?"

"Oh, come on. She's obsessed with Sassy."

"So what?"

"Jen Meadows."

"Just 'cause you've got a big crush on her."

"Shut up!"

No one could agree on any obviously superior contenders or the necessary characteristics. But everyone seemed to share the assumption that there could be only one BDOC. Someone had the idea of holding an election. Someone else said, "If nobody springs to mind automatically, then there just isn't any BDOC this year. By definition!" Several people agreed. But others thought an election would be a lot of fun, so we persisted. I volunteered to write an article for the *College News* to solicit nominations, and Maria, one of the staff members for the paper, said she would see that it ran.

Developing the list of BDOC qualifications wasn't easy. My roommate, Madeline, helped me, and our training in sociology (mine) and anthropology (hers) enabled us to distill all our friends', acquaintances', and hallmates' vague and contradictory ideas into definitive statements. The next issue of the *College News* contained this article:

Who Will Be the Next BDOC?
by Ruth Wielgosz and Madeline Bergstrom, with the advice of many others

Put your fears to rest—a BDOC selection process has been set into motion. In case you were wondering, BDOC stands for Big Dyke on Campus. She is a lesbian or bisexual woman who possesses that *je ne sais quoi* of having reached the ultimate in dykiness, a state that is hard to define but easy to recognize. In making your nominations, please take into consideration some or all of the following characteristics, which we feel are important qualifications:

1. Has lots of attitude, very self-confident.
2. Terrifying yet fascinating.
3. Everyone knows she's a dyke.
4. Sexy.
5. Unattainable, or nearly so.
6. Many people have crushes on her, and many more feel too unworthy.
7. Visually impressive, especially in regard to hair.
8. Inscrutably cool, always in control of the situation.
9. Everyone knows who she is, has heard of her or recognizes her, and most have an opinion about her.

10. Nice enough for it to break your heart that she's too cool for you.

Please submit nominations to Ruth, C-1050, and we'll make up a ballot for the election. Make sure you get the permission of your nominee; willingness to take on the responsibility is essential.

✳   ✳   ✳

What we felt but couldn't quite express as a general rule was that a BDOC doesn't have to be well-liked or even likable, but she has to be respected. Lee could not be the BDOC because we despised her (justifiably or not).

Soon, however, I realized I'd made a big mistake. I should have offered to contact the nominees myself to ask them to run because no one had the guts to tell her nominee she was nominating her—probably because everyone wanted to nominate their crushes. They would tell me "I'd love to nominate so-and-so, but I could never tell her!" I guess I didn't have the guts either, because I wrote the following article for the next issue of the *College News*:

Alas, BDOC Hopefuls
by Ruth Wielgosz

Well, I hate to disappoint everyone, but there weren't enough nominations to hold the BDOC election. I did not foresee the problem that many people were too intimidated by the women they wanted to nominate to dare ask their permission. Under these circumstances it would be unfair to allow less intimidating candidates to run for the position. Apologies to all three of you who were nominated. You definitely had winning potential, even if you aren't very scary. I can't reveal any names, but among those too scary to be asked were a well-known member of the administration, a professor, someone who already claims to be BDOC, and the lesbian poster child of the *College News*.

In addition, some people raised the concern that this might become a mere popularity contest, with everyone voting for her friend. Although I think our integrity is greater than that, it is undeniable that unconscious biases might have affected voting. Another valid point which has been raised is that the very need to have an election proves that there is no

BDOC, for, by definition, her identity should be obvious to all. I prefer to think of the situation as one of too many choices, rather than too few....

In any case, until this year I was not aware that there could be only one BDOC. This is a needless limitation to impose on ourselves: the more BDOCs, the better. Was Norma less of a BDOC before Emilie graduated? I don't think so! So go for it, everyone: you can be a BDOC too, if you want to. Personally, I think it would be too much effort; I need to concentrate on finding dates for this weekend.

✳ ✳ ✳

The "well-known member of the administration" was the college president, about whom, predictably, rumors persisted that she was a closet case on the basis of flimsy evidence. The professor was definitely not a closet case: She and her partner lived on campus, and her partner was the queer student adviser. The woman who wanted to nominate her but wouldn't tell her was a married staff member who seemed to be flirting with the idea of coming out. "Someone who already claims to be BDOC" was Lee; she did have some admirers. The last failed nomination, the "poster child," was Maria, the *College News* staffer who had been at the original discussion in Thomas Great Hall. She had referred to herself by that title in print a few issues before.

I secretly hoped some people thought I was a BDOC, but realistically I was too low-key and craved social acceptance too much. Also, it made me nervous to think of strangers knowing who I was and having opinions about me, whereas a true BDOC wouldn't care. I guess some women have that *je ne sais quoi* and others don't. I'm pretty much over it now. Being intimidating is no longer one of my goals, at least not most of the time.

Trial by Fire

by Susie Bullington
University of California, Santa Cruz

"Did you have oral sex?"

"Yes."

"Did you touch each other's breasts?" he continued.

"Yes," I said shaking, looking frantically at Anita. I couldn't believe this was happening. It seemed like a bad dream, and if only I could step out for a minute, it would all go away.

"Petting to orgasm?"

"Yes," she blurted.

Was that true? Did she have an orgasm? I wasn't sure I had. Anita looked straight at Lance unflinchingly. My stomach dropped. I wanted to grab her, make her look at me, take her away from this awful, cold, white room. I wanted to remind her who we were together, but instead it was like I was invisible.

I looked at Lance, his face red and damp. Why was he doing this? "I think we should finish this in separate rooms," he said. "I want to make sure Anita has a chance to speak, since I know you have a tendency to speak for her."

No! my heart screamed. *Please, Lord, don't separate us. This is the only chance I've had to see her in the past two weeks. This might be my last chance to see her. Please let us do this together.* I felt the tears rising.

"I don't think that's necessary. I'll let her do the talking," I pleaded, trying not to sound desperate.

Anita said nothing. I squirmed in my seat, telling myself not to panic. Lance debated. I began to argue, but finally he agreed it would be easier to go through this only once. Thank you, Lord.

I was shaking as he continued his interrogation. "How did this first start between you two?"

As Anita began to explain the private details of our relationship, I couldn't listen anymore. My mind reeled, and I wondered how I could have gotten myself into this situation.

When I first joined Inter-Varsity Christian Fellowship, I felt I'd found a home. Inter-Varsity members were the first people I met when I arrived at UC, Santa Cruz. Even before I'd met my RA, Inter-Varsity members were lugging boxes from my parents' car up to my new dorm room. Nervous about fitting in and making friends, I felt relieved to meet such outgoing people who seemed to take a genuine interest in me. Although I wasn't in the habit of going to church, I went to an Inter-Varsity bible[1] study/ice cream social my first week of college. I was pleasantly surprised to find a God so much more real and exciting and like me than anything I'd encountered accompanying Grandma to Mass in high school. Inter-Varsity bible studies talked about life in the dorms, the balance between relationships and schoolwork, and other issues I was dealing with as a college student.

I spent all my time with my new friends and quickly became well-liked, especially by the older students who acted as bible study leaders. Being away from home I felt lucky to have found a family of caring people who shared my goals and commitment to making the world a better place. In Inter-Varsity, we talked about real issues, not just the superficial topics of high school. I'd finally found my niche and felt, at last, joyful and filled with peace. I was surrounded by people I felt sincerely liked me, people I loved and trusted completely, and I devoted myself to the fellowship. I sat with my Inter-Varsity friends in class, went to fellowship meetings every night, and on weekends went to the quad dances where we all danced in a circle. I was growing in my faith every day and witnessed changes in my personality. Previously painfully shy, I became incredibly outgoing and felt vigor and purpose in my life. I was "on fire," my friends said, and I was being groomed for leadership, the headliner in a circle of up-and-coming new students.

Anita was also a part of this young cohort, albeit a resistant one. She and I were in the same dorm and bible study group that first year. We didn't hit it off right away, but by the end of the year we had become close enough friends that we decided to room together the following year. Our dorm room became a center for fellowship members, as I held prayer meetings there twice a week and Anita was in the new crop of bible study leaders. I'd been passed over for this honor because older leaders felt I was "too emotional." This could hardly be said of Anita, who was cool and reserved to the point of aloofness. When I'd see her in the cafeteria after a long day at school and ask how her day was, she'd respond suspiciously, "Why do you want to know?"

Because she was so closed and cautious, I was intrigued and deeply moved when slowly she began to trust me and open up. Though officially Anita was my bible study leader, in truth we began to act more as co-facilitators, meeting to prepare and plan activities, and mentoring the younger students together. She respected my sensitivity, and I admired her boldness and self-respect. She was a strong woman who spoke her mind, qualities I didn't see in myself. Through our spiritual partnership and budding emotional closeness, our relationship grew to be primary for both of us. We spent the majority of our time together, which thrilled me, and her spiritual mentors were delighted she finally had someone with whom to be vulnerable.

I went home that Christmas vacation and hung out with Melissa, my best friend from high school. Throughout most of high school, I'd wrestled with intense feelings for her, wanting to be more than a "best friend" but not knowing quite what. One evening over break, after a particularly intimate discussion in the car, she left me with an intense embrace that stirred all kinds of sexual feelings within me. Feeling confused, anxious, and despicable, I went the next day to the Christian bookstore and purchased *The Healing of the Homosexual* and covertly devoured it over the next several days. But I needed to talk about it with someone. Anita was home with her family nearby, and we'd been seeing a lot of each other. Sitting on the floor in my room, I finally took the risk and broached the subject with her. I showed her the book and told her about Melissa. I nervously asked, "What are you thinking?" She wasn't surprised by my revelations and was more understanding than I'd ever dreamed. "God is big enough to deal with this," she said. "Let's pray together," and she took my hands as we bowed our heads. She remained concerned, however, that I was attracted to her. I lied and told her I wasn't.

Back at school our friendship grew, but I was tormented with guilt over the depth of my feelings for her. Friends inquired about the cause of my sleepless nights and restless disposition, but I couldn't reveal my shame. It was especially difficult because my relationship with Anita had become more physically expressive with our growing trust of each other. Sitting close in bible study, holding hands at prayer meetings, and exchanging back rubs after long study sessions aroused intense confusing feelings in me.

Finally, one night after a late discussion in the hallway, I confessed my feelings. Anita was calm and reassuring but strangely quiet, so I felt insecure. "What are you thinking?" brought only serious glances in my direction. I didn't know if our friendship could withstand this kind of revelation. When we were finally getting ready for bed, I was terrified I'd blown it and ruined the intimacy we shared. I was already grieving that things would never be the same between us again. In my dismay I asked her if I could sleep with her in her bed because I was upset and scared. My knees caved from relief, excitement, and fear when she agreed. My stomach twisted into knots as we lay in silence for a long time in her twin-size bunk bed, my body half hanging off the side because I was afraid to touch her. I lay still, barely breathing, watching her sleep.

When she spoke I was startled but even more shocked by her words. She whispered to me, "If we could do anything, no holds barred, what would you want to do?" The question was at once terrifying and exhilarating. My heart spoke for my mind, which was in a stupor. "I'd like to kiss you," I whispered. I thought this was the obvious answer, but she pulled away and shook her head. "Kissing is too intimate," she asserted. Disappointed and a little hurt, I asked, "What would you want to do?" "Touch your breasts," she whispered. My breath caught in my throat. This was serious! Though I didn't understand why she was so curious about my breasts—most times I tried to forget I had them—I acquiesced, and the talking was finished. We made love all night, Anita in control, dictating every move. I barely felt my body as I reeled in surprise, fright, excitement, and disgust.

When sunrise came, it was like a spotlight illuminating our shame. What was the night before too good to be true, now seemed a horrible nightmare. The smell of vagina made us sick to our stomachs. We took vigorous showers without speaking and set out walking around campus in the early-morning chill. It took a long time before we could say anything. Mostly we needed to get out and walk. I couldn't believe what we'd done and felt scared. What would happen now? I would've liked to share my feelings with Anita and comfort her, but she was too upset. "Do you realize what we've done?" she practically shouted. I knew what she meant.

Had we risked our entire salvation for one night in bed? The possibility was too frightening to even discuss. I secretly wanted to ask Anita what she thought of our night together, but she could speak only bitterly and fearfully of the spiritual consequences of what we had done. We vowed it would never happen again.

Two days later we broke this vow and found ourselves in bed together again. This began a pattern we would follow for the remaining short weeks of our relationship: Every other day we would have sex with each other, and every opposite day we would be racked with guilt and anguish. The days we were sexual were sweet. Our trust and intimacy grew; Anita even told me she loved me. We made plans to go to Africa someday. I began skipping class because I couldn't bear to be away from her. I would do anything to be alone with her, not necessarily to be sexual, but to be able to behave with the intimacy of lovers. Anita derided us for being selfish. We were supposed to be ministering to others in our group, especially those we were discipling.

Anita felt especially guilty about our sexual relationship. I'd been involved with the church for only a couple of years, and those were in high school, but she was raised in a black fundamentalist church, and religion was the foundation of existence. The spiritual repercussions of what we were doing troubled her deeply. One afternoon after a particularly satisfying encounter, we emerged from our room and headed to the cafeteria for lunch. As we walked out into the sunshine smiling, we were immediately alarmed to find the quad area deserted. There was an eerie silence, and no one was around. Anita ran back inside, panic stricken. She was certain the rapture had come while we were "sinning" and that we had been left behind. We later learned that the United States was on the verge of going to war and everyone was huddled around the television in the rec room.

The weekly worship and bible study meetings no longer left me with joyous peaceful feelings. My conscience wasn't clear, and I felt Anita's troubled spirit beside me. The fellowship leader gave a sermon about the prophet Nathan confronting David about his relationship with Bathsheba, and I felt as though the spotlight were on us, as though everyone could see our shame. Amy, the song leader, sang ominous hymns of sin and punishment, and I saw Anita, with tears streaming down her face, mouthing the words: "With what shall I come before the Lord and bow my head before God on high? Shall I come before Him with burnt offerings?

Will the Lord be pleased with thousands of rams? Shall I give my first born for my transgression, the fruit of my body for the sin of my soul?" Each time, as soon as the service concluded, Anita ran home, and I found her lying on her bed sobbing and moaning. I tried to comfort her, but she could barely speak, lamenting between the sobs, "What have I done? What have I done?" certain of her own condemnation.

Anita had been pleading with me for days to talk to someone about our "problem." I didn't want to cause her further anguish, so I considered it. I felt divided because I liked the closeness of our relationship and wanted to keep it special and between us. But she kept saying we couldn't deal with it on our own, and after a couple of weeks I began to believe she was right. Clearly we couldn't stay away from each other, and spiritually we couldn't reconcile our actions with our faith. Three weeks after our first night together, we set about deciding whom to confide in and finally chose a mutual IVCF friend we thought would be wise yet sympathetic.

I felt apprehensive about our meeting with Amy but also a little excited. I had such intense feelings for Anita, and finally I got to tell somebody. However, when we explained to Amy how we had become "involved," our smiles disappeared as she grew serious. She took control, asserting, "You two must be separated right away. This type of sin must be dealt with swiftly and seriously. Susie, you'll stay with me until we can find you another place to live." Stunned, I wanted to blurt, "Wait, we were just kidding!" But it was too late. Our secret was out, and the prescription couldn't have been harsher. "The separation must be complete," she told us, and so Anita and I were forbidden to see or talk to each other. Amy helped me pack my essential belongings to stay temporarily at her apartment and told me if I needed anything else from our room, a friend would have to retrieve it for me. Amy also insisted we share our situation with Lance, the Inter-Varsity paid staff person assigned to our college.

Shocked at losing the most important person in my life over the course of 24 hours, I lay awake on the floor of Amy's living room, sobbing in agony and isolation night after night. I felt so lonely, as even Amy became aloof and would no longer change clothes in front of me. I walked to a pay phone in the middle of the night and called my parents. Dad could tell something was wrong, but I just said, "I miss you guys." I couldn't tell them how awful it was or why. I walked to the ocean and stared at the waves, contemplating what it would feel like to step off the steep cliffs. I wandered around campus aimlessly, skipping class for weeks, with no room to go home to. All I could think of was Anita, wondering how she was doing. I wanted to see her and hold her again.

Other friends provided no solace after our initial meeting with Lance. He warned us that the younger students were not mature enough to deal with this, so we were forbidden to speak about what had happened. The older student leaders had already turned their backs on me after a special meeting was held for Anita and me to "share" our situation. When I explained what had happened, Gordon, one of the bible study leaders, burst into tears in what I thought was a remarkable display of compassion. I later found out it wasn't compassion but fear that had prompted his reaction, as he was having an affair with a male member of the fellowship and was afraid he would be found out next.

The three older members of the group reacted with indignation and disgust. They felt angry and betrayed that this had been going on behind their backs. They demanded to know how this could have happened. Especially, they inquired, how could this have happened to someone as respectable as Anita? They quizzed me: Had I ever had these types of feelings before? Honestly, I answered "yes" and told them about my struggles in high school with Melissa. That provided resolution in their minds: I must have seduced Anita in some way. My mind cried out that the opposite was the case, but Anita never said a word. The last of the bible study leaders, Jack, was also strangely silent. I later found out that he and Gordon had also had an affair the year before.

One by one, each of my longstanding friends called me to regretfully inform me that they wanted to support Anita through this since they would be in the leader group with her. I felt hurt and rejected, but they said they couldn't actively be my friends because of the awkwardness of the situation. This included my new roommate, which was probably the hardest to take. Not having Anita to talk to and losing all my friends meant a lonely existence for me. Further changes came about as a result of our confession. Anita was asked to step down from her position as bible study leader, and our close-knit group was disbanded as members were relocated to other groups. I was replaced as music leader as well.

So here we were again with Lance for another long humiliating session. We spent nearly as long recounting our relationship before the judgment of others as our relationship had lasted. "You must confess every sin in detail to be fully cleansed," Lance said. As I heard Anita explaining our final night of lovemaking, I knew it was going to be my last chance to fight for this relationship. I felt desperate, angry, and helpless. We'd already agreed to stop being lovers; we only wanted to be friends. But Lance and Anita echoed the biblical refrain, "If your right hand is causing you to sin, you must cut it off to save the rest of the body." I was spiritually undisciplined, they said, and could not accept what must be done. As Anita nodded her head, I sat there numb. I wanted to scream, "Why are you doing this?" to Lance, to Anita, to God. Instead, as we finished, I got up quietly, with tears streaming down my face, and said good-bye to Anita for the last time.

A couple of weeks later, Anita moved to a new dorm in the upper quad, and I was back on campus. She steadfastly obeyed the advice of her Christian elders, and despite seeing each other in the cafeteria and at Inter-Varsity functions, she never spoke to me again. Our lack of closure haunted me. Everything had happened in such a whirlwind. Anita and I never had a chance to discuss what had resulted from our talk with Amy or how we felt about any of it. I began to feel crazy, as if it had never happened, as if we'd never become lovers, as if I'd imagined the whole thing. Anita's silence stung the most. I felt rejected and betrayed, and part of me has never forgiven her for giving in so easily. In an effort to gain some understanding about our relationship, I contacted her once after we had graduated from college, figuring we were no longer under the control of the Christian fellowship. But she was distant, and when I brought up our relationship, she said she'd only made love with me because she knew I'd wanted to and she didn't want to disappoint me. The last time I heard about her, she was married and working for Inter-Varsity.

My own relationship with Inter-Varsity was short-lived. Losing Anita hurled me into a deep depression. I dropped all but one of my classes for the quarter, quit the basketball team, and contemplated taking time off from school since I couldn't bear seeing Anita around campus without being able to talk to her. Suicidal thoughts plagued me. Members of the fellowship became concerned about my bitterness toward God, even holding special prayer meetings for me. I was referred to a male Christian counselor who, upon hearing about my suicidal temptations, chided, "Do you want to lose your salvation over one person?" But I could never again trust a God who would so cruelly take away something that mattered so much to me. The joy and peace that had opened my heart and brought me out of myself had vanished.

Despite all this I continued to participate actively in Inter-Varsity for several months, still trying to find acceptance and approval from those who had rejected me. Two incidents, however, eventually made me angry enough to leave the fellowship. I became friends with another woman in the fellowship and experienced continual harassment from leaders in the fellowship about this new relationship. Various leaders came by my room to confront me, and, in another "trial," I was forbidden to study alone with this woman or visit her at night. The leaders also undermined my friendships with women in a fellowship support group. I knew I wouldn't be able to have female friends if I stayed. All of the indignations I'd faced eventually became too much, and I officially left Inter-Varsity. I've not been able to bring myself to participate in another church or Christian organization since.

Despite the pain associated with my time in the fellowship, leaving was difficult. I'd invested so much of myself that without the fellowship I felt lonely and aimless. Every Wednesday night I would stand on my dorm balcony and watch my former friends walking to bible study.

Within a year, however, I found a new home on campus in LBQ, Lesbian/Bisexual/Questioning women, among whom I still considered myself "Questioning." The quarter I left Inter-Varsity, I took my first women's studies class, and becoming a feminist completely transformed me. I learned to actively take responsibility for my life instead of passively letting things happen, and I started to try to accept myself, my whole self, instead of fighting myself as I'd done in the fellowship. I began to see a lesbian therapist who helped me make peace with my past. The first time I went to LBQ, I was afraid to let people touch me. I knew I had feelings for women, but I wasn't one of "them." But as I kept returning to the group, I saw that lesbians were not scary monsters but interesting women and potential friends. I played on their softball team and began to see a home for myself in the gay community, among people who were similarly committed to making the world a better place. As I began to accept myself as a lesbian, my pride in being queer began to grow. Over the course of two years, my career goals transformed from Christian missionary to gay activist. I began speaking on panels around campus, telling my painful coming-out story, even with Inter-Varsity members in the audience. I'm publishing this piece in my continued fight to own my life and tell my own truth.

1 For personal reasons, the author has chosen not to capitalize *bible* throughout this piece.

the politics of silence

christopher m. bell
University of Missouri

This essay is dedicated to Joey, whom I trust will understand when I (mis)pronounce her name as "Joy."

Sitting in an impersonal and nondescript examination room in the student health center, I listened to the intermittent banter outside the door and the cascading rain outside the window. My thoughts drifted to my relatively stable physical well-being during my 23-year sojourn on this planet. As I'd been a stranger to major surgery, my health history consisted of bouts with minor aches, a pesky cough here and there, and the sniffles. But just two months before, I'd been diagnosed with mononucleosis, an affliction that I, at that time, heralded as the worst experience in my health history. I languished for four days in University Hospital, dehydrated, disoriented, and dismayed at my failing health so close to the commencement of the school year. After sufficient respite I improved slowly and began the school year on a wave of anticipation.

Several weeks into my studies, I noticed my lymph nodes were as swollen as they had been in the hospital. Ever cautious, I made an appointment with the student health center to have them examined. The doctor said the swelling may have derived from a variety of reasons and suggested I have my blood tested for several ailments, including HIV.

Two weeks later on a depressingly rainy day, I returned to student health to receive my test results. After an interminable wait, the doctor entered the room carrying a file folder. She sat across from me, placing the folder on the desk beside us, and asked how I was "doing."

"Fine," I lied, my eyes riveted to the manila folder containing my future.

"Well, Chris," she said, taking my hands into hers, "all of the tests came back negative, except one."

I swallowed and said nothing. Tearing my gaze from the folder, I focused on the doctor's eyes.

"The HIV-antibody test came back positive."

Not a sound escaped from me. I didn't even blink. I merely held her gaze and waited for her to continue. For the next 20 minutes the doctor talked about "next steps." I instinctively responded to her counseling with a series of disinterested "uh-huhs." At one point, when Dr. Diagnosis confessed she had never given anyone positive results, I made a mental note to invest in a "Gee, I know it was tough for you, but you did swell" greeting card for her.

In retrospect, I see my attitude had been grounded in the juvenile belief that somehow she wasn't speaking to me. Although we were the only two people in the room and she was steadily holding my perspiring palms, I was convinced she was speaking to someone, anyone, other than me.

I was born in St. Louis, Mo., a fact I find neither unique nor compelling, save the pronunciation of my home state has a peculiar affinity with *misery*. I learned at an early age to blaze my own path and accept the circumstances of my actions. Sometimes I was successful and content in my endeavors; more often I was dejected and disconcerted. Regardless of the outcome of my decisions, I thrived on being in control of my life. For instance, after high school graduation I opted to enroll in an undergraduate institution far outside my hometown. For reasons that escape me, I selected Colorado State University and eagerly embarked on my collegiate career.

Whatever expectations of college I'd conjured in my hyperfastidious imagination were quickly usurped as I, within days of arriving, was paralyzed by a severe case of depression. I never fully recovered from that depression (it has unpredictably revisited over the past six and a half years); thus, I returned to St. Louis in the middle of my inaugural semester in an effort to (re)focus my life. My mother encouraged me to continue my education by enrolling in a university closer to home. After giving this idea due consideration, I embarked on take-two of my collegiate escapade, Central Missouri State University. For the next three and a half years, I matured on a personal level via coming out as gay as well as on a more conceptual level by developing a greater appreciation for "multicul-turalism" and "diversity," concepts often conventionalized, now poignant-ly lucid. My undergraduate experience was satisfactory overall; as a result, I left CMSU, degree in hand, prepared to pursue a master's in English at the University of Missouri.

If this account were penned by a Disney screenwriter, my story would end on this sanguine note. Happily ensconced in graduate study, it appears I have carved a niche in academia. The requisite obstacles all college students endure have been hurdled, and I have become a stronger, more confident individual in the process. Nevertheless, my story, instead of ending, expands as a direct result of the episode in the student health center.

Never one to address a crisis by losing all composure, I left student health that day and calmly walked across campus toward the university's women's center, where a safer sex seminar was scheduled as part of Gay, Lesbian, Bisexual Pride Week. Treading along the campus paths, I passed various students reclining on the grass, walking to and from the library, and talking with one another. I assured myself that I was just like them, that nothing had changed. I also noticed the leaves were changing colors. *How fitting,* I thought. *As the inner mechanisms of the trees prepare to survive another winter, so I call on my faculties to arm themselves for my own quest for survival.*

Upon arriving at the women's center, I spotted various friends, including Tina McDaniel, president of the Triangle Coalition, the university's lesbian, gay, and bisexual undergraduate organization. Without pausing, indeed, without giving the idea much consideration at all, I advanced toward Tina and asked her to join me in the hall. Sensing the urgency in my voice, she agreed. We exited the women's center through the back door and stood in the empty hallway facing each other.

"Tina," I began, maintaining for both our sakes as much composure as possible, "I'm going to tell you something, and I want you to know it's OK to react any way you choose."

Slowly and sagely, she nodded.

"I just came from student health, where I was told that I'm HIV-positive, and I'm going to need your help." Taking in Tina's widened eyes and slightly parted lips, I continued. "I'm not going to be able to keep this to myself—you know the kind of person I am. So if you don't mind, I'd like to address the Triangle Coalition next week." I stopped talking and waited for Tina's response. I didn't have to wait long, as she, without hesitation, embraced me. As we stood in the hallway behind the women's center, several students filed through the front door. Their laughter and banter drifted out, adding a twisted conviviality to my confession.

"Of course you can, Chris," Tina said. "I think it would be a wonderful thing for you to do."

Making plans, we talked with each other for a few more moments, then re-entered the center. While Tina participated in the safer sex seminar, I slipped out the back. I went home, read a few *Canterbury Tales*, and slept. The next day I attended class, ate, and chatted with friends. In other words, I continued through life. What else could I have done?

The following Tuesday, nearly a week after my diagnosis, PJ, an editor friend from the school newspaper, approached me in the women's center.[1] She was writing an article about people's sexual behavior in the age of AIDS and requested my feedback. I paused for a moment to reflect on the irony of the situation. It had been six days since my diagnosis, and PJ was asking me about the disease that would, I believe(d), eclipse my life. At that point, I'd shared news of my diagnosis with a handful of people; yet I knew I would eventually inform a much larger contingent. Never a believer in karma, serendipity, the Easter Bunny, or other psychobabble, I was nonetheless intrigued by the coincidence of this opportunity. Chalk one up to the muses, I surmised.

PJ came to me for a single quote and left three hours later with enough material for a comprehensive cover story about my diagnosis. Subsequently, I was faced with the daunting task of apprising my close friends about my situation prior to the story's publication three days later. I didn't have enough time to formulate a concise strategy, so whenever I encountered someone in whom I wished to confide, I had to gauge the situation for an acceptable level of appropriateness.

The evening before the newspaper's publication, I addressed the Triangle Coalition. Standing in front of 70 people, I affirmed my HIV-positive status. With every nuance of grace I could muster, I spoke for ten minutes, informing my attentive audience of my faith in the future. I told them everything would be fine but emphasized I could not make it alone.

"I know I'll need your help in the next few weeks and maybe the next few months," I confided. "So I've come up with a trinity of emotions I'd like to hone and call my own. If you can help me adhere to this trinity, I'd be grateful. The first emotion is compassion. Because I need love, because I need to give love, I'd like to maintain a compassionate demeanor. I want to cherish others as they cherish me. The second emotion is hope. Because I believe there will be a cure for this virus, because I have no choice but to believe that, I dare to hope. Finally, there must be laughter. As laughter is the one thing that has sustained me through the rough times in my life and since I haven't laughed much in the last week, I need you guys to keep me laughing. Because, like author Zora Neale Hurston, 'I love myself the most when I am laughing.'"

Concluding on that note, I walked to the back of the room and collapsed in a chair. I was unsure if anyone understood how difficult it had been to articulate my feelings, to expose my essence, without breaking down. But I did it because I wanted to. Doing so gave me ownership of a potentially self-destructive situation.

The next day, nine days after D-Day (Diagnosis Day), my face and story were splattered all over the homecoming edition of the school newspaper for 20,000-plus students and countless faculty, staff, alumni, and community members to scrutinize. For the most part, I was pleased with the story and my representation.[2] Grounded in confidence and hubris, the article was devoid of sorrow, gloom, and other recidivist aspects of despair. *Maybe it'll make a difference in someone's life,* I thought.

Indeed, on the day of publication, a complete stranger approached me outside the English Department office.

"You're Chris Bell! You were in the *Maneater* today."

"Yes, I am and yes, I was."

"Oh, my gosh, I'm so glad I ran into you. I think you're so brave coming forth like that."

"Well, I dunno. I've always thought bravery is a not-so-distant cousin of stupidity...."

"Oh, no. It wasn't stupid at all; at least, I don't think so, and none of my sorority sisters who read the story thought so either," she said.

"Thank you. What's your name?"

"Danielle. I'm late for class, but would you mind if I hugged you?" Without waiting for a response, she embraced me, then walked away.

Not more than ten minutes later, while browsing through the CDs in the university bookstore, I heard someone clear her throat. "Excuse me."

"Yes?" I looked across the display rack into the eyes of a person I'd never met.

"Are you Chris Bell?"

"Yes."

The young lady walked around the display rack and stood next to me. She placed her hands on her hips and slowly wagged her head back and forth at me. "You know, man, coming out in the paper like that…you have balls of steel."

A bit taken aback yet grateful for the sentiment, I stammered a response, then continued browsing through the CDs as she confidently moved on.

Reflecting back on that day, the day I became a cause célèbre at the University of Missouri, I remember experiencing a tumult of emotions. Fear, hope, inner peace—I felt them all. Most of all I was happy I'd acted in as forthright a manner as possible. Never in my life had I known such an overwhelming sense of assurance and self-control.

Since I publicly acknowledged my diagnosis, my experience has been overwhelmingly—forgive the pun—positive. My heterosexual friends have embraced me without hesitation, and lesbians and bisexual women have been wonderful. Gay and bi men, however, require some explanation. Most of these individuals have been supportive; nevertheless, since the time I arrived on campus—and came out—two years ago, some gay/bi men have outed themselves to me while they remain closeted to others. Some of these individuals avert their eyes when they spy me in the library, the food court, or other campus venues and exchange empty inflammatory rhetoric about me behind my back. In my estimation they have little regard for my well-being or lack thereof.

Certainly, these individuals are irrelevant, but their actions are significant. These individuals, when looking at me, seem fearful, which probably stems from subconscious self-loathing. "He outed himself and acted like the typical faggot," their actions suggest. "And look what's happened to him. He got AIDS!" Never one to allow negativity to go unchecked, I am nonetheless nonplussed by this "explanation" because it is both unfounded and trite. Neither my own nor most others' openness about being gay is a death sentence. If anything, my openness about my sexuality—and, I anticipate, my openness about carrying HIV—has allowed me to live with much more candor, self-respect, and integrity than before.

While on the subject of people's reaction to my status, I must address the intersection of race and sexuality. As an openly gay African-American student at a predominantly white institution, I have often been pressed by other, presumably heterosexual African-American students to justify my sexuality. "Isn't it enough that you're black?" they ask. "Why do you want to add to your discrimination?" These individuals level these charges at me only when they are on their home turf, namely, the enclave of the food court, where mostly African-Americans sit, dine, and chatter. Usually I am discounted by these individuals who do not, by their admission, view me as a legitimate black person because of my sexuality. When I acknowledge their presence, they ignore me. My response to their charges is that being openly gay and openly HIV-positive is a clarion call to my "bruthas" and "sistahs" who view homosexuality and HIV/AIDS as something that affects only white people. As my race is a viable part of my identity, so is my sexuality and, now, my seropositive status. Diminishing one aspect diminishes me.

Two weeks after the school paper's publication, my boss, the director of freshman composition, expressed disappointment with my decision to "go public" and pointedly "suggested" I take the semester off from teaching. "Consider the effect all this is having on your students," he said. I didn't want to stop teaching, but I believed he knew what was best, so I complied. A few hours later it hit me. As my role in that decision was at best negligible, I had lost control. This loss of control was heightened by the increasingly addictive, incredibly surreal sensation of performing for my own personal and invisible audience. While the spectators held their collective breath, waiting for my breakdown, I confounded their expectations by making it through each day. And I'd been so active in communicating my HIV status to others that I hadn't adequately dealt with it myself. When I was relieved of my teaching duties, not having anything else to focus on, I self-acknowledged for the first time: "I'm HIV-positive!" Three weeks after receiving my test results, my brain finally began to process the implication of the diagnosis.

Since I was no longer teaching and lost all interest in the classes I was taking, I saw no need to venture to campus at all. For the next three and a half weeks, I lounged on my living room sofa, bathing infrequently and subsisting on cookies, chips, and water. During this time I charmed myself into believing my life was over. *Why cling to life? There's nothing left.* I thought. *My dreams deferred, I have an imminent appointment with death.*

Then one day I got sick of myself and made a concerted effort to move on with life. I received assistance from Joey, a person I've recently anointed as my solid ground, as well as through literature, where I frequently, during times of nearly insurmountable depression, seek solace. Many of my most rewarding reading experiences have come from the literary frenzies I engage in when unable to undertake other tasks. This time, I read virtually any title the university bookstore carried as well as texts from the university library's holdings—from works with little literary but invaluable inspirational merit (Patti Labelle's autobiography) to Oprah's Book Club selections to feminist tracts (Rebecca Walker's *To Be Real* and her mother Alice's *In Search of Our Mothers' Gardens*) to Langston Hughes. During the last month I have focused solely on Hughes, reading his complete poems, both of his autobiographies, as well as a two-volume biography of him. It is interesting I have grafted to Hughes at this time. A luminous figure, Hughes recounts the rhythms of all people, representing their dreams and detritus, their triumphs and tragedies. His is a lesson in the rudiments of survival, a construct of immense appeal to me.

Likewise, as Hughes portrayed people who cannot acknowledge unerring certainties and prime truths as atavistic, I am disgusted by those both in and outside academia who pretend AIDS does not exist or that they are somehow immune to the reality of this pandemic. Consequently, this statement brings me to the title of this essay, the politics of silence. HIV/AIDS is the only disease I know of that carries a politic, a proscribed mode of dictates. This politic states that in the face of death and despair, human beings should create and maintain silence. We are seduced into adhering to this silence because of its apparent ease, thereby creating an even more stringent protocol to which people feel obliged to cater. We are so enthralled with this silence that we allow a shroud of propriety to govern (read: dominate) our compassion. As a result, people are embarrassed and/or ashamed by everything associated with HIV/AIDS because of the potent silence attached to the disease. Certainly not all people. But too many.

A few days after emerging from my depressive funk, I received a phone call from Dr. Mary Bixby, facilitator of a Learning Strategies course. I had known Dr. Bixby for some time and revered her for her good humor and forthrightness. After inquiring about my welfare, she asked if I were available to participate on a panel in her class that day. I accepted. I felt no need to mull it over since I viewed the opportunity as an effort at combating the silence shrouding HIV/AIDS issues on college campuses, the alleged breeding grounds for intelligence and inquiry.

That afternoon, in front of an auditorium of 200 first-year students, I discussed my diagnosis and fielded questions. Most of them had read the *Maneater* article and were pleasantly surprised when they saw I would be speaking. I enjoyed this interaction because the students' questions were carefully crafted and engaging.

How did you contract the virus?

"I had unprotected sex with my partner of a year and a half. For the first month or so of our relationship, we used condoms, but we grew out of that practice somewhere along the way. Though I wish we had used protection the entire time, I have accepted my part in the situation."

Do you regret getting tested?

"My life would be different if I hadn't received a positive diagnosis, but I'm glad to know I have the virus so I can take steps to stop its potential spread among partners I might have."

Have you told your family?

"My parents divorced when I was 3, and I haven't seen my dad since then. My mother is aware of my status and it has in no way altered her love for and support of me."

That night, while working on a paper, I paused to check my E-mail. Abby, one of the students from Dr. Bixby's class, had sent a touching letter apprising me of how pleased she was that I had come to her class. She wrote that she'd sent a copy of the *Maneater* article to a friend at another university who had just come out. As I responded to Abby's letter, I thought about how easy it is to educate one another simply by sharing our stories. I pondered the necessity of self-expression, especially in the face of adversity and reticence; for as Sir Francis Bacon augured 400 years ago, "Silence is the virtue of fools."

Likewise, in the early days of the AIDS pandemic, ACT-UP[3] advocated the inclusion of HIV/AIDS concerns into our international dialogues because they realized that "SILENCE = DEATH." Over the years, this notion has figured into demonstrations, educational materials, and lectures;

accordingly, the statement has become clichéd to some. But perhaps it is clichéd because it reveals the truth that silence indeed equals death. In essence, I have chosen to speak about my HIV-positive status not because I seek laurels but because I understand the longevity created when the human voice counters silence.

Since receiving and acknowledging my diagnosis, I have benefited from immeasurable positive reinforcement. I would be remiss, however, not to mention the following, which I am still trying to reconcile.

I returned to my apartment one evening after finishing a speaking engagement and retrieved my messages. While I played them back, the phone rang. The caller, Mariah, was a friend whom I'd met the previous summer when we were members of the Rape Awareness Week steering committee. She asked if I would be willing to meet with her to discuss an important issue. I agreed to meet her for lunch the next day. After hanging up I replayed my messages, curious as to what was on her mind.

When we met, Mariah was characteristically upbeat. After discussing current events for a while, she calmly informed me that she had been to student health and had tested positive for a potentially life-threatening sexually transmitted disease, though not HIV. I thought back to when I had confided in Tina McDaniel and how difficult it must have been for her to hear my confession. With that in mind I summoned my compassion and finessed the situation with Mariah as best I could.[4] She thanked me for my concern, then asked if I thought it would be a good idea for her to do as I have done; that is, to come forward and educate others. For the remainder of our conversation, I shared with Mariah the highs and lows of my going public. When our conversation ended and she stood up to go to class, I hugged her.

A week after my conversation with Mariah, while I was volunteering in the gay, lesbian, bisexual resource center, a friend entered. Noting that we were alone in the center, he sat next to me and told me he had just come from student health, where he had tested positive for an STD. A few days after this conversation, a young woman left a message on my answering machine asking me to meet her at the women's center. The next day she confided that she too had tested positive for an STD.[5]

These conversations have caused me to ponder the extent of STD education on college campuses. Too often emphasis is placed on prevention, which is admittedly important. But having heard the stories of these three people, knowing there are certainly others like them, I feel the university does not sufficiently support and acknowledge the presence of students, faculty, and staff who have contracted STDs. The majority of people on college campuses tend to dismiss individuals with STDs, automatically perceiving us as lifelong members of the international fraternity of the walking wounded.

Recently, and for several reasons, I have decided to postpone my academic pursuits, one semester before the conferring of my master's degree. First, there is my growing perturbation at some of my peers' persistence in complaining about affectations of minute infinitesimal importance ("Should I study for my sociology midterm before or after I get baked?" or "Can I wear my teal blue Doc Martens with this shirt?"). Measured against these ideals, my reservoir of patience, usually at a premium, is rapidly running dry.

Secondly, recently I have felt a need to remove myself from compromising environs. Though I revel in the support I have received from friends, I am wary of individuals such as the director of freshman composition. Instead of affirming my decision to be straightforward and honest, some people have attempted to foist silence onto me. These individuals' devotion to silence speaks of a desire to invalidate me, to make me a voiceless invisible man. Clearly these kinds of people march to their own beat, the peccadilloes of neglect and the politics of silence. On the contrary, I dance to a rhythm of realization and control. While I called on my voice to counter silence, the band played on, playing nothing.

There are numerous strategies for living with HIV/AIDS. A relative newcomer to this arena, I have forged the path I believe best for me. I do not recommend that every person plaster his or her face over their school newspaper or handle a positive diagnosis in any of the other ways I have. I did what worked for me; if asked to do it all over, I would do it exactly the same, because it was right for me. I have no regrets. Moreover, since my diagnosis four months ago, my perspective on life has altered to the point where I find it vital (read: life-affirming) to place myself in positive environments. Appreciative of every waking moment, I no longer have time for other people's cruelty and negative eccentricities. I want to live in an atmosphere of free-spirited whimsical joy and good humor. As I avowed to the Triangle Coalition, as well as in a presentation to a campus Greek organization, more than anything I love myself most when I am laughing.

1 By now, you're probably wondering why I, a (gay) man, spend so much time at the women's center. I am in the process of developing a feminist ideology. Thus, I frequent the women's center to research, engage in feminist theory discussions, and most importantly I like it there and feel welcome.

2 The article may be located at: http://www.themaneater.com/971017/news/16story1.html. Please bear in mind that, despite its title, the *Maneater* is the school newspaper, not a Larry Flynt publication.

3 AIDS Coalition to Unleash Power: an organization founded in 1987 to increase drug testing and media coverage of AIDS issues.

4 My consternation was magnified because I didn't know a single thing about Mariah's particular STD.

5 That none of these individuals tested positive for HIV in no way diminishes the severity of their situations. Statistically, HIV-positive individuals contract other STDs prior to HIV. My bout with mono is a prime example.

Wearing the Dress

by Andrew T. Gray
Occidental College, California;
New England Conservatory of Music, Massachusetts;
University of Texas-Austin

*T*he *black dress has been hanging in my closet for a week. I've decided to wear it tomorrow. See, I just bought these fabulous three-inch heels, and I've got to wear them ASAP. The dress is sleeveless, low-cut, and drops straight to my ankles. Look out, University of Texas!*

Three years old: I'm playing with a doll when my dad comes into my room. He rips the doll out of my hands and screams, "You don't want to grow up to be a sissy, do you?" My innocent play has become malevolent. I'm now acutely self-conscious. Is petting the dog a "sissy thing to do"? What about kissing my mother good night?

Five years old: I want to be a witch for Halloween. My grandmother makes my costume. When she brings it over, I'm disappointed that it's a pants suit and not a dress. But even by age 5 I know better than to show my feelings. Little boys shouldn't want to wear dresses, even on Halloween.

Seven years old: End of recess. "OK, class, line up. Boys on the right, girls on the left," the teacher orders. Oh, God! I hate this. I've been play-ing with my friends, who are girls, while the boys play soccer. I don't like being in the boys' line. I don't belong there. My friends get to stand in line together. Why must I be separated?

Upon entering college I explained these childhood memories to myself as part of my homosexual experience. Now in my final year, I know these events have less to do with my sexuality and more to do with my trans-gendered identity. Growing up in a small Texas town taught me that males who walk and talk the way I do—in an "effeminate" manner—are "fags." I admitted I was the "fag" other students had been calling me when

I finally came to terms with my sexual attraction to males halfway through my senior year of high school. During freshman orientation at Occidental College, I came out as gay to every person I met. People were accepting, and I felt free for the first time in my life. I could finally, and without shame, be who I was...or so I thought.

First, though, I'm going to shave. If I had more courage, I wouldn't mind showing chest and underarm hair. But I'm too steeped in popular culture to think I look good in a dress with body hair popping out everywhere. After the first stroke of the razor across my lathered chest, I realize this is going to take a lot longer than expected. An hour and a half later, I have a smooth chest (I should have trimmed it with clippers first). I pluck a few hairs off my back and gaze at myself in the mirror—beautiful! Huge pecs, well-defined biceps and triceps, bulbous delts, enormous lats hanging in a V from my back....

At first, the gay community of Los Angeles provided me with the liberation I sought (compared to Friendswood, Texas, *any* place was better). But it wasn't long before I realized that many of the same prejudices that plague the straight community also pervade the gay one. For example, just before entering a gay bar, one of my friends asked me, "Can't you at least pretend you've got something between your legs?"

"What do you mean?"

"Look, if you want guys to talk to you, you've got to act more butch. Stay standing against the wall; don't move or talk too much...you're too femme."

All of a sudden I felt like I was back in high school. I became obsessed again with controlling the way I moved and spoke, trying with all my might to make myself a desired part of my new community, to act like there was "something between my legs."

After shaving my legs, I run into my bedroom and slip into the dress and heels. I strut into the living room and model in the mirror. With the heels, I'm 6'2", 180 pounds of voluptuous muscle. What I see excites me.

My sophomore year at Occidental, I did drag for the first time. I had fun but was taken more as a joke than as a serious drag queen. As a friend put it (trying to be helpful, I'm sure), "You could never *really* do drag. Your face, your body—everything's too big and muscular. You'd look ridiculous."

Passing as a biological woman would have been difficult for me; my mannerisms, however, which even my most concentrated efforts barely affected, prevented me from passing as a "normal" (masculine) man. So I decided to rebel against both sides. Several weeks after my first attempt at drag, I borrowed a skirt and wore it to all of my classes. I didn't don a wig or make up or try to hide my "masculine" body. I marked myself as not being a "normal" male and felt good about it.

The next morning I wake up filled with nervous anticipation—will I go through with it? Yep. I'm "dressed" and "heeled" and about to walk out the door. This is not the first time I've worn traditionally feminine apparel to UT. I've been wearing skirts once or twice a week for several months, but for some reason people can dismiss a skirt as a sort of kilt. My friend Sue says, "Well, my uncle lives in Scotland, and he wears kilts every now and then, so I guess your skirts are OK."

This dress will not be OK, and that thrills me.

I've always been a "bottom." From age 13, I've been putting various small things inside me to aid my masturbatory fantasies. My mental sex scenario usually consists of my getting fucked by a huge football-player type; I imagine myself as a much smaller person (neither male nor female). Throughout my college years I've been trying to rid myself of the shame surrounding my "bottom" status. By the end of my sophomore year, I considered myself an out and proud bottom. Then, an experience forced me to question my supposed shamelessness.

Halfway through my third year at Occidental, I transferred to the New England Conservatory of Music in Boston because I thought I wanted to be an opera singer. In the dormitory I had a tiny room and a roommate who almost never left. On one unusual occasion, though, he did go out for the evening, so I decided to make the most of the opportunity. I began to masturbate, using a can of mousse as a dildo and facial moisturizer as lubricant. The top of the mousse can came off inside me (don't ask why I never thought that would happen). I tried for over an hour to pull or push it out, but I couldn't. It was totally stuck, and the more I tried to twist it around, the more it hurt. I started to bleed. Reluctantly, I realized I needed to go to the city hospital.

As I approached the head nurse of the emergency room, I was filled with a shame and fear like none I'd ever known. From the look on my face, the nurse could tell I needed privacy. We stepped behind a sheet hanging from the ceiling.

"What's the problem, sir?"

"The cap of a bottle is stuck inside my anus."

"How did it get there?" she asked politely.

"I put it there." (Probably the four most difficult words I have ever uttered.)

She sent for a doctor who turned out to be extraordinarily nice about the situation and tried to make me feel less embarrassed. In fact, all of the medical personnel were considerate. Why, then, was I so hysterical? I knew that getting the cap out wasn't an issue of life or death. (The doctor reached in with his fingers and pulled as hard as he could. The cap had created a suction inside my large intestine, and it came out with minimal bleeding.) It was the nature of the injury that humiliated me. Not only had I been caught masturbating but masturbating in a way "normal" males never do. Yet, if I didn't think of myself as male, why feel "male" shame?

I'm driving myself to school today. I usually take the bus, but I'm afraid of having to stand during the 20-minute ride in these shoes. I park in the campus garage and sit in the car for a moment to muster up my courage.... Well, here goes! I open the door, step out, and plop my backpack onto my shoulders. I make my way to the stairs, and a couple of cars pass. I keep my eyes straight ahead; I don't know if the people in the car notice me—I tell myself they don't. I walk down the stairs and run into some students. They're speaking a language other than English, so I have no idea what they're saying, but they definitely notice me. I again focus my eyes straight ahead. I walk briskly to the sidewalk, realizing the six-block hike to class is going to take an eternity.

I start down 24th Street and the hard stuff begins. I can see people hundreds of yards away walking toward me with perplexed looks. The first woman who passes me starts laughing, and so do I; I guess it's my nerves. A group of male athletes are talking in a huddle off to the left in front of a science building. I hear an "Oh, my gawd!" and a "Holy shit!" from two of them. I'm unsure how to handle these outbursts and stares. Part of me wants to stare back and ask what they're looking at. But I'm afraid I won't be able to keep a straight face.

Because I wasn't sure I wanted to be an opera singer, I transferred to the University of Texas after one semester at New England Conservatory so I could, as my parents put it, "figure out what the hell [I wanted] to do and stop wasting money." My transgender tendencies were quickly pushed into the closet due to my fear of Texas. Thanks to an English class, contemporary lesbian cultures, taught by an out and proud lesbian, I read Leslie Feinberg's *Stone Butch Blues*. The book gave me a language with which to discuss my transgendered self. I hadn't expected that. I had noticed a "butch-femme" section on the syllabus and thought how boring that part would be. I didn't think I'd have anything to relate to. Was I ever surprised! I got more out of that section than any other in the class. Although I had never wanted to identify as male, I thought I had no alternative. Discussing Feinberg's book not only showed me I had a choice but also gave me a vocabulary with which to describe myself. The term "transgender" came up many times during our discussions, and for the first time I thought, *That's me; I'm transgendered.*

I immediately began searching for more books that might speak to my experience, and although the texts were scarce, I did find a few. Kate Bornstein's *Gender Outlaw*, which chronicles her journey as a male-to-female transsexual, inspired me to begin my life as an out transgendered person.

I'm arriving in a more heavily populated area of campus. Surprisingly, I feel more comfortable here. Yes, more people are staring at me, but I can also see people not staring at me, which soothes me. I walk into the building of my first class and a burly football player holds the door for me—not so much out of kindness but out of shock. I walk up the stairs and head down the hall. My French professor approaches from the opposite direction.

"May I ask why?" she implores.

Oh, shit, I haven't thought of any fast answers—there are so many reasons.

"Because I felt like it."

"Oh, I see. Well, whatever floats your boat."

Some people claim I cross-dress as an immature way of getting attention. But if everyone stopped paying attention, I would still do it (and it would be *so* much easier). Most days, though, I live in traditionally male clothing and pass as a gay man. I enhance my "masculine" body by lifting weights so that when I go to bars, others will view me as an attractive guy.

I walk into class, and most of the other students are seated. They gasp. They've seen me in skirts and never said much, but this get-up apparently requires comment.

"Andrew, that's a great dress!"

"Look at those shoes."

"You look terrific."

All these responses come from women. One lone man responds, "You look good."

Their positive remarks completely shock me, but I'm also acutely conscious of the blank stares from the other half of the class. Are they horrified and hiding it well or just not interested? French proceeds as usual, but I can't pay attention. I replay in my mind all the looks people have given me that morning. When class ends I approach my professor. I'm not satisfied with the explanation I gave her earlier.

"Actually, there are other reasons why I'm dressed like this."

"OK." She looks up with a serious expression.

"It's a manifestation of society's internalized misogyny that people think it's OK for women to dress like men but not acceptable for a man to dress like a woman. 'Why would someone ever want to be like a woman?' our culture seems to be saying. By cross-dressing I'm drawing attention to this sexism. I'm saying I want to be like a woman. I want people to ask what's so perverted about that."

"At least you're not doing it just to be weird." My teacher smiles as she exits the classroom.

At a bar in Austin around Thanksgiving of my fifth year, I met this totally hot guy. He'd just gotten out of the Navy and was as "straight-acting" as could be. We had a great weekend of sex that led me to think he might be "the one." I dismissed his conservative political views and lack of interest in queer issues as part of his "butch" demeanor. I thought maybe it's true that opposites attract. I spent ten days with him in Seattle over winter break and slowly divulged my transgender identity to him. He didn't understand where I was coming from; the more I tried to explain, the more annoyed he became. He wanted a "normal" guy. I was upset with myself. Why did I have to be so fucked up?

Since I left Seattle, he has not contacted me. Sometimes it hurts; mostly it makes me yearn for someone who understands what I'm going through. I'm tired of people imagining how hard it must be. I want someone who *knows* how hard it is.

Suddenly, I'm filled with fear. I don't want to venture across campus. Why can't I just stay here in French class? But I march out the door with my head held high and briskly walk toward the geology building. I remember my friend Kristen is in this class, which makes me less scared. I walk up to the door, and she's standing with a smile on her face. I grin back, feeling suddenly at ease.

Being with a friend makes all the difference in the world.

I'm not part of a transgender community. No one I know considers themselves transgendered. When I first arrived at UT, I attended a queer organization's meeting and hated the experience. Close to 100 people were there, and everyone seemed to know each other. No one spoke to me. At Occidental, only ten to 12 people had been at each queer meeting, and it was impossible to attend without talking to other people. But at UT I didn't know how to break into the sprawling queer scene, so I gave up for a while.

Once I began coming out as transgendered, however, I decided to give UT's queer organizations another chance. At the beginning of the spring semester of my fifth and final year, I attended a few more meetings. In spite of its pro-diversity stance, the campus lesbian and gay community didn't welcome me with open arms. At the queer meetings my questions and comments were viewed as tedious and annoying.

A lesbian/bi/gay campus group meeting I attended:

FACILITATOR: What do we as gay people have in common with each other besides our same-sex attraction?

ANDREW: I take offense to that question. I don't think same-sex attraction is a universal similarity among all queer people. What about pre-op transsexual men who are attracted to women? After their surgery they'll be lesbians, but now they're technically heterosexual men. I consider them queer and part of the queer community even though they're not technically attracted to the same sex. And what if I were to get a sex-change to become a woman? Would I suddenly become straight and no longer be a part of the queer community? I don't think so.

FACILITATOR: How does everyone feel about what Andrew's saying?

STUDENT 1: I disagree with him completely. I don't have anything in common with transsexuals. If they want to form their own community, that's fine, but I don't care to have anything to do with them. I also hate the use of the term "queer." It's degrading; it's like an African-American calling himself a "nigger."

FACILITATOR: Anyone else? I'm sure we don't all feel this way. Does anyone support what Andrew's saying?

(A few heads nod; a couple of people turn and give supportive looks, but no one speaks up.)

STUDENT 2: Can we get back on track and talk about what the gay community has in common? That's what I came here to discuss. I say it's a perfect sense of style!

(Laughter around the room.)

Another lesbian/bi/gay campus group meeting I attended:

FACILITATOR: So what's the general consensus? Do we support the assimilation of gay people into the mainstream?

STUDENT 3: I think our community, and maybe even minorities in general, tend to view assimilation as a negative thing. I don't necessarily think it has to be that way.

STUDENT 4: I agree. I don't think any of us in this room are that different from mainstream society. Most of us are not flaming queens; what we do in private shouldn't be an issue in our everyday lives. We're no different than straight people in most ways.

STUDENT 5: I think assimilation is the best way for us to gain positive recognition and respectful treatment. I hate to say it, but I think the leather daddies and drag queens hold us back.

ANDREW (who is wearing a skirt): I can't believe you people are saying this! I'm not "mainstream." I'm a flaming queen! I wear dresses; I refuse to call myself a man, despite having a penis. That's what makes me queer: my inability and lack of desire to assimilate. What I do in private has little to do with it. Why do I bother coming to these meetings?

FACILITATOR: Andrew, I think it's important that you come to our meetings. You provide a different, valuable perspective, and I'm sorry if you feel unwelcome. But I think you sometimes attack others for not thinking exactly as you do. It's great you wear whatever you want, but I have no desire to cross-dress. The idea of walking around campus, or anywhere, in a skirt doesn't appeal to me. You need to accept that not everyone is just like you.

ANDREW: Why?

FACILITATOR: Why what?

ANDREW: Why don't you want to wear a skirt?

FACILITATOR: Um…uh, I don't know.

My next class is chamber singers. I've been in this choir for two years, so I know all the people in it. I expect an overwhelmingly warm response from my "friends."

Garth, who's usually supportive, walks in. "Why are you dressed like that?" he scowls.

"I wanted to."

"Whatever," he mumbles and walks away.

OK. Keep your cool, Andrew. One of my best friends, Scott, comes in snickering. "I can't believe you did it." He laughs a little harder.

Millie sits down and doesn't say a word to me. We always talk. Why is she being like this? Carl comes in and ignores me. I force him into conversation. He suggests I take off my watch, since it's "too big to be worn with a dress," but he makes no encouraging comments.

After choir I rush to my car and drive home. I had planned to go to my English class in the afternoon and then to a lesbian/gay organization's meeting, but I can't stay on campus any longer. I'm drained. At about 4 P.M. I walk into my apartment and take off my shoes. God, my feet hurt. I lie down on the couch and turn on the TV, exhausted from just seven hours on campus.

The next morning I ponder whether to wear a skirt. I know I can't do it. Yesterday took more energy than writing a 50-page research paper or running a marathon. I don't have the fortitude today. Although I hate passing as a nontransgendered person, I'm not tough enough to be "out" all the time. I open my closet door and slip on some jeans and a T-shirt. The skirt can wait until Friday.

Too Strong a Homosexual Presence?

by AJ Tschupp

Trenton State College, New Jersey

It was late February. I was finishing up my recruitment interview with the field hockey coach when one of the players knocked on the door. "Ready for the tour?" Jen asked, smiling. It appeared my interview was finished, so I shook hands with the coach and followed the junior-year player out the door with my mom and stepdad close behind.

As we walked around the Trenton State College campus, Jen pointed out the dorms and dining halls and briefly talked about the team. She mentioned the number of players on the roster, where some of them lived, that many of them were psychology majors like I would be, and gave me other background information. As the tour progressed I noticed my parents weren't quite keeping up with us, and soon they were lagging far behind.

"So, do you have any questions?" Jen asked.

I'd already asked about how the team got along and if they socialized together off the field. "I can't think of anything else right now."

"Nothing at all is on your mind?" she persisted.

I smiled nervously and shook my head.

She sighed and leaned in a little closer. "In case you're wondering, there are no dykes on the team." I detected a hint of pride in her voice about this "fact."

"Uh, um…OK." I didn't know what to say. I was still a timid young woman who couldn't see herself as anything but heterosexual, but I was shocked she would say such a thing to me, a complete stranger. She laughed, and shortly afterward we finished our tour.

That's what I remember most about how I was recruited to become a goalie for the Trenton State College (now known as The College of New

Jersey) NCAA Division III field hockey team. Originally from Long Island, N.Y., I was one of only a handful of out-of-state students in a school of 6,000. My outsider status made me feel a bit out of place, and it continued on the field, both in field hockey and later in my second sport, lacrosse.

During the first season I quickly learned that the team was determined to dispel the stereotype that all women field hockey players are lesbian. These messages were often subtle but still pervasive. Teammates would ask each other almost weekly if they had boyfriends, and they rewarded those who did with praise and attention. The all-female dorm, Decker Hall, was jokingly referred to as "Dyker Hall." Derogatory words about gays or lesbians, such as "faggot" and "lezzie," were used whenever homosexuality was mentioned.

Before practice one day, two juniors and a senior began "teasing" another junior teammate, Laurie, calling her "lezzie." They persisted for more than five minutes, nearly driving Laurie to tears as she yelled at them to "shut up!" because she was "not like that." The rest of the team laughed. I was quiet on the team as it was, but for a reason I could not yet identify, I was bothered by the comments and did not join in.

At the beginning of winter break, I was diagnosed with Epstein-Barr, an illness referred to as chronic mono. Due to an enlarged spleen and extreme fatigue, I was prohibited by school doctors to join the lacrosse team in the spring as I had intended. But since I loved sports, I wanted to remain involved, so I did the statistics for each game. This kept me in contact with many of the players and coaches from hockey, but no longer on a daily basis.

Spring semester I enrolled in an introductory women's studies course that opened up a whole new world to me. Here was a safe environment to discuss topics ranging from the definition of feminism to abusive relationships to lesbian baiting. Finally, I'd found something I liked even better than athletics: a home of supportive, rather than competitive, women. Never had I heard lesbianism discussed openly without snickers or sneers.

Before class one morning I was flipping through the TV channels in my dorm room. I stopped on a program showing news clips of a recent gay pride parade in Washington, D.C. I was mesmerized. For the first time in my life, I allowed myself to think for more than ten seconds that I could relate to these people. I could relate? Oh, my goodness! I really could relate. These people did not scare me. What was I saying? I identified with their fight for recognition and equality. I looked at them and felt myself identify.

For the rest of the semester and throughout the summer, I spent what felt like every waking moment thinking, judging, reflecting, questioning, and contemplating my sexual identity. I became more withdrawn at home, constantly reviewing my last 19 years, looking for signs to prove what my sexual identity was. Afraid to mull things over with my parents, I sought counseling in hope of finding an objective listener. I didn't encounter the warm supportive therapist I was hoping for, but her devil's advocate stance did help me solidify my defense of why I believe I'm a lesbian.

Lesbian. The word tied my tongue in knots worse than any tongue twister. By the end of the summer, I had accepted my homosexuality but felt more comfortable using the word "gay." I may have been comfortable with it, but what would my homophobic team have to say? I learned from the past year it was wiser not to give them a chance to say anything about me. I made the decision to protect myself by hiding in the closet. And I hated every minute of it.

Before fall semester even started, we were required to participate in a hockey camp. Older males from England showed up to coach my team, and my teammates and I would coach local high school girls. A few months earlier doctors had said I could play again. Four of us gathered at the apartment of two teammates, Carrie and Noelle, both juniors. They began to talk about Marie, one of our teammates as well as one of the only older players who talked to me.

"Can you believe Marie is rooming with Karen this year?" Noelle said.

"You know Karen, right? The softball player? You gotta watch out for those softball players! They're all dykes on that field," Carrie laughed.

The other players assumed Marie was a lesbian because she had short hair and didn't wear makeup, but she had told me she was straight.

"Well, I don't think it's fair they get to room together but I'm not allowed to room with my boyfriend," Noelle said.

The others echoed her sentiments. "Yeah, no one thinks anything of it because they're two girls," someone said.

I kept quiet, shaking from nerves and anger. I was angry not only at their bigotry and ignorance, but also at their inaccurate assumption about our teammate.

At the end of the week, a party was scheduled with the camp's male coaches. I was physically exhausted from coaching and practicing intensely for five days in 90-degree heat. Mentally, I was exhausted from hiding my new identity from teammates, making sure I didn't say anything that might give me away. I wanted to go home and rest before the semester started.

"Why don't you come to the party?" Terry asked.

"Me?" I asked, surprised to be included in a team activity.

"I'm sure there's a coach left that we can hook you up with!"

"Oh, well, you know, I have a long drive back to Long Island. I think I'm going to head home after the last session." My polite refusal was answered with looks and whispers.

As the season progressed, looks and whispers were also hurled behind the back of one of the assistant coaches whom the players called a dyke based on her masculine dress and mannerisms. I became closer friends with Marie, and the team ignored us more and more. They were most obvious after away games when we'd stop somewhere for dinner and no one would sit with us or near us. My paranoia grew when I realized the looks and whispers were taking place behind my back too.

At the time, I had been seeing an on-campus counselor. I was still looking for support for my new identity, and even though I was growing more and more comfortable with it, I was struggling with depression. Although the depression was multifaceted, my lack of belonging on the team definitely played a major role.

One day I was called into the head coach's office. "I know one of the goalies is going to counseling," she said. "It's you, isn't it?"

"Yes," I replied, stunned she could discover such a private matter.

"You know you can talk to me about something that's bothering you, don't you?" she said in a demanding tone.

"Yeah, I guess so." I wondered where she was going with this. There was a silent pause that I wasn't willing to fill.

"Do you have something to tell me?"

"Not really." I wasn't about to partake in an interrogation and was dismissed from the office. Although I hated hiding in the closet, I didn't feel safe enough to risk more alienation by my team. Maybe my coach wasn't trying to get me to share my new identity, but my team's opinion on homosexuality certainly wasn't inviting me to be more open and honest. They had already ostracized me because I didn't drink alcohol while in season and because I was always studying. I wasn't about to risk further stigma by revealing my sexual identity, so I chose to remain silent.

By spring of my sophomore year, I was beginning to transform from shy and closeted to outspoken and proud. This change was encouraged by the women's studies minor I was now pursuing, supportive friends I was meeting in these classes, and my first lesbian relationship. Then I had an activation of my Epstein-Barr virus, which my doctor said is most often triggered by stress. I knew the stress of hiding in the closet every day was getting to be too much, and I couldn't relax and have fun like I used to. My illness gave me a legitimate reason for quitting sports, although I still wanted to play because I loved field hockey and lacrosse. Still, I was growing tired of hiding.

The question I faced was whether to quit sports altogether. My mom, to whom I had come out the past November, and my partner both knew how unhappy I was in the program and suggested I consider quitting. I knew it was an unhealthy environment for me, but after playing sports for eight years I had a difficult time deciding. I knew, however, what had to be done for my health, and when I returned to campus I told the coach that my spleen was too enlarged for me to play hockey.

"I'm sorry to hear that, AJ."

"Playing two sports takes too much out on my body. So, with sadness, I'm quitting both lacrosse and field hockey."

"I know it must've been a tough decision, but you need to take care of your health first."

We shook hands, and I ended my athletic career with a sad heart but a feeling of freedom. It was one of the most difficult decisions I'd ever made. For eight years, I'd identified myself as a scholar-athlete. Now the athletic component was gone. Although I'd been miserable much of the time on the field, I still felt proud wearing a college athletic team uniform. I thought it gave me status, but I realized that meant nothing if I didn't fit in on the team.

My mental and physical health finally took precedence in my life, and for the first time in my college career I had time for other interests. The Trenton State College women's center became my home away from home. I had moved off campus the summer before my junior year, so the center provided me a quiet, safe, and supportive place at school for the next year and a half. Between the women's center and GUTS, the Gay Union of

Trenton State, I slowly but steadily built a network of support with new acquaintances and a few professors.

I became active at the women's center, dedicating a lot of time to help with programming, and soon I ran for executive board positions. Yet it was never a competitive or judgmental atmosphere. Unlike my experience with the women's athletic teams, this new all-female environment provided me with support, acceptance, and the freedom to discover who I was and what I could become. As I gained support I found the courage to take risks, and as I took risks I was gaining support. This included running for and being elected president of the women's center February of my junior year. I also found support when I enrolled in a women's studies course in the nursing department.

Halfway through the semester I was assigned to give a presentation on female sexuality. A week before it was due, I stopped by my professor's office. I had come out in a paper I wrote earlier in the semester, but I was nervous talking to her in person about it.

"Hi, Dr. Cosgrove. May I ask you for some advice on my presentation next week?"

"Ask away."

"Well, I was thinking of discussing lesbianism as a major aspect of female sexuality."

"So what's the question?"

"I want to come out to the class. Do you think they can handle it?"

"I don't care if they can handle it. They need to hear it. I don't think your safety is at risk, and I'll be there if there's a negative response. But I think it's important for you to do it and for them to know it affects a classmate personally."

I breathed a sigh of relief and smiled. I felt excited but was nervous, since I couldn't anticipate my classmates' reactions. It felt good, however, to know my professor was on my side.

The next week I eased the topic of lesbianism into my presentation. I had some butterflies but mostly felt confident. "Can anyone tell me some of the stereotypes about lesbians?" I asked. Everyone looked around. "Come on, we've heard them all. You can say them."

"Butchy," someone shouted.

"Unattractive," another called out.

"Wants to act like a man."

"OK," I said, "now that we've named some stereotypes, how many of you believe you know someone who is lesbian? If you know a woman who is lesbian, raise your hand." A few arms went up. I walked around the crowded room. "Your hand is not up. Would you put it up? Yours too." They looked perplexed but followed my instructions.

"Is everyone's hand up? Look around the room. You look confused." I smiled. "I had all of you raise your hands to show that you know someone who is lesbian, because you all know me." Hands came down, and astonished looks came across most of their faces. With a single nod my professor signaled her approval of my coming-out method.

When it came time for written student evaluations at the end of the class, I received both genuine support and positive feedback. Classmates noted my "bravery" and "courage to be honest" as well as my "mature manner" in discussing the subject. This support in an all-female class contrasted starkly with what I'd felt on women's athletic teams.

Their positive response helped encourage me to speak at the Take Back the Night Rally in April, organized by our women's center. Our executive board wanted someone to speak about sexual identity, but we couldn't think of a professor to take this role. I offered to speak on the subject, and they excitedly supported me, giving me even more courage. Held on campuses across the country, Take Back the Night is a rally for women to empower themselves and feel safe. On that warm Wednesday night, I introduced myself as president of the women's center and began the event. Speakers from both on and off campus addressed a variety of women's issues such as domestic abuse, and sexual assault and abuse. The vice president of the women's center then introduced me as the next speaker.

Nervously clutching my note cards, I stepped up to the podium, hoping my shaking legs would hold me steady. I looked out at more than 250 faces as I began. "I'm here to speak about a form of oppression," my voice cracked, "that I face every day. You may be thinking that, aside from my gender, what could a white middle-class American like myself face? But I face something that forces me to live a double life. While my immediate family knows me as one person, my extended family only knows a facade. My classmates know me as an 'out'-spoken person, while my coworkers know someone else. My mom is scared to death that I'm giving this speech, because she fears someone will beat the shit out of me in the parking lot. I face all of these oppressions because I am lesbian."

Lesbian. I'd said it! I'd said it to a crowd of 250 people! After two years I was able to use the "L-word." I'd decided it was important to me to separate from the word "gay" because people associate that word with males. And I realized that which we do not say, we do not acknowledge. I continued my speech, explaining homophobia and its partner in crime, heterosexism. I spoke of my exasperation to the comment, "You just haven't met the right guy" and jokingly asked the heterosexual women present if they just hadn't met the right woman.

A year earlier I had quietly participated in the rally wearing my pink triangle T-shirt, wanting to speak during the open-mike session but being too scared. Explaining I'd finally found my voice, I'd hoped this night I could help someone else do the same. Though I didn't say it, I realized that wanting to help someone was one of my drives for speaking. I'd never felt I had anyone to relate to, so I hoped someone in the crowd could identify with me. I was feeling more confident in myself and my identity, so it was important for me to share it, even with strangers.

Though I realized this event would be in the school paper and that my former teammates might see my picture and read about me, for the first time in my college career, I hoped they would. I knew I was growing and becoming a successful student leader. I was proud of myself and my identity and no longer needed their approval. This was a major turning point in my personal growth.

As the rally continued, I was showered with overwhelming support from both students and professors, many of whom I'd never met before. Echoing the comments I'd been given for my presentation in the nursing class, women's center members bombarded me with congratulatory hugs—and they hugged me without fear of what people might think of their sexual identity, which I often saw on my athletic teams. Their affection was based on sincere warmth and friendship.

I felt more confident than I'd ever felt in my life. I was also enjoying my growing comfort with public speaking and felt I had more and more supporters as I became the most visible and vocal lesbian on campus. But I wasn't pleasing all of the people all of the time.

After hearing rumors from my women's center faculty advisers that there had been complaints about the rally, I scheduled a meeting the August before my senior year with Shelly Carter, an administrator from the Office of Student Life.

"I'm glad you could make it," she said. "I want to discuss some ideas with you about the upcoming Welcome Weekend activities for first-year students."

"That sounds good, but first I was wondering if we could talk about Take Back the Night, because I'm hearing some people might have had concerns. I thought it was a complete success, so I'm curious what the problem was."

She shifted in her chair and sighed. "Well, after the rally several students told me they felt like it had been for lesbian and bisexual women only, which made them feel out of place."

"That's absurd." I was stunned. I thought back to that night and realized that other than myself, only one other person—a bisexual woman—spoke about sexual identity. And that was out of 25 speakers.

Shelly calmly continued, "These students complained that there was too strong a homosexual presence."

Not knowing whether to cry or scream, I laughed. *What about the 364 other days of the year when there's a strong heterosexual presence?* I sarcastically asked myself. I was speechless.

"The women's center is growing, and right now it has a good image on campus," she continued. "This could help you recruit first-year students. My advice is to focus on the positive programs you and the board have put together. I know you've done some things on female sexuality, but I'm concerned the center has too much of a lesbian focus. Maybe you could tone that down. There's already a Gay Union for those kinds of topics. Get the new students into the women's center before you bring up those issues. Showcase your other programs first, OK?"

"I get your message," I answered sharply. I was exasperated and struggling to not take her comments as a personal attack, but it was difficult for me to control my defensiveness. I was fuming that we were discussing the comments of a handful of students when there had been a crowd of 250. I knew I had the support of the women's studies faculty, but I was unsure whether other administrators shared Shelly's view.

I smiled and nodded to appease her but did not follow any of her advice. I didn't share the details of the meeting with the rest of the executive board until after the semester had begun. Thankfully, they too were shocked at the complaints and even more disappointed by Shelly's "advice." We agreed that it was against everything we stood for to have me be more reserved or to avoid doing programs related to sexuality simply because there was already a gay and lesbian organization on campus. So I continued to wear my backpack with my lesbian and feminist buttons. I continued to speak openly about my partner in front of new and returning members. My openness did not hurt the "image" of the center. It was an example of the diversity among our collective group of women and a testament to the open and accepting environment of which I'd become a part.

I continued to grow into my role as an outspoken student leader. I sometimes felt like a pioneer, because I had no one after which to model myself. Though this wasn't always easy, it made the accomplishment of each goal much more rewarding. Such was the case when I sought participants for my senior psychology honors thesis. I'd developed an interview to assess identity development in lesbigay college students but had difficulty finding potential participants, since few students were completely out on campus. And the Gay Union was small and did not offer a large sample. Several in the group were unwilling to participate. But my professor was extremely supportive of the topic from the minute I presented it to her. Like the nursing professor a semester before, my psychology professor felt that the research needed to be done and that the faculty needed to hear my ideas. With limited resources I managed to find ten people willing to participate.

Each of the ten interviews was fascinating in its own way. The students relayed their life stories, their struggles and triumphs. After answering my questions for more than an hour, each one always jokingly asked me to share my story since I knew everything about them. Often I did share my experiences, including coming out to my parents and brother. Just as they were interested to hear about the support I'd received, I was compassionate to those whose families did not know or were not supportive. While I'd experienced struggles in college as I came out, I was intrigued with my interviewees who had come out at a much younger age. Despite the differences in backgrounds, we all were struggling together to survive and grow at Trenton State College.

My college career ended much differently than I'd envisioned. I went from a reserved athlete to an outspoken feminist lesbian. Though the all-women's athletic "culture" offered me little support or appreciation of differences, the network of psychology and women's studies professors and my peers at the women's center showed me that all-women environments can provide a safety net while taking risks. These women gave me the courage to spread my wings and try new things, and I'll always be grateful for their positive role in my identity development and my ability to internalize the word *pride*.

An Unfailing Sufficiency

by Owen Garcia*
Brigham Young University, Utah

There was no question about it. I was destined to attend Brigham Young University. My father had earned his Ph.D. there, and my mother had worked on her master's degree there. The school had actively recruited me, luring me with an early admission and a full scholarship for the first year. But my desperation was more compelling than any of these reasons. I was a devout Mormon who was well aware that I was gay, and I needed help available only at BYU, serious spiritual help. I knew that in a place as reputed within Mormon circles for academic and spiritual superiority as BYU, surely I would find what I needed.

BYU is not only the hub of the education system of the Church of Jesus Christ of Latter-day Saints (the LDS Church) but also the center of spiritual socialization for young adult Mormons. Within the church, BYU is known as a playground for young men and women to date and possibly enjoy a romance before they enlist in the LDS service and spend two years as proselytizing missionaries. In fact, the immense pressure to prepare for one's mission and to find a spouse often seems to supersede the importance of academics at BYU. The whole social system there is meant to provide ample opportunity for any worthy man or woman to find their eternal companion after their missionary service ends.

And worthiness is key. Marriage is the consummate purpose of mortal existence and the preeminent ordinance in Mormonism, for which all young single Mormons should always strive to be worthy. Celestial marriage is so significant an ordinance in Mormonism that it is conducted only within the sacred walls of the House of the Lord, the temple, and there are only about 50 temples in the world where worthy LDS couples can be married for eternity. And worthiness to enter the temples is not easily achieved. Certainly not every member of the LDS Church can maintain temple worthiness at all times.

I wanted to be worthy like that. I wanted to be worthy to go to the temple. I wanted to meet the perfect woman who'd be my eternal companion (since eternal companionships are only heterosexual). I wanted to serve the Lord and his church by going on a mission. I wanted to excel in my studies and do it among my LDS peers. *Why shouldn't I be able to?* I said to myself. *Just because I have sexual fantasies about men doesn't mean that I can't. Besides, with enough faith, I should be able to overcome this temptation.* I believed BYU would provide an environment in which my attraction to men would attenuate and in which my will to be temple-worthy would be rewarded by God himself.

I grew up in Rhode Island, so going to BYU was not only a major step in the direction of religious dedication but also a major departure from home. I'd already come out to several friends during my last year of high school, all of whom were remarkably supportive and far more comfortable with my sexuality than I. As much as I believed it wouldn't be, walking away from that kind of support was traumatic. Not only that, but even though I'd never discussed it with them, my parents knew about my sexuality. I knew my parents were understanding, but on some level I needed to vilify them. If my parents had been overtly accepting in addition to my friends, then there would have been no hope for me to live up to God's expectations. As mixed up as it sounds, I believed God would never be as accepting as my parents. After all, my parents were mortal and imperfect.

Maybe I should have talked with them about it before I got on that plane to Utah. Once I boarded, though, I burst into tears. I was so inconsolable that the flight attendants could do nothing for me. Two of them crouched, asking, "Are you OK?" Of course not! I was realizing that my unconditionally loving parents, who could've been such a boon to me, were now going to be 2,000 miles away. I felt alone and afraid.

My first housing assignment was in an on-campus apartment building normally reserved for upperclassmen because it was the closest to campus. I asked for this building because I have a mobility impairment. I walk slowly with some pain, a result of juvenile-onset rheumatoid arthritis. Not having to walk far was a necessary accommodation. Almost everyone in the building was a junior or senior, and most of them had already served their missions and were yearning for their next rite of passage, marriage.

My first-semester roommates did their best to include me in their zealous pursuits of women, but they soon noticed how disinterested I was. It took them several weeks before they caught on that I might be queer. And once they grew suspicious, they set a trap that scared me shitless.

I was home alone one night. The other guys had all gone to a friend's apartment. The phone rang, and I answered it, hoping it might be for me.

"Is this Owen?" the voice on the other end asked.

"Yes."

"Great. This is Pierre. Do you remember me?" he asked in what seemed a Parisian accent. "I was your substitute French TA today."

I had, in fact, had a substitute French TA that day, though I thought his name was Michel. But I could be wrong, I thought, so I said I remembered.

"Well, this is difficult for me…I'm not sure I should be doing this, but…I think you're cute, and I was wondering if you'd like to go out sometime. I don't know, maybe for ice cream." This, I should add, is a typical line at BYU. The quintessential first date in college, going out for coffee, would be taboo since coffee is forbidden in Mormonism. On the other hand, two men going on a date is also forbidden! As innocent as ice cream would be, it wouldn't make up for what he was proposing.

My mind went into overload. Was this man really gay? Did he just ask me out? Michel—I mean Pierre—was hot, and I was both thrilled and mortified that this guy was asking me out. I'd never even talked to another gay man before. Was this happening? What if I said yes? Of course I wanted to. Of course I knew I shouldn't. What if this wasn't what it seemed? Wait a minute—how did he know I was gay? I'd heard rumors that BYU security officers often entrapped and expelled those men and women they suspected of moral misconduct, and this would certainly qualify. What should I do not to blow my cover? I wanted to say the right thing because if this weren't legitimate, I didn't want any retribution to come of it. And if it was….

After a long pause I got up the nerve to ask the shielded question, "Um…are you sure you have the right person?"

He burst out laughing and screamed, "Owen! That's so hilarious!" His accent was gone. "You should have heard yourself, buddy. Ha! Do you know who this is?"

"Uh, no," I stammered, partly from fear, partly from irritation, and partly from serious disappointment.

"This is Tom! Ha ha ha ha!"

My roommate? "Real funny, Tom." He explained that he was joking, but I knew it was more than a joke. I'm still not sure how he knew I'd had a substitute French TA, but that was proof that this was serious business. I felt threatened all the time that my inner turmoil was a visible scourge that would leave me vulnerable to teasing at best and outright persecution at worst. After all, that had been the fate of lepers in the Bible. If I could only have enough faith that Christ could heal me too, I'd have no reason to be afraid. But after Tom's phone call, I felt more frightened than ever.

I immediately called my parents. Only they could help me. They were already aware that I was disappointed with the overly social atmosphere at BYU and that I'd hoped my studies would demand more of me. They had even heard me complain that I felt I didn't belong to any in-groups yet, and that was frustrating me. But that night I had to tell them the rest. I told them I was coming home to Rhode Island because BYU wasn't what I thought it would be. It wasn't spiritually supportive, and, moreover, I didn't fit in.

My mom was the first to recognize this as the moment of truth. She put on her sweet "everything will be all right," trusting, and understanding mom voice. "Why don't you tell us what's really wrong, honey?"

Pregnant pause. That was permission enough. So, I began, "I'm gay, and I thought this would be the right place for me to deal with it, but it turns out to be so superficial that I can't cope with anything." I started to cry. "I can't stand it. I thought I was doing the right thing by coming here. But I need to go to some other school where I don't have to be all alone."

My mom took up where she left off, unfazed, in the same tone of voice. "Honey, I'm so glad we're finally talking about this. The first thing I want you to know is that I love you. The next thing is you should always feel welcome back home, and if you ever want to bring someone home to be part of our family too, he will also always be welcome here." Mom was ten years ahead of me, it seemed. I wasn't even sure I wanted to date men. After I told the story of what had happened with Tom, she understood. I was scared of my sexuality. At that, my dad got to the point and asked, "What do you think you need to do?"

This was when my pursuit for help really began. In the course of our conversation, my parents raised some good points. My dad explained how disadvantaged I would be if I didn't finish my first semester at least, and my mom described what conditions would be like for me at home. And, they continued, I was right after all. BYU and the surrounding city of Provo is a community full of resources for Mormons that cannot be found elsewhere. I knew I shouldn't walk away without exploring what might be out there for someone like me. Counseling was the first logical step, we concluded, and it would be free through the counseling center on campus. Counseling seemed a reasonable, safe, and neutral idea in the midst of my crisis and the fervent religiousness that pervades BYU.

At the counseling center, I was told, "Many men report great success with a program we call reparative therapy." They added that even though homosexuality was no longer considered a diagnosable disorder, it was still a behavior one could overcome. Through counseling with an appropriate male figure, I could repair my weak male self-concept, which was what had led me to believe I needed male partners. The guiding belief of this reparative therapy is that no one is innately or naturally homosexual but that homosexual attraction compensates for a deeply felt need for a different male self-concept. According to the therapist, I was a promising candidate because I was ego dysdonic, or self-hating, which is the first condition for success in the program. Even more promising was that the program was under the direction of men who have faith in Jesus Christ, which was proclaimed to be the determining factor in whether one will successfully change. All I needed was faith in Christ and a new male self-concept and I would no longer be tempted. Wow.

I didn't go home, not with a promise like that. Instead, I plunged myself into reparative therapy. And within two and a half years, by my junior summer, I'd convinced myself I was no longer in need of another man to make me whole. I was whole in my relationship with Christ and was ready to start dating women. "Saying it makes it real," I was told, so I voiced this miraculous change in my life to my closest friends. When I came out to my friends as a recovered homosexual, I received great praise and immediate superstar status for being diligent and valiant, an example and a witness to the truth of the Gospel of Christ. Even more amazing, I was approached by a friend of a friend, Nathan, who asked me how he could get into this therapy too. When we spoke about my triumph, we were exhilarated with the prospects: He could finally find freedom from his compulsions as I had; I could reinforce what I'd learned for myself by helping Nathan; and we could be there for each other and watch each other so neither one of us would "slip up."

Within weeks of our pact, I moved into a new on-campus apartment. It was summer, and a bunch of first-year students had flocked to BYU to get a head start on their academic careers. Ryan and his friend from their hometown in western Utah were assigned to my new apartment. Ryan was gorgeous, though I wouldn't have told anyone at the time. I didn't even tell Nathan right away. Instead, I convinced myself that I merely admired certain qualities of his character, like his humble silent strength. His innocent playfulness, his gentle and sweet...laugh, his...tanned...sculpted...body. No! I was certain I had no need for Ryan. I thought my relationship with Christ would be enough to carry me through my life without being tempted so easily. Why was I so drawn to this guy? Why couldn't I will myself to be happy with women? Why did I want to hold him, to touch him, so badly? Why was I forbidden? What was wrong with me?

The next part of this story is hard to tell, the kind of thing one doesn't want to talk about, even though sometimes it's best to. Certainly you won't understand the degree of pain we all went through my last year at BYU if I don't tell you. But I'm pausing here to emphasize that I'm not proud of what I did. Nobody should have to live through it, either as victim or perpetrator. I'm telling this story so others can learn.

On more than one occasion that summer, I went into Ryan's room while he was asleep to grope his body and genitals without his knowledge. When he woke up on one occasion, our worlds exploded, and nothing was the same after. Everything was a mess, and no one was prepared to deal with it. Our friends agonized for both of us. Ryan's parents were enraged. Ryan wanted it to be behind us, immediately. Nathan was on his way to New Zealand because he was straight enough in his own mind to finally serve a mission. Our new bishop barely knew either Ryan or me, so he was unsure what disciplinary action he would take, even though the letter of the law was that any "sexual predator" who poses a threat to the safety of other BYU students should be expelled. My parents were frightened. And I was lamenting. I slipped into confused depression. My constructed heterosexual identity had been obliterated.

The summer ended right around this time, thank God. For a two-week break, we separated. Ryan went home to his family. I went home to Rhode

Island. When we reconverged at BYU for that fall semester, we started picking up the pieces. Ryan didn't want it to be such a big deal, and I didn't want to feel like I'd destroyed his life. I promised my bishop I would go back into therapy and promised Ryan I would do anything he wanted or needed to respect his privacy and wishes. Bless his soul, he tried hard to forgive me, and to demonstrate it he called me on occasion to say hello. Sometimes we'd stay on the phone for hours, rebuilding what I thought was a recovering friendship. I was so encouraged, in fact, that I started taking liberties. I'd call him. I'd offer to help him with such-and-such. I'd make time to see him. I started to plan my time around seeing him again. In fact, I became so obsessed with making everything all right that by the end of October, I'd made everyone who was apprised of the situation terribly uncomfortable and highly suspicious of my motivations.

Now I was harassing Ryan, and his friends didn't like it. Ryan was too tender-hearted to say he didn't like it himself, so Missy and Sara decided they needed to intervene on his behalf. When I received their phone call, asking me to come to a "pow-wow," I started to feel unbearable guilt and disdain for my continuing weakness. When, in the meeting, I was told that Ryan's truest desire was that our friendship would dwindle away, my greatest pain was my self-disgust for clinging to a defunct dream. That night, out of Christian love for my welfare and Ryan's, I was cut off. Ryan's friends gave me mandates, backed up by threats of reprisal, never to contact him again.

I was now almost entirely alone with little in which to believe. I no longer felt Ryan was healing. I no longer had unconditional support from our mutual friends. I didn't have Nathan's understanding friendship handy. I didn't have my parents as I needed them; they were, after all, 2,000 miles away. I kept trying to believe in something, but little came of my will to believe. I did keep pouring my heart out to God in prayers. I kept bearing my soul to my bishop. And I beseeched the Holy Spirit, hoping my attraction to men would, after years of suffering, be wiped out.

I found some distraction in school. When offered a chance to teach philosophy to students at a local performing and fine arts high school, I leapt at the chance. I could redirect myself into my studies and maybe make a difference in someone else's life. So I taught with passion. And I grew close to my students. It was a small private high school that encouraged socializing between teachers and students, so sometimes we would go to movies together or even have dinner at one another's homes.

On one of these occasions my youngest student, a 12-year-old boy, came to my apartment to meet me before we headed to his parents' house for dinner. Ryan saw me walking out of my building that day and immediately believed I'd be a threat to this young boy. I wasn't to be trusted, and someone had to be told. Ryan, Missy, Sara, and others all believed I had deceived the bishop. Why else would a predator be allowed to continue at BYU? Mormons are compassionate, but they'll never allow mercy to rob justice, as the saying goes. I must've deceived the bishop in some way; I must not have been telling the whole story. They needed to go above his head, and their report precipitated a series of events that eventually led to a final and lasting judgment. The bishop's ecclesiastical superior was also a vice president of the university, and the heavy hand of justice came crashing down from the administration building.

It wasn't fast, but it was severe. School had just ended. I had completed my last year at BYU without further incident, minding my own business, struggling to suppress my sexuality with both the Lord's and my therapist's help, and abiding by the conditions that were set that long-ago night at the pow-wow. My teaching had miraculously benefited my self-confidence, and I was making strides again in therapy. I even felt God had forgiven me for fondling Ryan and that God was pleased with my progress. That is, until I received a phone call from the office of the vice president. I was told I had to come in; otherwise my graduation would be in jeopardy.

"Owen, are these accusations true?" he asked, showing me a letter Ryan had sent him.

I confirmed them and added that the bishop had been fully aware of my transgressions. "Why am I here, exactly?" I asked.

"Is it also true that you've had an extracurricular relationship with a 12-year-old boy who lives in the community?"

Wait a minute! Was my socializing with my students being interpreted to be sexually motivated and morally corrupt? It was. And despite my best attempts to describe my relationship with my students as legitimate, the vice president still seemed intent.

"I don't know what to say, Owen. I feel I can't fairly adjudicate without knowing more. There's a proper and formal way to go about that, as you know. We'll have to have a meeting of the Disciplinary Council." Three days later one was held in my honor.

Unsurprisingly, the council found that my behavior of nearly a year prior was so unbecoming of a member of God's true church that I was to be disfellowshipped. Disfellowshipment is not as extreme as excommunication, and the difference is that under the former I would retain my membership in the church but lose my right to participate in ordinances, and I would be censored at meetings. My disfellowshipment would last six months, after which I could receive full standing in the church again so long as I met the conditions of my disfellowshipment. I was still allowed to graduate, however.

The ruling wasn't the most significant part of that evening, though. I had almost been prepared for that. But I hadn't been prepared for the vice president's claim on God's behalf. I remember his words exactly: "Heavenly Father has not accepted your sacrifices." How did he know that? He claimed inspiration, but how did he get it? With such limited knowledge of what had happened in my heart over the last four years, how could he claim to know God was unsatisfied? The most significant part of that evening was the little thought that crept into my mind after he'd said those words: *I don't need you to tell me what God thinks.* In the moment when it seemed God had betrayed me and that I'd lost everything I had strived for at BYU, I began to realize what I *really* needed to learn at BYU: to love myself, even if I'm queer.

I went to BYU believing I needed its resources. I came out to my parents because I felt I needed their permission to come home. I went into therapy thinking I needed to change my sexuality. I professed my straightness because I needed others to tell me it was true. I clung to Ryan because I needed someone to love, to touch. I needed, I needed, I needed. I needed so much, and it was never enough. What I never had, though, until the night of the Disciplinary Council meeting, was myself. What I needed was neither forgiveness nor healing. I needed what Walt Whitman calls an "unfailing sufficiency." Thanks to the bittersweet intentions of my peers who tried hard to help me, even though I was a sexual deviant in their eyes, and even thanks to the prejudices, scorn, and judgments of BYU's officials, I learned I could rely only on myself to find the truth. When I fully embraced that idea, I started to trust myself...my queer self. You could say I went to BYU wanting God to provide a way for me to deal with or overcome the burden of my sexuality. But I came away from BYU believing that way is within me, that self-sufficiency depends on me, that I can love my queer self, and that is enough for me now.

   *This is a pseudonym. The author wanted to use his real name to demonstrate his commitment to telling the truth and taking responsibility for his actions and to display his confidence in the growth he has experienced since these events occurred. The editors, however, feel the pseudonym is necessary to protect the identities of other individuals (also identified by pseudonyms) in the story.

Out in the Boondocks

by Brandi Lyons
New York

Choking back tears I watched my parents drive away. I was trying hard to be brave, but I was scared as hell. I'd never been on my own. What the hell was I supposed to do? I suddenly missed them. I wanted to be taken care of, watched over, loved. Here I was in the middle of the Adirondack Mountains, with the nearest grocery store ten miles away and the closest so-called hospital another five miles from that. And I didn't know anyone on this small campus. A rush of panic came over me. My face felt flushed, my mouth dry, and my palms sweaty. *Oh, my God, what am I doing here?*

"Hey, you all right?" A woman's voice brought me back to reality.

Struggling to catch my breath, I turned to see a smiling girl. I guessed her to be about my age, perhaps a little older. She had short sandy hair and bright blue eyes that sparkled in the sunlight.

"I'm Justine. You look like you could use a drink. I've got iced tea in my room. You're welcome to it."

I realized I'd been staring at her and tried to regain my composure. "Oh, uh, yeah, thanks. That would be great." I felt like an idiot but followed her anyway. She led me upstairs. In this dorm, freshmen like myself lived on the bottom floor and sophomores on the second. I was excited that we lived in the same dorm.

"Here we are. Come on in." She held the door for me as I walked into her room. Upon entering I couldn't help noticing the rainbow flag hanging above her bed. I tried to scan the rest of the room without being obvious. In my peripheral vision I spotted a pink triangle on the opposite wall and a DYKY T-shirt on a papasan chair across from the bed. I felt my face get hot again but tried not to show it. I'd never known a gay person before. I didn't know how to react.

"Here's some tea." She handed me a cup and must have read my face. "I hope you're not freaked out by all of this."

"Oh, no. Not at all. I just…" I had no idea what to say.

"So are you a freshman? I've never seen you before." She casually changed the subject. I was grateful.

"Yeah, I got here today. My parents just left."

"Oh, so that's why you looked so confused down there." She smiled. "Don't be freaked out. It'll all fall into place. You have to go with the flow of things at first. You know, until you get comfortable. You'll find your niche." She motioned for me to have a seat.

"My niche? I don't know; I've never fit into any niche." The thought of it made me nervous.

She laughed. "I know what you mean. Everybody's always been a little afraid of me, I think…I guess I'm not an all-American girl."

I looked at her short hair, her dark blue tank top that was a few sizes too big, her sports sandals, and her cut-off army shorts. I couldn't help noticing that her legs were in need of a shave. She was anything but an all-American girl, and I loved it. I wished I could look like her. I wished I could have her confidence. Something about her made me like her right away. We continued talking until dinner time, then she suggested we go to the student lounge instead of the cafeteria because the food was much better. I got a piece of pizza, my staple food, and she got a salad.

"Ah yes," she commented, "the only vegetarian meal you'll ever find on this campus—lettuce and carrots." She grinned to let me know she was joking. Her eyes lit up when she smiled.

We sat at a table in the corner where we could look outside. The sun was beginning to set over the lake, and the entire sky was orange.

"That's why I chose this college." She pointed to the sky. "You've never seen a sunset until you've seen one in the Adirondacks."

I smiled because I didn't know what to say. She didn't seem to notice my sudden nervousness.

"Do you like hiking?" she continued. "There are some great trails around here. We should go sometime, if you're interested."

"Yeah, I'd love to go hiking." I thought I sounded a little too enthusiastic and privately wondered why I felt such a need to impress this woman I'd met just a few hours before. But I liked her a lot, and I wanted her to like me too.

Justine and I instantly became friends. We talked about everything. She told me about her past girlfriends, and I told her about my failed relationships with men. She warned me about professors, who to take and who to avoid; I'd cook her vegetarian meals whenever possible. She introduced me to her friends, and I'd introduce her to anyone new I'd met. We accompanied each other to parties and went on hiking expeditions. I felt like I'd met a long-lost sister. The closer we became, the stronger my feelings became. I tried to hide them from her because I didn't want to admit that I too might be a lesbian. I was confused and scared. I thought that if I told her my feelings, it may change the way she felt about me, in turn changing and quite possibly ruining our friendship. I couldn't take that risk.

I pushed my feelings aside day after day, week after week, even month after month. But I thought about her constantly. I'd catch myself daydreaming about her in class. I told myself the feelings would go away if I didn't acknowledge them, but they grew stronger. My heart skipped a beat when I saw her. I'd get that warm feeling in the pit of my stomach whenever she came close. Her touch put me over the edge, and I fantasized about sleeping with her.

"Don't you agree?"

I came crashing back to Earth and realized I'd been staring at her. I had absolutely no idea what she'd been saying.

"Oh, yeah. Definitely." It was a feeble attempt, but it was all I could muster.

She smiled that smile that said she knew exactly what I'd been thinking. She had caught me, and I was frantically trying to cover it up.

"You know, it's OK," she said, touching my leg.

"What's that?" I tried my best to act innocent.

"If you want to talk to me about something, it's OK. You can tell me anything." She looked into my eyes, and I melted. I could no longer deny it. I wanted her.

"I know, but I think some things are better left unsaid."

"You'll never know what could happen if everything is out in the open."

"That's what scares me. It could be horrible." I had to look away.

"But it could be wonderful." She put her hand on my knee again. Every nerve ending in my body was alive, and I was short of breath.

"But what if you don't feel the same way I do?" I couldn't believe we were having this conversation. I couldn't believe I was still capable of having a conversation.

"Brandi," she took my hand, "I do feel the same way. I've felt it for a long time. But I'm not going to push the issue. I know you've got a lot to deal with. I've been there. When you're ready to talk about it, we can. Just let me know. I'm not going to push you, OK?"

All I could manage was to nod my head. I was so nervous that I was shaking. I didn't know what to do or say next.

Justine let go of my hand and stood up. "I hate to leave, but I was supposed to be at a study group for accounting about 15 minutes ago," she explained while I tried to calm down. "Do you mind if I stop by later?"

"I'd like that." I stood and walked her to the door.

"Pick up a movie or something. I'll bring the ice cream." She smiled and kissed me on the cheek. "See ya then."

Taking a deep breath I closed the door behind her.

Although we saw each other every day and talked about everything and anything, the subject didn't come up again for another three weeks. It was mid-February, the night of Justine's 21st birthday. A bunch of us had gotten together for a small party in my room. We had baked her a cake, and as the evening wore on the cake and most of the alcohol were gone.

"Well, guys, I'm going to call it a night." Jeff, our last guest, stumbled toward the door. I'd met him about four months before in my English literature class. We had become fast friends, "coffee buddies," as he called us. Every Tuesday and Thursday we met for coffee in the student lounge and discussed the world's problems. He usually griped about women, and I usually pointed out how useless men are. He was a great guy, and I was happy he had come to Justine's party.

"Justine, do you need a ride home or anything?" he offered.

She smiled. "Actually no, I live upstairs. But thanks, and thanks for coming. It was nice meeting you." She got up and shook his hand.

"We'll have to get together soon. Maybe for coffee?" he suggested.

"Sounds great."

He excused himself, and she walked over to take her place next to me on the bed. She touched my leg, and my heart skipped. I wasn't sure if it was the alcohol, but I hadn't been able to take my eyes off her all night. She had caught me looking more than once but never acknowledged it.

"Thanks for the party." Her hand moved to my thigh.

"Justine, I..." I couldn't get any words to come out.

She chuckled. "You're so cute when you're nervous. Don't worry, we'll just chill out, OK? I don't want to go home and be all alone." She stood and moved to the stereo and started looking through my CDs. I appreciated her attempt to change the subject, but this time I didn't want her to. I was ready to talk about this.

"Justine, can we talk? I mean, seriously?"

"Of course we can. What's the matter?" She spun around to look at me.

"How did you know you were gay?"

"Oh, God, I just knew. I had crushes on girls, not guys. Women interest me, men bore me. Men are useless!"

"But how did you know you wanted to sleep with women?"

She stared at me. I knew she was trying to get inside my head, and I tried my best not to let her.

"You know, I denied it for a long time. I kept pushing away that feeling."

"What feeling?"

She hesitated, then sat next to me on the bed. "The feeling you're having now. The feeling you get when I do this." She placed her hand on my thigh again, and my heart stopped.

"I pushed and pushed," she said, "but no matter what it always came back. And it came back stronger each time." She moved closer to me, and I thought I would melt. I couldn't breathe. "You can't push it away forever. You just need to relax and go with it." Her hand moved as she leaned closer. I was shaking as our eyes met. "Close your eyes and surrender to the feeling. Don't fight it anymore." I did as she said, and when her lips touched mine it was heaven.

The kiss left me feeling light-headed, happy, excited, confused, and nervous at the same time.

"Are you OK? I shouldn't have done that. I'm sorry," she said.

"No, it's OK. I wanted you to do it." I paused, trying to find the courage to say what I really wanted to say. "I, um," I tripped over my words. "I want you to do it again."

Her shocked expression didn't help calm my nerves. "Are you sure?" She looked into my eyes. I'd never been so sure of anything in my life. We kissed again, and as our tongues met, my nervousness was swept away, leaving me with a passion I'd never felt before. The next two hours went by incredibly fast and unbearably slow at the same time. The feeling was so intense, I lost control of all thought. I could concentrate only on this kiss, this touch, this moment in time.

We lay in each other's arms after we made love. Consciousness slowly drifted over me, and I began to process what had happened. Thoughts raced through my head: *Does this mean I'm gay? How will people react? Am I making the right choice? Do I have a choice? Should I continue to deny my feelings? Is that even possible?*

"Any regrets?" Justine's gentle voice asked, and I suddenly grew aware of her skin touching mine. God, she felt good.

"None at all." I kissed her forehead before nodding off to sleep.

Justine and I dated for the rest of the school year. We were together 24 hours a day, seven days a week. Since she was out to the entire campus, it wasn't long before rumors started to fly. People pointed and whispered behind our backs. Some started to avoid us, while others went out of their way to aggravate us. People I'd thought were good friends suddenly were too busy to hang out. Invitations to parties dwindled and eventually stopped coming altogether.

I was frustrated, hurt, and confused as I walked out of my calculus class expecting to meet Jeff for our coffee break. I couldn't wait to hear what advice he could give me.

"Man, am I ever ready for that coffee!" I exclaimed as I walked up to him.

"Brandi, I can't today, OK?" My smile faded. He backed a step away as I approached. I noticed his eyes were darting around, falling anywhere but on mine.

"Oh, bummer. Why not?"

"I just can't, OK?" he snapped at me for the first time ever.

"All right, then Thursday?"

"No, I don't think we should do this anymore." His eyes were on the ground. I was confused.

"Why? What's the matter?" I couldn't keep the hurt out of my voice.

"Brandi, people are talking. You and Justine this, you and Justine that. I don't know if it's true, but if it is, I don't want to be a part of it."

"A part of what, Jeff? What are you saying?" My voice rose as I became defensive.

"Look, don't take it personally, OK? I like you and all. It's just that..." He stopped short.

"It's just that if I'm a dyke like Justine, then you don't want to hang out with me. Am I right?" I was so hurt and so stunned that I didn't know what to do.

"Well, what are people going to think about me if I hang out with you? They're going to think I'm gay."

I almost smacked him. I couldn't believe what he'd said. "You know what, Jeff? Don't worry about it. I wouldn't want to blemish the reputation you've got going here." I spun and walked away from him as fast as I could. What an asshole! I hated him for what he'd said.

Throughout the next few weeks, Justine and I were bombarded with more of the same attitude. Sarcastic remarks such as "You just need a good man like me!" often took the place of friendly hellos. People stepped into our path to try to intimidate us. One day while we were walking to the gym, a car drove by, and the driver screamed an obscenity and gave us the finger. We encountered so much hatred that I was becoming scared. But Justine had a way of ignoring it, pretending it wasn't there. As much as I tried, I couldn't do that. I needed to get away from it all. Justine, bless her soul, had the perfect solution: a long weekend at Whiteface Mountain, just the two of us.

"Hon, can you fit this in your bag? There's no room in mine." She held up her fleece jacket and looked at me with that pathetic, helpless look I loved so much.

"Yeah, here, give it to me. Are you ready?" She handed me the jacket, and with one last run down the checklist we were out the door.

"I thought maybe we could stop at the café and grab some hot cocoa first," she suggested.

"That sounds good. Let's put our bags in the car first."

We walked in silence the rest of the way to the parking lot. I could hardly wait to get on our way and off campus.

"Oh, my God!" Justine's voice broke the silence. We saw it at the same time. I dropped my bag in the snow and walked cautiously to my car. All the windows were smashed, the tires flat, and the lights broken. "Oh, my God!" she said again.

I couldn't speak. I couldn't breathe. All I could do was look. I walked to the passenger side to examine the rest of the damage—more of the same.

"Honey, come here. Look." Justine was staring at the hood of my car.

DYKE had been scribbled in the snow across the hood. My jaw clenched shut, and my hands were in fists. Every muscle in my body was tight. That was it. That was the last straw. Someone was going to pay.

"Brandi—"

"Don't touch anything, Justine. Leave it the way it is." I started to walk away, back toward the dorm.

"What are you going to do?" She ran after me.

"Have the son of a bitch arrested!" I walked into my room, slammed the door, and picked up the phone. I was so angry, I couldn't even talk to the dispatcher. Justine took over, apologizing for my attitude. *My* attitude? I had every right in the world to have an attitude.

"They should be here soon," she said as she hung up the phone.

"How the fuck are you going to apologize for my attitude?" I lashed out.

"Honey, come on. Let's just relax."

"Justine, I can't relax! That's my fucking car out there!" I was pacing back and forth. My heart felt like it was going to beat out of my chest. I was short of breath and dizzy, and had to sit down before I fell down.

"Fuck!" I screamed. Then the tears came. I couldn't stop them, though I tried like hell. When Justine put her arms around me, I cried harder. "I can't do this anymore, Justine. You know, it's not enough that everyone talks about us. It's not enough that we have no friends left on this damn campus. Now they've got to trash my car? What's next? I don't even feel safe here anymore." She tried to comfort me, to no avail. I wanted to go some place where I could feel safe, somewhere I could be with the person I loved without fearing for my life. I hated this school. I hated this town. I hated the world.

When the police arrived 20 minutes later, Justine and I met them in the parking lot. Without two words to us, they examined my car and the area surrounding it. They searched inside and out, and finally, after 15 minutes, one of the officers turned to us.

"Is this your car?" he asked unenthusiastically.

"Yeah, it's mine. Is there anything you can do?"

"Well…I'm not sure. They didn't leave any fingerprints, so I'm assuming the suspects were wearing gloves." he explained.

"The suspects?" Justine asked. "You mean you think it was more than one person?"

"We counted five sets of footprints. I'm assuming two of them are yours?" He looked at me and I nodded.

"Any suggestions about what we should do now?"

"Well, this type of violence is usually random. Usually a bunch of guys out raising some hell. But in this case, judging by the accusation on the hood, it was most likely directed at you personally." He was stating the obvious. "In which case I advise you to use extra precaution. Make sure to lock your doors, and try to travel in groups of two or three. I wouldn't recommend being alone."

His warning struck a fear in me I had never known. I assumed someone was out to hurt us. The thought brought tears to my eyes. I had to walk away to hide them.

I suffered through the next week, terrified to leave my room, even to walk to classes. I'd jump at every noise I heard. I couldn't eat or sleep, and Justine was no help at all. None of it seemed to faze her. She said I was overreacting. I felt completely alone, and was convinced the only thing that would do any good was for me to get out of there. I was debating whether I should quit school when the phone rang.

"Is Brandi there?" It was a male voice I didn't recognize. My defenses went up immediately.

"Who's this?"

"This is Greg Cassil. I'm an English professor here at school." He sounded sincere.

"What can I do for you?"

"I've heard about what's been going on recently."

"Yeah, who hasn't?" It had been the talk of the campus for the last week.

"I want to help. I'm gay too, and was wondering if you'd like to help me start a support group for other gay and lesbian students."

"That sounds great, but I don't think you'll find anyone else who qualifies." I was incredibly skeptical.

"You'd be surprised at the number of students who have approached me. I have a list of seven names so far. Yours would make eight."

Ironically, such a tiny number seemed unreasonably high. But if this guy was for real, it couldn't hurt to hear him out. I listened for another few minutes as he explained the details. The club would be open to anyone with the understanding that it supported gay and lesbian lifestyles. They'd meet twice a week in Greg's office, starting the next night at 7:30. I was still skeptical but decided to give it a try.

"I guess I don't have anything to lose. See you tomorrow night," I agreed and hung up.

The meeting went better than I could've imagined. Eleven people attended, including myself and Justine. I recognized a few people from around campus but had spoken to only one of them before. Her name was Jill. She was in one of Justine's classes and had come to her birthday party. Jill and Justine started talking immediately about what they wanted out of the group. The rest of us sat and listened, occasionally adding our own thoughts. Some of the ideas included hiking trips, mountain biking expeditions, guest speakers, and, if possible, a dance or two.

Then Greg spoke. "I'd like to see this group recognized as an official club by the Student Government Association. Does anyone else want to get involved politically?" He looked at me as he finished his question, and I smiled.

"I know this is the first time in a long time that I've actually felt safe on this campus. I want that to continue," I said, and Justine winked at me from her spot next to Jill.

"Something needs to be done to stop the kind of violence that Brandi and Justine have experienced," Jill said. I felt a twinge of jealousy when I saw her hand touch my girlfriend's knee.

"I just want to be accepted for who I am," Justine added.

"Is the student government something we'd all be interested in? If we become an official club, it not only means funding for all of the events we've been discussing, but also we could get an amendment written in the student handbook, something specifically against hate crimes. Violators could be suspended as well as prosecuted," Greg explained. He'd obviously put a lot of thought into the group. I admired him for taking such initiative.

The meeting lasted two hours, at which point we all made plans to meet again in three days to plan our first event, a camping trip to Whiteface Mountain.

"Brandi," Greg called to me as I was leaving. "You got a sec?"

"Of course," I said, watching Justine walk away with Jill. "What's up?"

"What did you think?"

"I can't believe all of these people!"

He laughed and nodded his head. "Having people with similar feelings around you will help a lot. When I heard about your car, I knew something had to be done. I couldn't keep quiet any longer."

"You'll never know how much that means to me. I was contemplating quitting school."

We talked in his office for another half hour. It felt good to actually be listened to and understood, and I felt comfortable with him.

A few weeks later Justine and I broke up because she started a new relationship with Jill. Although it was hard, it was comforting and helpful to have a support group to turn to.

Throughout the next three years, Greg and I became best friends. We worked together as coleaders of the club, organizing camping trips and other events. We helped the group start a PFLAG branch in the neighboring town, convinced a local dance club to make Tuesday nights gay night, and finally, after two years of petitioning and begging, the group received recognition as an official club by the Student Government Association.

It was a lot of hard work and took a lot of time, but it was time well spent. We had finally created a space on campus where gay students could feel safe. They could feel comfortable being open, and they always had somewhere to turn if things got to be too much. Knowing I'd helped to create it was an amazing feeling.

I remember Greg's final words to me at graduation. "Brandi, you're the only one who's going to make you happy. Go out there and do it."

Out and Proud

by Daniel A. Sloane

University of Pennsylvania

When I enrolled at the University of Pennsylvania, I had just begun to explore what it meant to be gay. Even though I'd known I was gay all through my high school years, they'd been years of denial and self-hatred. I'd never confided in anyone, not even my closest friends. When I finally came to terms with myself and who I was, I realized the next step was to come out to Wendy, my best friend of six years. I guess you can say things went smoothly. We hugged, we cried, and that summer we checked out guys together. And even though I couldn't have asked for a better friend, I still felt alone. I wanted to be around other gay people like me. So during my first week at Penn, I attended a Lesbian, Gay, Bisexual Alliance (LGBA) event.

I'd never been so nervous. My legs wobbled and my eyes darted back and forth as I made my way to the meeting. I paused outside the door, afraid of who or what would be inside. Was I doing the right thing? Would there be other people like me? Did I really belong there? Yes. Once again I was affirming who I was, this time to people I'd never met. I pulled myself together and walked through the door. For the first time in my life, I was with other people like me. They had gone through the same experiences, felt the same emotions, had the same worries. And they were gay. We introduced ourselves and told our stories. I felt exhilarated and was eager to spend more time with these people. After the meeting I picked up a copy of the *LGB Community Resource Guide* and the *Philadelphia Gay News*.

I'd been sharing a dorm room in Hill House, a predominantly freshman residence hall at Penn. When I returned to my room, I put the papers in the bottom of my desk drawer, figuring I'd read them later when it would be safe and private.

The following Monday I returned from class to find two pornographic pictures of men on my desk. The pictures were printed from a computer, and on the bottom of each page was a distinct mark that my roommate's printer always made. Across each picture FAG BOY was written in black capital letters. I was terrified. My heart raced as the tears welled up in my eyes. I immediately threw the pictures in the trash and ran. I had no idea where I was running to or what I would do, but I knew I needed to get away—and fast.

As I sped down the steps of the dorm and across the college green, I felt terror building in my stomach, and as soon as I reached a place where no one was around, I stopped running and threw up. Then I sat down and cried. I sat there and cried for hours, wondering what I was going to do and trying to figure out what had happened.

Who had put those pictures on my desk? My roommate, Dylan? He was the only person I could think of. After all, they had come from his computer. How had he found out? Had he looked through the papers in my drawer? He must have. And as I started to piece things together and answer my own questions, my fear changed to anger. I'd been violated. My private space had been invaded, and I felt exposed and vulnerable. Everyone has a barrier they feel safe behind, a line that can't be crossed. But I no longer had that. I needed someplace safe to go.

The campus lesbian, gay, bisexual center was the only place I could think of. I'd heard about a social they were having that evening and decided to go. Some of the same people I'd met before were there. When I told them what had happened, they suggested I come back the next day and speak with Bob Schoenberg, the director of the center.

I met with Bob the next day and told him about the pictures. He took action immediately. That same day he made phone calls and promised to see it through to the end. Bob spoke with Steve Feld, at that time assistant dean of Hill House, and with my grad fellow and resident adviser, Senthil. For the first time, I felt someone was on my side. Bob told me I needed to file an incident report with Senthil.

I stood there and nodded, but inside I was petrified. I didn't want to be a victim. I didn't want to file an incident report. I didn't want to be gay. I wanted to run far away. Away from my roommate, from my dorm, from Penn, from homophobia, from everything. But I realized I had run long enough.

I returned to my dorm that evening and met with Senthil in his room.

We talked for a little while about what had happened; then I filled out an incident report. Senthil then called my roommate into his room. It was the first time I'd seen Dylan since the incident. He seemed nervous and uncomfortable. My being gay never came up in the conversation, but it was obvious he knew. He swore he knew nothing about the pictures. "Maybe someone broke into our room and did it," Dylan suggested. He couldn't even look at me.

There were no signs of forced entry, and nothing was stolen. Between the two of us, we had a TV, VCR, stereo, refrigerator, and hundreds of CDs. Who would go through all the effort to break into the room and leave homophobic pictures on my desk without stealing anything? Why not just slip the pictures under the door and save the trouble? It didn't make sense, and that was becoming clear to everyone.

After Dylan left, Senthil and I talked some more. He suggested that perhaps Dylan was going through my things, and when he found the papers in my drawer he had a "freak" reaction. He had probably never dealt with someone gay before and flipped out. The pictures that were left on my desk could have been his initial response, and maybe now he regretted it and was trying to cover it up.

I had no definite proof, and any accusations would be premature, but still I felt uncomfortable. I'm sure Dylan did too. I knew I needed to talk to him and sort things out. There was no space for homophobia in the 13- by 9-foot room we had to share.

As I walked back to my room, I realized people in my dorm suite had heard about what had happened. I heard their whispers and felt their eyes follow me. I was very scared. Again I felt all alone. But I promised myself I wouldn't run. I needed to stay and deal with this. This is who I was, and these were the problems I would have to face—if not now, then later in life.

Dylan was in our room when I returned. We talked for about an hour. I explained how it took me years to get used to being gay and that I didn't expect him to be able to deal with it right away, but I did expect him to be understanding.

"I expect you to respect my privacy," I said, "as I have respected yours. And I expect you to let me make the choice of whether I want other people to know I am gay."

He tried to be open and honest with me. Dylan told me he felt uncomfortable but was trying to be understanding; he needed some time. I told him I was still the same person he had been living with and became friends with during the past two weeks. Nothing had changed. He just knew something more about me.

That night I don't think either of us slept. I stayed awake staring at the ceiling, still unsure about everything. Should I trust my roommate? He had seemed sincere. Did people in my dorm know? Would they treat me differently? Would I have to deal with more homophobic attacks? I was full of unanswered questions that frightened me but still hoped everything would end quickly and without any more trouble.

My hopes held true at first. For about a week, Dylan seemed fine, becoming much more comfortable around me. We even went into town for dinner one evening, and he was able to joke about the situation. But a few days later, I noticed Dylan was starting to act strangely again. For three nights in a row, he didn't sleep in our room. He told me he had been at parties or crashed at a friend's place. He began avoiding me and brushing me off. When his parents called, instead of engaging in a friendly conversation as they had several times before, they hung up after I identified myself as Dylan's roommate. After a couple days of this strange behavior, I confronted Dylan.

"What's going on?"

"What do you mean?"

"We were getting along great, and you told me things were OK. Two days later you refuse to sleep in the room, you avoid me as much as you can, and your parents hang up on me every time they call. So what's going on?"

Dylan fixed his eyes to the floor. "I told my parents you're gay," he said quietly. "They yelled at me for being so stupid and for listening to what everyone else is telling me." His voice grew angry. "They told me there are only two ways of dealing with homosexuals. If you can be friendly, live, or even associate with someone who is gay, then you must be gay too. If you're not gay, the only thing to do with gay people is to bash them."

I couldn't move. I was frozen by his words. His voice got louder, and he looked directly at me. "They asked me how I can sleep in this room knowing there's a fag next to me." Suddenly he was quiet again. Almost apologetically, he said, "They want me out of the room immediately."

I guess Dylan's parents weren't familiar with Penn's room-changing policy, which indicated that Dylan would have to wait until October 16, the published lottery date, to qualify for a room change; after all, this wasn't a dire emergency. Dylan's parents were furious when they found out. There was no way in hell their son was going to "sleep in that room knowing there was a fag next to him...." They promptly called the assistant dean of the dorm, Steve Feld. He reminded them of the policy and told them he'd look into the situation but that they'd have to go through Residential Living. So they called the vice provost, who also directed them to Residential Living. After that they phoned both the provost and the president, whose secretaries also directed them to Residential Living.

Dylan's parents told him that until everything was worked out, they didn't want him sleeping in the same room with me. If they found out he went against their word, they threatened to drive down from Smalltown, Mass., and take him out of school and back home. Under the weight of his parent's ignorance and bigotry, Dylan cracked. He slept in the lounge for one night until he discovered there was an empty room down the hall that was unlocked and began sleeping there.

"I think you're looking at me during the night" was his excuse.

"Don't flatter yourself!" I joked. He didn't find it amusing.

After learning about Dylan's parents' ultimatum, I needed to talk to someone. I was concerned and scared about the situation. The next day I contacted Bob at the LGB center and then went to talk with Steve Feld. Steve had spoken with Dylan and said he had seemed OK with everything. He had also spoken with Dylan's parents, and he supported Residential Living's decision to deny the room change.

"How are you feeling about everything?" Steve asked me.

"Three weeks ago if someone told me I'd be where I am now, I wouldn't have believed them in my wildest dreams. But I'm here...and I plan on staying."

I wanted to be strong, but I was tired, both emotionally and physically. I'd been through so much in the past two weeks. I kept telling myself it would all be over soon and that I could get on with my life, but when I returned to my room the next evening, I found the following note on my bed:

Dan,

I feel bad writing this, but I don't know what else to do. Yesterday I lied to you and Steve Feld. I was just so relieved to find out it was OK to question your sexuality (every straight person does at one time or another), and I realized I could never be attracted to a man, no matter if I could tell if they're good looking or not (I mistook this as being weird). Because of this relief, I didn't feel anything bad for the first few hours. I was so relieved that I could never be like you. But then the uncomfortableness and unbearableness set back in last night. But I still knew I could never be attracted to a man. So I searched and searched (painfully I thought I was lying to myself but wasn't) and came up with the answer. Even though I know I'm perfectly straight, what my dad convinced me of is true, in my eyes, and no one will convince me otherwise. I may be prejudiced in your eyes, but not in mine. No one will change this....

—Dylan

I decided it would all end here. I couldn't tolerate any more. I went back to Steve Feld, this time determined to settle everything. I didn't say a word. I simply handed him the letter. He read it once and then again and then looked up at me. "What do you want to do?"

"I haven't slept in two weeks," I said. "It's only the beginning of my first semester, and already my grades are suffering." I paused and took a deep breath, fighting back tears. "I want my life back." I didn't want to have to deal with my roommate or his parents any longer. "But I'm not moving out of that room. This is their problem, not mine."

"Then I'll go ahead and arrange temporary housing for Dylan until something definite can be decided."

Two days later Dylan's parents drove from Massachusetts and took Dylan home to get away for a few days. One week later his parents returned to Penn, without Dylan, and moved his stuff out of our room. Dylan had withdrawn on a "medical leave." I didn't know what to feel. I was glad they were finally out of my life, but at the same time I realized that Dylan too had become a victim of homophobia.

There were lots of questions and rumors going around my suite after Dylan left. Senthil didn't know how to respond to them. He wanted to respect my privacy, but at the same time people were asking about Dylan. So at our next meeting, I came out to my entire suite and explained what had happened. Most of them sat quietly and nodded their heads. Others looked away. No one said a word.

I returned to my room after the meeting, waiting for the homophobes to strike. Sure enough, there was a knock on the door.

"Come in."

Two guys from around the corner entered. I was shaking, wondering what they would do first. "We came to tell you how impressed we are with your courage," one said. "It took a lot of guts to stand up there and tell your story. If you need anything or if anyone messes with you, tell us and we'll kick the shit out of 'em."

About five more people came to my door that night, each with a similar message. I was overwhelmed by the amount of support I had received—from my suite, my friends, the LGBA, the LGB center, and, most importantly, the administration. They stood behind me all the way, from Bob Schoenberg and Steve Feld right up to the president herself. I want to commend and thank the university for the wonderful job they did to help resolve my problem.

It took me quite a while before I felt I'd regained control of my life. I'd been outed and felt extremely vulnerable. But I wasn't about to go back into the closet I had hidden in for years. I refused to stand by and silently watch other gay youth suffer through similar experiences. This is why I decided to share this story—in the hopes that it may provide guidance to those embarking on the journey of coming out and educate others about the real threat of homophobia gay youth face every day.

The Iconoclast

by Sapphrodykie*

Howard University, Washington, D.C.

"You want to be discreet. Keep your hair long and dab on a little of that Revlon Coffee Bean lipstick you like so people won't think you're a boy. Wear some of those Blue Blocker sunglasses with the reflector lenses so folks don't see you looking at women. Don't ruin your reputation. You hear me talking to you?"

"Yeah, Mama, I hear you."

I hung up the phone and went to my 11 o'clock. I'd been watching this girl, learning her ways. She always came to class late, and it seemed as if she wanted everyone's attention on her. She definitely had mine. I stared at her so hard sometimes, I thought I'd burn a hole in the back of her head. I fantasized about what was under those flannel shirts—a sports bra or one of Victoria's secrets? What was inside those Doc Martens? Some Touche D'or fire-engine red toes or a desperate need for a pedicure? She had never talked to me, had never even looked my way. Her name was Love.

In my junior year, on one of the last few days of that class, I got up the nerve to sneak the *Blade*, D.C.'s gay, lesbian, bisexual, and transgendered community newspaper, out of the box on campus. I headed to class early so I could read it before anyone arrived. I heard someone coming, so I immediately hid the paper and took out a hairstyle magazine. It was Love.

Love displayed her usual boldness. She sat down and cocked her leg up in the chair beside me. I glanced at the V imprint between her thighs. I noticed the crooked smile she gave me, and I could hardly breathe. I knew I was attracted to women, but I'd always assumed the women I'd be interested in would be like me: girly, with hair tucked neatly behind their ears, sun dresses, 2 ½-inch heels, makeup, and smelling like my Paloma Picasso perfume. Love showed me where my true attraction lay. Her short hair hidden under a baseball cap, she didn't wear a trace of makeup and wore jeans every day. She walked like a boy, and when she gave me the look it seemed as if she was one. Class started, and all of a sudden Love lost interest in me.

I had arrived at 2425 4th Street NW in Washington, D.C., mid-August of my freshman year. I was at the capstone of black education, the Mecca, and I thought I was *bad*. I was ready to take on the world, but like any "fresh fish" I was confused. I knew I would be graduating from Howard University in four years with honors and two degrees, and I knew what sorority to pledge. What I didn't know was myself.

When I came to college, I had a steady boyfriend, and we were great for each other. But I was with him only because everyone expected me to have a boyfriend. He deserved someone who would love him with the intensity of Louisiana hot sauce, not my table black pepper, so we eased away from each other, and that was OK.

I'd always been intrigued by women, and at times my desire was so strong and unyielding that the guilt felt almost unbearable. My freshman year I joined Oxala (*O-sha-la*), a campus organization for gay, lesbian, bisexual, and transgender students. I looked to the group for reassurance and as a resource because I was constantly consumed with thoughts of women, the way they smelled, their softness. Oxala, I soon learned, was the only welcoming and safe place on campus for gay, lesbian, bisexual, transgender, and questioning students.

"You just need some good dick!"

Howard University is not the place to be if you want to walk across the yard and hold hands with your lover. It's a school where parents send their daughters to find a husband, and men come to take advantage of the 14-to-1 women-to-men ratio. Homosexuality is viewed as a sin, and if you want to be anybody on campus or survive the full four years, you'd better be anything but gay—a crackhead even, because at least then you could be rehabilitated.

"Female faggot!"

Once I started attending Oxala meetings, I learned from my peers that epithets like these are common on campus, as are more subtle forms of hatred. Oxala fliers are torn down ten seconds after they have been put up, people suspected of being gay are ostracized, and openly gay professors don't exist.

"Don't talk to me! Your breath probably smells like pussy!"

Howard students have said they'd rather see a woman with a man who beats her than with another woman. Closeted gay students avoid eye contact with those who are out. The promotion of homophobia has caused gay students on campus to live in shame and fear.

"Dyke!"

Fall semester of my sophomore year, I went into a major depression because I didn't know who to be or what I wanted to be. I felt awkward around my female friends because some of them were appealing, and I tried not to make too many male friends because most of the ones I already had wanted to sleep with me, and I wasn't interested.

I made an appointment at the university counseling center that fall because I needed reassurance that I was normal. When I met with the psychologist, I told her I thought I liked women the same way my girlfriends like men, that I wanted to touch them, and that I loved being surrounded by them, but not in the sistahfriend fashion. I didn't feel strange telling her because I'd never have to see her again, and my files were confidential. I expected her to refer me to others who felt the same way I did or give me the phone numbers of organizations that helped people questioning their sexuality.

Instead, she told me that what I was feeling was unnatural and that if I put on a little more makeup and got my head out of the books more often and went on a date, maybe I'd feel like the other girls. She also suggested I go home for a while because my "female desires" were just symptoms of my being homesick and missing my mother. I went back to my room in tears.

By the fall semester of my sophomore year, Oxala began to dissolve because no one wanted the responsibility of running the group, so I again had no one to turn to. I spent a lot of time in the gay and lesbian studies section at Borders and Lambda Rising bookstores trying to understand exactly what I was feeling.

As I began to explore further, I found that rejection didn't come just from the heterosexual community. I went to The Edge, a black gay and lesbian club, on ladies night, and no one talked to me. When I said hello to someone whose eye I thought I caught, she said, "What are you doing here?" Then she eyed my long hair, made-up face, and skirt. "You don't look gay. Oh, you're from Howard. You're probably lost. Howard is in that direction," she informed me, pointing down the street. I was totally thrown off. I felt isolated, even though I was surrounded by my kind. Was it because of my femininity or did I really not belong? During the remainder of my sophomore year, I didn't come up with any answers.

Junior year, Oxala meetings resumed, meeting off campus at a coffee shop, and new faces appeared. I began to spend more time in the gay community. I found myself looking at pictures of nude men to see if I would feel a tingle...nothing. I went to women-sponsored cultural activities and loved being immersed in estrogen. Despite the lack of support I felt, I finally decided to accept that I am a triple minority: black, female, and lesbian.

Because of the homophobic atmosphere on campus, I knew I couldn't tell my friends, so I stopped returning their calls. I was tired of telling lies about my fake boyfriends. I knew they'd freak if I told them how I felt when I saw Love in class. Or about how when I had seen Love in the library at the end of the semester, I'd wanted her to press me up against the wall and penetrate my mouth with the same tongue I imagined gliding across my nipples. I was at a school with 11,000 students, yet I was all alone. Wanting to find support from someone, I decided to come out to my best friend at school, Bella, at the start of our senior year.

When she arrived on campus after the summer break I went over to her new home to help her unpack. "Bella, did you know that I like women?" I asked as I helped her hang up her Express originals and open dusty boxes from three months of storage.

"What?" she said as she backed toward the door and began to put kitchen dishes in her underwear drawer.

"Bella, it's OK. Are you all right? I've wanted to tell you, but I was scared. Remember that time I dragged you to an Oxala meeting and told you it was for a research paper on lesbianism for my women's health class? Well, that was true, but why do you think I chose that topic?" I asked as I approached her and grabbed her hand.

She pulled away. "But what about Noah? And you always talk about that fine boy on the basketball team, and...girl, quit playin'!" She laughed then.

I told her it was true and picked up the *Webster's Dictionary* off her floor. I turned to the F's and began to read her the definition of *friend*: "a person attached to another by feelings of affection or personal regard; a person who is on good terms with another; a person who is not hostile." That day I asked Bella just to be my friend, but things were never the same. I had always flirted with her; I never hid my looking at attractive women; and I purposely left my lesbian anthologies and herotica books lying around. She'd already known but stayed around because she wasn't sure. I guess I gave her the perfect opportunity to stop being my friend.

My new motto was "Fuck the World." I was tired of not being who I really was. Deceiving myself was the worst. I had to love myself for me and not live for everyone else. My happiness depended on my accepting my sexuality. I put up posters of women loving women, pictures of beautiful bare-breasted dreadlocked women. I ordered a subscription to the Black Lesbian Support Group newsletter, wore my rainbow ring necklace, put my rainbow button on my backpack, and cut off all my hair. Around this time Sasha, my roommate during senior year, moved in. She had an honest curiosity about my choice of decor and seemed to be OK with living with a lesbian.

Mid-September, Love walked into Room 236 of Locke Hall and became a part of my "Black Social and Political Thought and Theory" class. I hadn't seen her since April, that time in the library. I thought I was going to faint. I pushed my chair close to hers and wrote her a note:

I don't want to offend you, but I was at an Oxala meeting and someone was describing who I think is you. I don't know if you're in the life or not, but I was wondering. Please don't get upset if I'm off, but it just seemed like they were describing you. If I'm being too forward or personal, I apologize. Again don't be upset.

I slid Love the folded page. After class I asked her if I was right in my assumption. She said yes, so I asked her out. We became great friends, and on November 1, she became my woman. We began to spend more time together, even in my room, and I decided not to hide our relationship.

Soon it became clear that while the posters on my side of the room had been tolerable to my roommate, my being in a relationship with Love was not. She and her friends started saying that the interlocking women's symbols on the wall were rainbow-colored because we were all mixed up, but then added "I'm just joking" to the end of their statements. "I can't stand living in here with this bitch," I overheard Sasha say on the phone one night. "She'd better not put her bulldaggin' hands on me!"

Sasha had been living with me three weeks when I came home one day to grab tickets to a step-show only to find my side of the room trashed. Water had been poured on my bed, the posters on my wall were wet, my step-show tickets were missing, and the word DYKE was written on my picture of Barbara Jordan. Nothing was wrong with my roommate's side of the room. When I confronted Sasha about it, she said she and her friends hadn't done a thing; she denied it all. About a week later, an hour before sunrise, she got out of bed and began to pack her bags. She moved out the same day.

My involvement with Love became "queerly visible," and because of that I began to lose my friends. They stopped calling, didn't invite me out anymore, and avoided me on campus. Some of my so-called friends stopped coming to church because, they said, since I had become a chapel assistant, the church was now a "sinners' haven that promoted homosexuality."

Men on campus began to view my sexuality as some sort of kinky sex game in which they either wanted to be the referee or a tag-team partner. Women on campus viewed me as a threat because they thought their men would want me; occasionally a woman thought I wanted to turn her out.

I became a recluse and left campus only to go to the Oxala meetings. I was taking about five medications because every aspect of my being seemed to hurt. Love was my world; her support was tremendous, but with all sorts of aches and pains, I practically lived in the health center. When it was time for my annual pap smear, the question came up.

"When was the last time you had sexual intercourse?" the nurse asked.

"Uh, about three years ago."

"Seriously? Three years, and no kind of sex?"

"No, I don't do that," I said sheepishly.

"You're not doing that lesbian sex thang are you?"

"No."

I had a terrible time getting up the nerve to open my legs for the doctor because I thought if she looked, she would be able to tell. I was embarrassed because the nurse's tone made me feel dirty, and the way she said "lesbian thang" made it seem that my ails were from my being intensely pleased with "making mushy" with a woman instead of letting a sweaty pig of a man grunt on top of me.

Since my roommate moved out, I had a double room to myself and decided I didn't want another homophobic Howardite to inhabit my space. There were no more singles available, and I knew I couldn't afford one if there were. My dorm director, Ms. Macabre, and I had worked in the chapel office together the semester before, and I respected her and considered her a friend. Because of that, though, I felt I couldn't talk to her. I decided to make a confidential appointment with the director of residence life and explain my desire not to have another roommate.

I entered the Rev. Joles's office about two weeks after my roommate had moved out. He apologized for running behind schedule, offered me a seat, and asked how he could help.

"I live in the annex, and I'm in a double by myself because my roommate moved out. I want to know if I can stay in there without getting another roommate if I have extenuating circumstances," I mumbled, certain I sounded like an incoherent toddler.

"It's against Howard University's regulations to allow a single student to occupy a double room if another student is in need of housing, but what's the problem?"

"My roommate of two years decided she no longer wanted to live with me, and my new roommate moved out because...I'm sorry, I feel uncomfortable."

"Go ahead, it's OK."

Come on girl, get yourself together, I thought. *If you're going to pull this off, you have to sound grown-up and confident.*

"I'm a lesbian," I said, "and my roommates didn't approve and had problems with my lifestyle." I told him how my side of the room had been trashed. "I can't live in an environment like that. I can't afford a single, no one else will be moving in so late, and I don't want to have to explain myself to anyone or deal with their attitudes or their friends."

"Oh, well now. Let's see. Why did you tell them? Maybe if you hadn't said anything."

"I've lived for 20 years without saying anything. I felt they had a right to know because if I respected them enough to be honest with them, they would respect me enough to at least be friendly. My roommate talked about me at night on the phone when she thought that I was asleep. She told her sister about intimate times between my girlfriend and me that she had read in my journal. She slammed doors and at times didn't speak to me. I began to dread her even coming home."

"I don't mean to come across wrong, and please forgive me for my stupidity on the subject, but are you sure you're gay? You're so pretty, and I've seen you speak in the chapel. Men probably follow you around," he whispered.

"Don't worry, your questions are OK. Yes, I'm sure, and I know I can be with a nice man. I've had relationships with men before, and they weren't what I wanted."

The Rev. Joles told me about other gay students who had been treated badly by roommates and who had decided to move off campus. Such incidents caused the number of students in residence halls to decline, and something needed to be done, he said. He told me that if I helped him come up with ways to better relations between gay and straight students in the dorms, I could keep my room. He would also give Ms. Macabre a signed approval form and tell her that my reason for remaining in the room was confidential. I felt I'd won a small battle.

I suggested to the Rev. Joles that they should make sure the RAs were aware that homosexual, bisexual, and transsexual students do reside in university housing and come up with some sort of sensitivity training. I also had read in the *Blade* that some schools offered gay floors on which students could elect to live. It would also be a good idea, I told him, to sponsor programs that dealt with homophobia and discrimination, especially in the black community.

About five days after my meeting with the Rev. Joles, Love and I eased out of a peach-scented bubble bath. She lit our candles, I put on Maxwell's *Urban Hang Suite*, and she laid me down. As Love slid between my thighs, the phone rang.

"You have to vacate your room by 5 P.M. tomorrow, or I'm going to have to lock you out of your room. You're no better than anybody else, and you will not get special treatment!" Ms. Macabre screamed so loud, I had to move the phone from my ear. "What are you talking about, 'confidential'? And what did you do to your roommate to make her leave? How dare you go over my head just to get your way!"

"Ms. Macabre, I'm sorry." Love held my hand, and I felt fear creep in.

"I didn't mean to go to Rev. Joles to purposely avoid you, but I felt weird talking to you about it. I didn't want you to look at me funny or start disliking me."

She asked what was so top-secret and such a big deal and what could possibly be a reason for me to have my own room.

"It's not about the room. I just couldn't deal with having another roommate. Can you imagine what it's like being in the same room with someone you know dislikes you? It's too uncomfortable. Ms. Macabre, I'm gay." For some reason, I expected compassion.

"So! You need to call your mother and ask her to overnight you the extra $1,200 or move into Meridian Hill. I heard a lot of gay students live there."

"My mother doesn't have any money, and I can't move anywhere, especially in 24 hours," I said on the verge of tears.

"Well, you're gonna have to come up with something." She hung up the phone.

Love gave me the comfort of her arms and reminded me that Rev. Joles had approved my living there. I called him at 9 A.M. the next day, and Ms. Macabre called an hour later and told me she had had a change of heart. Ms. Macabre and I used to be friends, but we never spoke again the way we used to.

One month later Oxala and the Women's Action Coalition invited me, as the president of one of the largest women's groups on campus, to co-sponsor a forum on sexism and homophobia. I presented the idea to my executive board to see if they wanted to participate. Once again I felt my worlds colliding.

"What? No, we ain't sponsoring no program with no gay nothing!"

"Ladies, the program is not gay-oriented. It's about unfair treatment based on gender or sexual orientation. The mission of our organization is to promote educational and political upliftment to African-American women and to help eliminate prejudice and discrimination. That's what sexism and homophobia are based on." I tried to sound unwavering.

"Yeah, well, we don't want our group's name on any fliers that might make us look like a bunch of lesbians. You might because we all see your rainbow key chain, and we don't know if you're trying to come out or what, but...."

"Excuse me?" I retorted. "My sexual orientation is none of your business, and whether we do the program is based on a majority vote. If you elect not to do it, that's fine, but understand that as so-called leaders you should attack these issues instead of contributing to the problem."

The majority voted not to participate or serve as sponsors, and professors and community leaders who had originally said they would speak declined. The program was canceled.

After spring break a member of the Howard University Board of Trustees printed an article in the school paper on how discrimination against homosexuals should not be viewed along the same lines as racism and sexism. Homosexuals have a choice, he argued: Don't be gay and you won't be discriminated against. Attitudes precisely like his made the atmosphere at Howard intolerable for me.

Most people say their college years were the best days of their life, but mine were the worst. I went to a historically black college because I'd gone to white schools all my life. I wanted to be embraced by my people; instead most pushed me away. All I had wanted to do was belong, but I didn't seem to fit in anywhere. I looked like the all-American, well-educated, middle-income, man-marrying, baby-popping, business-suit-wearing, white-picket-fence-wanting black female, but felt like the butchy femme, lover of androgynous women and pussy that I really am. I had dealt with racism and sexism, but homophobia was new; some of it was internalized, which made me feel inadequate as a lesbian because I often felt too scared to be down with the cause.

Howard University held its 130th graduation ceremony on May 9, 1998, and I was a part of it. I did graduate with two degrees and with honors, as I'd planned, but I never did get to pledge a sorority as an undergraduate. Three years in a row, they rejected me because I wasn't "of the right character." (What really hurt was that I'd seen some of the closeted sorority members at the gay clubs dancing right next to me, yet they still ignored me on campus.)

I had come out to the dean of the chapel just prior to graduation, and he expressed his pride in me. He asked me to be mistress of ceremony and address the graduates, parents, and university officials at the annual Howard University's Presidential Prayer Breakfast. Before the breakfast I was also presented with numerous awards from campus organizations for my outstanding dedication and service.

My grandmother met Love after the graduation exercises and knew instantly that she and I were more than friends. She calls me periodically to quote Bible scriptures on homosexuality but constantly sends me her love and admiration. I haven't come out to my entire family, but those who do know don't question it.

Love has helped me to accept that I am a lesbian and that it will be hard loving her and trying to be loved by society at the same time. She heals me and teaches me. She helps me prevent past emotional injuries from recurring and shows me that I am strong enough to battle those to come. I reach for her at night, and she says "Baby, I'm right here." I pray that my beautiful woman will be by my side for the rest of my life.

I decided to accept my homosexuality in college, and because of that I lost many friends. In the acceptance of a dynamic African-American lesbian, I found myself. My undergraduate experience was everything but nurturing, and unfortunately the general intolerant attitude toward homosexuality seemed to be welcomed. My response? "I am the resurrection and the light. *Whoever* believes in me will live, even though he dies; and *whoever* lives and believes in me will never die. Do you believe this?" John 11:25-26.

*Sapphrodykie is a pseudonym.

How to Find Your Major

by Julie A. Holland

Purdue University, Indiana

It's finally here, fall semester of my senior year. I won't be graduating in May, but technically I'm a senior. This is going to be a great year. I've been looking forward to it for a long time not because I'm closer to graduating, which is nice, but because of who my roommates are this year, in particular, Gina. All of us—Gina, Amanda, Sue, and I—are friends, but Gina and I are much more than that. Everyone knows Gina and I are close, but no one knows how close we really are.

We've been lovers for almost two years, and upon her request I haven't told anyone. In fact, she threatened to end the relationship if I ever told anyone, and since I don't want to risk having my world as I know it crash around me, I've done as she asked and have kept everything to myself. To do this I have pulled away from all my other friends and have focused on Gina and our happiness together. Now we'll be living together for the first time. I've been dreaming about this since the first night we made love.

I'm the last one to move into the apartment. My internship at NASA ended two days ago, and I still had to stop by my mom's to pick up the remainder of my things before I headed back to college. I'm glad I had the opportunity to work at NASA, but it was a rough summer being away from Gina. I drove 300 miles one way almost every weekend to see her. In the apartment my room is next to Gina's. I'm grateful for this since I wasn't here to claim it, and Gina is too paranoid about our friends finding out about us to have claimed it for me.

Once I finish unpacking I'll need to get ready for classes tomorrow. I know my professors this year won't waste any time before delving into the material. I'm sure I'll already be working on homework tomorrow night. I'm especially nervous about my dynamics class and Professor Howell.

I've been putting off taking this class, even though it's required. From the horror stories I've heard, I should receive more than enough homework from her—an ironic benefit of the class that will justify routinely staying up late "studying" with Gina.

※　※　※

We're about a fourth of the way through fall semester, and it's one of those typical late study nights. Gina and I usually study in her room on the bed. My legs get cramped when I study on her bed, but that's the price I pay to sit close to her. The typical night for us has become a late study session that lasts well after the time Amanda and Sue go to bed, and then I sleep in Gina's room with her. She sets the alarm for 5 A.M., at which time I drag myself into my own bed so no one is the wiser. We think we're so clever.

※　※　※

Five weeks into the semester with one set of tests completed, classes are going fine, even dynamics. The studying strategy is actually going better than planned. Not only have I been able to spend time with Gina but also the extra time I've been putting into studying has shown in my grades. On the outside Gina and I seem to be doing fine, but something is lurking beneath the surface. I feel like there's a demon ready to pop up at any time and rip everything away from me. But I don't know what it is or how to fight it. It isn't our friends, because they're still in the dark. I try to convince myself that I'm being paranoid and overanalyzing, and I try to put the uneasy feeling out of my mind.

But Gina has been talking to Tim, the guy next door, lately and more than just a "Hello" here, "How are you doing?" there. At first I didn't think much of it, but he's been stopping by more often. I don't like it, and I don't like him. Who does he think he is? He can't walk into my life, our lives, and take away everything I've worked so hard to protect. I tell Gina how I feel, and she reassures me that there's nothing to worry about.

"Julie, you know I love you. This is a good way to divert some attention away from us. It's been a long time since either of us dated anyone, and people are starting to talk."

"Oh, come on. Who cares what they say? We're graduating soon anyway, and then we'll be out of here."

"Julie, you know how I feel about this. Don't give me another guilt trip. You knew from the beginning that I didn't want anyone to know."

It doesn't take long. Only a couple of weeks after Gina meets Tim, she has a date with him. Our roommates are excited for her, and they keep telling me to quit being a suffocating friend. They have no idea what I'm going through, but that's my own fault. I'm the one who has isolated myself from them. I feel like my life is ending, seeping out of me slowly, and I try to scream for help, but nothing comes out. I'm the one who is suffocating.

✳ ✳ ✳

It's our two-year anniversary, and I'm wondering if we'll even spend it together. Although Gina has been dating Tim, she and I have still been seeing each other. She assures me that she still wants to be with me but says she also wants to be with Tim.

"I always told you it was just a phase for both of us."

"I know you've always said that, but you know it's not true for me." In my heart I'd started to believe, wanted to believe, that she felt the same way I did but couldn't admit it to herself.

"Julie, I'm not ending anything. I still want to be with you, and we will celebrate our anniversary. There's an equestrian event coming up next week, and we'll celebrate then. Try to be patient and understanding about my feelings. I want to be with Tim too."

I accept this because I have no other choice. One positive thing is the competition coming up. Gina is on the Purdue equestrian team, and whenever she has an away event we go together. I love these events because we can be completely alone. I need to focus on this and not on Tim. I know we'll get through this crisis. We have to. I can't imagine what my life would be like without Gina.

✳ ✳ ✳

During the past month my world has slowly crumbled around me. The walls I've carefully built to protect my relationship with Gina from our friends and the outside world are the same walls that are caving in on me now, and me alone. Gina has found a way to travel freely in and out of this isolated world we have created over the past two years. I don't have the same freedom; I'm trapped. I didn't create a back door, an escape. After I put up the walls, I made escape less likely each time I reinforced them. I never thought I would need to create a way out. When would I have wanted to? It has been my paradise.

Even when Gina is with me, I'm alone. She visits from time to time in what has been transformed from my paradise into my prison, but she never stays long. The only thing she leaves behind is the scent of her hair on my pillow, the same scent I know Tim is enjoying now as he leans in to kiss her neck. I hold my pillow against me every night, imagining she's here with me like it was in the beginning.

I've engulfed myself in my homework, especially dynamics, which has become my best class. It's the only thing I enjoy and that has kept me in engineering. I've even changed my area of study to dynamics and controls. I've tried to use this to pull myself out of my despair, and though it helps, it isn't enough.

✴   ✴   ✴

Almost every night I call my mom crying so hard I can't speak. We have the same conversation each time.

"Julie, what's wrong?" she asks in her caring mom voice.

"Nothing."

"Julie, you can tell me. Whatever it is, you can tell me."

"I don't know what's wrong."

"Is it school?"

"No."

"Is it Gina?"

"No, Mom, I don't know what's wrong. Really, I don't."

My mom thinks I'm losing my mind because I call her crying for no known reason. Maybe she isn't far from the target. I too feel I'm losing my mind. I'm afraid to tell her the truth, afraid to disappoint her, so I continue to hold it all inside.

Every night I cry myself to sleep with the sounds of Gina and Tim making love in the next room, and every morning I wonder why I should get up, because nothing ever changes. I can no longer see the light at the end of the tunnel. I'm convinced this is how I'm going to feel for the rest of my life, and I begin to evaluate how I can shorten the sentence.

Since I'm afraid of blood, the most promising option would be to overdose on something. I figure I'll take everything we have in the apartment, from Tylenol to sinus medicine to antibiotics. Gina is at Tim's, and Amanda and Sue are asleep. I carefully set everything I can find on the bathroom counter, sit on the floor, and look up through tear-filled eyes at my cure. But I just sit there, looking up at the pills and bottles. After a couple of hours, I carefully separate all of the pills and put them back in their respective bottles and return them to their cabinets. Not tonight. Maybe tomorrow.

❋　❋　❋

After going through this routine a number of times, I decide on another approach. I'll pull someone else into my isolated desolate world to keep me company until I find the courage to swallow my cure. I carefully choose the teaching assistant from my propulsion class, Doug. This is a well-thought-out choice. He's good-looking, nice, intelligent, and best of all graduating in less than a month. How serious could things get in one month? I don't want anything serious. I just want some companionship. I ask him out, and he says yes.

❋　❋　❋

It's Christmas break, and I'm staying at my mom's house for the holidays. Things with Doug have gone OK, but I don't feel any less lonely. A new problem has arisen, though; Doug has been talking about marriage. This is not what I had in mind. I try to put Doug out of my head because I can concentrate on only one problem at a time, and Doug's seems less threatening, at least from my point of view.

On break at my mom's house, I see Gina as often as she'll let me but not nearly as often as I'd like. Tonight I watch the clock anxiously because I get to spend the evening with her. She should have already been here. I see the dog get up and walk toward the front door, barking, and then I hear a car door close. I rush to the front door, and as I open it I see her walking up the steps.

"Hi." I give her a brief hug. We stay up talking with my mom for a while, and then Gina asks if she can use the phone.

"Julie, I need to give him a quick call. I already told him I would."

"You promised tonight was just going to be the two of us." My despair is evident in my voice.

"I know I did, and it is. I'm here, aren't I?"

She makes the call in the other room and talks for what seems an eternity. When she comes back I can immediately tell something is up.

"Now hear me out," she says before she even sits down.

"Oh, no, I don't want to 'hear you out.'" There's a sharp edge to my voice that surprises even me. I turn away from her.

She reaches for my arms and turns me toward her, not letting go. "Julie, I won't be long. I promise."

"Won't be long? Won't be long!" I want to yell at her to leave and not come back, but the words are stuck in my throat.

"I'm just going to his house for an hour. Then I'll come back. I promise."

I've heard her promises so many times before, promises she's not kept once, but what can I say? What can I do? Every day that goes by, she slips through my fingers a bit more, out of my life, but she still manages to have the same hold on me. I'm her puppet, and I do whatever she wants. Whenever I try to break away, she knows how to reel me in. I watch from the window as she leaves for Tim's.

One hour. Two hours. Three hours. Still no Gina. I know where Tim lives, so before I realize what I'm doing, I get into my car and head over to his house. I park on a side street and get out, standing by my car, staring at his house. I wonder what I thought I was going to do once I got here. I scratch out a quick, harsh note for Gina, sneak up to her car, and place it on her front seat. Then I go back to my car. Feeling conspicuous sitting in my car in a residential area, I drive to the park on the other side of his house. Sitting on the swings I watch his house, crying, trying to figure out how I came to this point. I'm ashamed of myself for being out here, for letting her control me, but still I can't make myself leave.

Four hours. Five hours. I see some sign of life in the house, and then the front light switches on. Gina comes out the front door and heads for her car. I watch her read the unpleasant note I left, crunch it up, throw it down, and then look around. I'm confident she can't see me; the park is too dark. As she starts her car, my confidence turns to panic as I realize that from her location, she's going to beat me back to my mom's. I run to my car and race home, pulling into my mom's driveway immediately after Gina does. She gets out of her car and stands there, staring at me. Why do I feel like I'm the only one who was in the wrong? She's been gone for over five hours, but should I have expected anything less? This is how it's been since Tim entered our lives, broken promise after broken promise. As I start to cry, she walks over to me and holds me.

"Julie, I'm sorry. I am. I fell asleep, I swear."

There's so much I want to say, but nothing comes out. All I can do is let my body sag into her arms. I can no longer do it alone.

※ ※ ※

The spring semester is about to start. Over the last couple of months, I've lost about 15 pounds. I don't eat much anymore. I don't do much of anything anymore. I just exist. I don't even think about committing suicide. I broke up with Doug. After he started talking about marriage and love, I felt it was the best thing to do. After seeing how upset he was and knowing what Gina has put me through, I decided not to date another man again. It's not fair, and I won't do to someone else what Gina has done to me.

I dive into my studies immediately. Academically, last semester turned out to be my best ever. It's amazing what depression can do for your schoolwork. Because of my success in dynamics, I'm taking another of Professor Howell's classes, "Spacecraft Attitude Dynamics." I don't think I've ever been this excited about a class. Doing well in her last class, known for its difficulty, boosted my self-confidence more than I could've imagined.

Scott, who is in two of my four classes, has become my regular study partner. I met him last year in another class but never got to know him. Now, though, we spend a lot of our free time together working on homework. Last night when he came by to study, he brought his fiancée, Holly. A psychology major, she also attends Purdue. He's been saying he wanted us to meet each other, that we would get along. I wondered why he thought this. Is she depressed too? As it turns out, she isn't. She's outgoing and pleasant, but I'm not very talkative these days and have no desire to make new friends. My life is still consumed by Gina, who I'm still seeing and who's still seeing Tim.

Tonight, like every other night, I'm studying with Scott, this time without his fiancée. "Holly mentioned on the way home last night that she was worried about you."

I put on my best shocked face, which wasn't hard, since his statement caught me off guard. No one usually pays that much attention to me. Certainly not Gina. "Worried? About me? Come on, Scott, she's using her psych classes on the wrong person."

"Well, I thought she was off-base, but she made me promise to tell you that if you ever need to talk to someone, you can call her."

"OK, Scott, you did your part, and now you can tell her you gave me the message."

"She also mentioned playing lacrosse and wanted to know if she could go to a practice with you."

I've been playing lacrosse for Purdue since I was a sophomore. I speak about it frequently because it serves as a good release, but apparently I've made it too appealing. I'm hesitant to let anyone into my world. I don't even have any friends on the team.

"Why? So she can study me further? Maybe get some extra-credit points in one of her classes?" I snapped at Scott, showing my fear before I could stop myself.

"No, she's really interested. You know, you seem a bit defensive—are you sure you're OK?"

"Sorry. I'm fine. I'm just tired. Yes, of course she can come to a practice."

✳   ✳   ✳

Holly has started coming to lacrosse practice with me, and to my surprise I've allowed myself to get to know her better. Scott was right; Holly and I do have a lot in common, and we're getting along great. She has even made me smile and laugh, things I haven't done in months, things I never thought I'd do again. I start to confide in her and lean on her.

Today, not unlike yesterday or the day before, I'm upset about Gina. Usually I can hide my feelings during the day while I'm around other people, but today is proving to be more difficult. Holly and I are sitting on my bed in the apartment when, all of the sudden, I start crying. Holly reaches over and holds me, obviously concerned.

"Julie, what's wrong?"

I don't say anything. I pull away from her and look at the floor.

"Julie, you can tell me. Whatever it is, you can talk to me."

I look at her and then quickly look away. I want to tell her, I want to tell someone, but I don't know if I can get the words out. I'm afraid that once I verbalize my feelings, they'll be even worse than before.

Holly reaches over and lifts my chin. "Julie, you can't keep holding this inside."

"It's so hard."

"What's so hard?"

"I...I'm in love with Gina." I spit it out like it's a bad taste in my mouth. Unconsciously I move away from her. She leans over and pulls me close and holds me. She tells me everything is going to be fine. All of my feelings that have been trapped inside come flooding out, and I tell her the whole story.

"Julie, you have to end it because obviously she won't."

"I tell myself that all the time, but I can't make myself do it. There are times when I have everything planned out, exactly what I'm going to say, and then when I see her I can't imagine not being with her, so I don't say anything."

"I know it's hard, but I also know you can do it, for yourself. You deserve more than this. There *is* more than this. I know you don't think so now. You think Gina is the only one, but I promise, you will find someone else."

✳ ✳ ✳

It's a week before Valentine's Day, and Gina and I are getting ready to go away for one of her equestrian competitions. I've always looked forward to these weekends, but this time is different. So much has been weighing on my mind. I know what's best for me. How couldn't I with Holly constantly reminding me?

It's the night after the competition, and we're at the hotel. We both need showers after spending the day around horses, but to Gina's surprise I shower alone. I don't say anything about it; I just jump in first. I'm avoiding the whole issue. It seems easier than saying, "I don't want to be with you anymore." I don't think I'm strong enough to do that.

After our showers we lie in bed cuddling, and she leans over to kiss me. Hesitantly I kiss her back. She moves closer and kisses my neck.

"Gina, I'm too tired tonight." I'm not even convincing myself, so I doubt she's going to buy it.

"Really?" There's confusion in her voice.

"Yes, it's been a long day." I kiss her and turn over. I can't look at her face and not give in.

"Well, OK."

I'm still awake, watching her long after she's fallen asleep. I feel a strange ache in my heart. It's a combination of longing and fear, but for the first time also some confidence and optimism about the future. I was able to say no, in a round-about way, and resist her. I know it'll be easier the next time and that I have turned the corner. I can do this. I deserve more than what she's giving.

✻ ✻ ✻

I've been avoiding Gina since we got back from our trip. She's trying to figure out what's up and is incredibly mistrustful of Holly. I think she's jealous. She's used to having me wrapped around her finger.

It's Friday night, one week since the trip, and Holly is at my apartment. I haven't spent any significant time with Gina. She's out with Tim right now but promised she'd be home early so we could spend time together. She hasn't given me any reason the last four months to make me believe her, but Holly seems worried that Gina is going to try to pull me back in.

"Why don't you spend the night at my house?" Holly asks.

"I don't think Gina's going to come home early, and besides, I can't stay at your house the rest of the semester."

"Then I'm staying here."

There's no use arguing. Her mind is made up. I'm relieved, although I try not to show it. We set up a place for her to sleep on the living room floor. As we finish, Gina walks through the door.

"Gina?" I can't believe it.

She quickly assesses the situation. "Julie. Holly." From the tone of her voice, I can tell she's not happy with Holly spending the night.

"Hi, Gina. Nice to see you again." Holly's being especially sweet.

"Julie, can I talk to you?" Before waiting for a response, Gina turns and walks toward her bedroom, expecting me to follow.

Nervous and scared, I turn to Holly for support, but I know she can't come with me. Gina knows it too. "Be strong. I'll be right out here." Holly says.

My confidence is a little shaken, but as I head for Gina's bedroom I keep repeating to myself that Holly is right out in the living room. I walk into Gina's room without knocking.

"Julie, I've missed you. I've been looking forward to spending tonight with you all week."

"Gina, listen."

"What?" She asks in a soothing tone as she wraps her arms around me. It feels good to be held by her again. It would be so easy to give in. I've missed her too.

Julie, I'm right out here. I can hear Holly's voice in my head. I can't give in. I must be strong.

"Gina, listen to me." I speak slowly, in a soft voice. I reach behind me and take hold of her arms by her wrists, gently releasing her grip on me. I bring her arms in front of both of us and hold her hands.

"Gina, I can't."

"Can't what?"

"I can't do this anymore."

"What do you mean, 'can't do this anymore?' What are you talking about? I love you. Tonight it's only us, like I promised."

"I love you too. I've never loved anyone like this, but I just can't." I begin crying, and she puts her arms back around me.

"Everything will be fine. We'll be fine."

Julie, I'm right out here.

"Are you going to leave Tim?"

She doesn't answer.

"That's what I thought, and that's why I can't do this anymore."

"Julie, come on, let's go to bed."

"No, Gina, I can't." I pull away from her and walk out of the room without looking back. I head for the living room. Holly is anxiously waiting for me.

"I didn't know if you were going to come back out."

"Holly, I hope I'm doing the right thing." The tears are flowing freely now. Holly holds me until I fall asleep on the living room floor with her.

✳   ✳   ✳

Holly has been incredibly supportive. After about a month, I come out to Amanda and Sue but tell them nothing about my relationship with Gina. They don't seem surprised. Maybe they did know what was going on, but none of us say anything, and I don't know if we ever will. Next I come out to my mom. She's also not surprised and is supportive. I didn't give her enough credit. I should've known I could tell her anything and she'd be there for me as always. The more people I come out to, the more I feel like a huge weight has been lifted off my shoulders. My classes are going well but not as well as last semester, although I'm much happier and healthier. I've found there are other things to live for, not just grades and not just Gina. Holly was right. Everything *will* be fine. And I know I'll eventually meet someone else. But in the meantime I'm going to focus on myself, my classes, and being happy. It's been a long time coming.

And Then They Came...

by Richard Joseph Andreoli
University of California, Los Angeles

*S*cratch, scratch, scratch...

I rubbed my crotch as I sat waiting at UCLA's student health services.

I can't believe this, I thought, squirming in my seat and constantly reciting my eighth-grade Sex-Ed teacher's words: "You can't kill them with scalding water. You'll just burn your business." In eighth grade we had laughed. Embarrassed, barely pubescent, voice-cracking laughs that disguised everyone's hidden fear that the next time we scratched someone might say we had crabs. But as I waited for the doctor, worried I'd infected the entire University Catholic Center, I thanked God I'd remembered those wise instructions, because right then I was in so much agony that boiling water sounded tempting.

Scratch, scratch, scratch...

I looked around the health center to make sure no one saw what I was doing. As a teenager I'd envied baseball players scratching themselves in public and everyone acting like it was no big deal. But when I'd do it on the playground, invariably some girl would see, tease me, and make me the topic of afternoon gossip.

Now, as an adult, I again cautiously rubbed my groin to relieve the itching, waiting to see who would begin sending jibes my way. I no longer felt like a 21-year-old man but instead had reverted into a nervous 12-year-old whose greatest fear was ridicule.

This wasn't how I'd pictured my Great Awakening.

College was supposed to mark the beginning of many great changes in my life. As a child I'd imagined I'd be uprooted from the mundane world I'd been forced to grow up in and be granted the opportunity to create a whole new image. In reality I'd simply be releasing the real me, allowing myself to live as the well-adjusted gay man I knew I was on the inside. I'd awaken what I was too scared to be in high school, or junior high, when my feelings toward other guys started to emerge. I felt I could enact that transformation only through a physical transplantation, and the day I received my acceptance letter from UCLA, I knew the time had arrived.

Scratch, scratch, scratch... But I never thought it would bring me such pain.

Everyone goes through changes when leaving for college, but the process is more complex for a gay person. In forming (releasing) this persona, it's like popping an annoying tightness from one's back and suddenly being able to move with freedom never before experienced. No more censoring dialogue or keeping track of who knows which version of a story. It's all about the freedom honesty offers, an honesty "normal" people never have to deal with.

For me, the releasing was slightly different. I'd been out to myself since I was 16 and began coming out to others at 18. By the time the UCLA letter arrived, I felt pretty experienced in the ways of gay culture. I'd had a boyfriend, a collection of tricks, and some solid gay friends. I was cute, which always helped me get my foot in the door for gay-related activities. I still hadn't done the circuit party scene, but I'd gone clubbing 'til dawn and done my fair share of drugs. If nothing else, I could fake a conversation with the gay "in" crowd. Socially, I knew I had it together.

Scratch, scratch, scratch... But I'd never had a "social disease" before.

My roommate was a gay orientation counselor named David. We met during orientation, when he told me he needed a roommate at his co-op next to campus. The Catholic Co-op.

For other homosexuals, living with Catholics might seem an itchy situation, but having been active in San Diego Catholic youth programs, I was comfortable being out and living in the Catholic community. David was out as well, so everyone at the co-op was accustomed to big queens. More importantly, in a house of 30 people, there was David, a lesbian, a bisexual, and myself; so much for the 10% theory.

Now, in a place where no one knew my past insecurities, I was no longer Richard; I became Rick. Shorter to write, butcher to say, and an amalgam of who I was and who I would be. The new name along with an update of clothes, a decision to work out, and a surge of consistent confidence would prevent me from ever feeling the shame I felt as a child and complete the picture.

Some picture! I thought as I fumbled with my fly in an attempt to prevent the passing nurse from seeing me pinch my pubes. The saga of the creeping crawdads began one month and one day after school began. I was leaving the offices of *TenPercent*, UCLA's gay newsmagazine, wearing glasses of rose-tinted confidence as I passed a tall muscular white guy with soft brown hair and a cute smile. He had a dough-boy look, but his youthful grin of a 5-year-old gave him an endearing glow. He was talking with a black woman I'd seen working for *Nomo*, the African-American newspaper that shared offices with us. He looked at me and stood there.

Contact! Point-five seconds: We both knew we were gay and interested.

I walked past, placing that added bit o' confidence and attitude in my stride. I knew he was watching, so I gave a quick look over my shoulder and let a slight smile slip out, as though I was shy and innocent. Once out of sight, I laughed, thrilled beyond belief. This was the first guy in L.A. who was attracted to me. Not only that, I thought he was fine.

In retrospect he wasn't all that; he wasn't even half that. Hell, he wasn't even a filet o' fish and fries. I was just a single guy, caught up in the excitement of L.A. gay life. Had I spent any time in West Hollywood and bore witness to the many handsome men, I probably wouldn't have fallen for him. But since I was into the adventure, living the life I was meant to live, I was impulsive. Because, after all, I was Rick now, and I was going to do what I wanted.

That night, David and I sat on our beds like junior high girls, cross-legged, drinking Cokes, and discussing this mysterious man in rapid snatches of conversation. "He's beefy," I said.

"Ooh, beefy!" David exclaimed. Twenty-years-old, David had had sex only once in his life and kissed a guy only three times besides that. Compared to him I felt like the gay stud of the universe. I liked that feeling, so unlike the awkwardness I'd felt talking about "chicks" when I was younger. David sat on the edge of his bed, enraptured with excitement, as though experiencing penis by proxy.

"Brown hair, great smile..."

"I love brown hair," he said, swigging from his can, not taking his eyes off me.

"And a fine ass..." My roommate was about to pop, totally riveted by my tale. "Bubble butt."

"No!" his voice shot to a higher octave, shaking the windows. He put the can on the floor and batted his fingertips on his knees. "And you didn't get his name?" David seemed more frustrated than I was. "I bet I know him!"

We made a plan, and the next day we staked out the patio outside Ackerman Union, waiting for the mysterious brown-haired man. David wildly waved "Hi!" to everyone he knew in a bold operatic voice, stopping each minute to ask if every somewhat cute dark-haired guy that passed by was the man I'd met. I acted cool, pretending to read from my abnormal-psychology book. This game was old hat to me rather than a rite of passage into the Land of the Homo as it was for David.

After a half hour David abruptly jumped up and screeched, "Hi, Mack!" It was the guy from the day before, and David did know him.... For a moment, this journey was no longer as fun as it had been the night before, when I had told David my story. I was no longer in the smug superior position, that of all-knowing gay male, because David knew this guy, knew his name, maybe even knew things about him. I no longer held all the cards in the deck, and as such I was no longer the star at the party.

Introductions were made, and I again used my shy-boy look. But Mack was ready this time to play into my game. If I were the cute blushing boy, he would play the aggressor. The man who called the shots. The top, at least in terms of this foreplay.

He sat and accidentally hit his thigh against mine. "Oh, sorry," he apologized in a voice so innocent I smiled. He knew how to play his game as well as I played mine.

I don't remember much of the dialogue, which in retrospect should have been a red light as to how boring Mack was. Indeed, when I now see Mack around campus, I wonder what my attraction was. He wasn't really that cute—straight mousy brown hair, a little too chunky, and with a constant lip curl as if he were positive the world had decided to take a laxative and shit on him, just to piss him off.

My attraction stemmed from this being a fabricated romance. Just like when I studied in England and hoped to fall in love with someone there, I now found Mack fascinating because it was part of the scenario. As an escape from the jeers and fears (realistic or not) that I experienced in primary school, I would concoct fantasies of romantic encounters. In reality, I wanted Mack to be as I envisioned. I wanted—and would have—a college romance.

It took only one date, on which I went to Mack's house. He prepared stuffed bell peppers with wild rice. It's funny how I remember that detail and little about the man who prepared it for me. Once dinner was finished we made no attempt at mindless small talk. We didn't sit on the couch watching *Tales of the City*, slowly reaching one arm around the other, kissing a bit, and eventually going at it before the first on-screen potluck dinner.

We cut to the chase.

I offered one thank-you kiss, which led to more and more. Within ten seconds he had my back pinned against the kitchen counter and was bearing down on me. Time for the games to begin!

A shame it sucked...so to speak. After sex, I usually experience a sudden numinous moment in which everything is totally clear to me. If the sex has been good and I'm completely present in both body and mind, carnal and spiritual, then I can relax and embrace the moment. A total sense of freedom envelops me, and I know peace. Life is as it should be. But if the sex is bad, if I've convinced myself to partake in something I know is purely physical and not completely centered, then I'm immediately bored beyond belief.

A dullness sprouts at the base of my back and spreads up my lats, into my shoulders and neck, then creeps over my cranium until it reaches my forehead. My brows and eyes begin to feel heavy, my cheek muscles slowly ache, my upper lip feels chapped and my chin chafed. I want to leave (or kick him out without offering a towel, depending on if it was my place or his), shower, snuggle into bed with my imagined mate, and dream of how fabulous I'll be once I'm the successful writer everyone calls "Rick." Indeed, the new name and image are all part of the fantasy.

That night with Mack was such a night. The encounter held no more excitement than masturbation; indeed, it was worse than beating off because once we were finished, I had to make small talk. Fortunately, Mack was as happy with the "hump-and-go" concept as I was, offering me a scratchy, somewhat clean towel to dry off with, then escorting me to the door.

At that point, unfortunately, it was too late.

That evening I got away with telling David (who'd waited up for me) that the date itself, "was OK. But, you know, when they're cute..." and I was now finding Mack less cute by the second, "they shouldn't speak." David laughed, and that was good enough. But the following week when I had to tell him about the crabs—and as his roommate, I had to tell him—was like that yearly dream I have about showing up for work wearing only under-wear. I'm not just ashamed and mortified but ultimately helpless.

"Oh, my God," he said, leaning forward to grab my arm. He then pulled back, eyes wide, because he was sure they could jump the two feet between us like a flea on crystal meth. "Oh, my God," he said again, in case someone wasn't listening. "No!" He hushed and decided that the most proper action would be to flop himself onto the bean bag. "Are you sure?"

"Yes." I was annoyed. I didn't want to get into it, but I had to maintain a certain amount of attitude. I'd created the image of aloof coolness in all things queer, so the only way to save face was to treat this as another facet of my life. As David huddled in the folds of the cloth-covered bean bag, I wondered if I'd sat in the same place while wearing boxers the day before, when I didn't know I had the pesky buggers. Thus began my fear that through David I might infect the whole Catholic Center.

"Do they look like…?" he couldn't even say the word. I nodded. "And they itch?"

"No, they're moving like ben-wa balls, and I'm orgasming as we speak." He gave me one of his "condescending queer" looks, like a TV mother gives her child when he goes for the laugh and she doesn't think anything is funny. I decided to lighten the moment. "If they didn't itch, I'd keep them as pets."

"Oh, my God!" he called again and giggled, then laughed, then stifled it with a fist in his mouth, then continued again in a muffled nervous squeak.

The next day, in a white sterile examination room decorated with posters for preventing venereal disease, I waited for the doctor, angry with myself because I'd given in to an urge that wasn't worth it; deep down I'd known that. I'd wanted Mack to be more than he was, and in seeing my imagination overrule my intellect so much that I was blinded into think-ing this dumpy boring guy might fit into my new "comfortably gay and all about me" personality, I began to wonder if the "new me" wasn't a recy-cling of the tired old package. *How tacky,* I thought. *How blasé; how much like '80s television.*

I wasn't happy with myself.

The doctor entered, looking straight at and into me. Contact! Point-five seconds, and from the glimmer in his eye we both knew the other was gay.

Neither a cruising glance nor a flirtatious leer but the simple acknowl-edgment that only one gay person can give another. Immediately I expe-rienced my first moment of relief since all this began. He was gay, so he should understand me; there was no need for shame. Professional, he immediately got down to business.

"OK, says here you've got crabs." I nodded energetically, trying to keep a positive attitude. I probably looked like I was excited about them or some-thing equally idiotic. He looked up at me over the file. "Anything else?"

"Not that I know of," I said, because as he asked the question I realized I didn't know what might be crawling down there besides those sharp-taloned creatures of the night.

"All right, then, drop your trousers and get on the table." He put down my file and began washing his hands.

I wondered whether to take off my shirt. I'd suddenly become modest. I'm not ashamed of my body, but I have two great fears when it comes to examinations that involve no pants: Will I get an erection while he's touching me (it doesn't matter if I'm attracted to him or not; the fear is there)? Or will the room be cold, making me shrink into my body so far that the doctor will think I should have gone to the women's clinic? I guess keeping my shirt on was a sort of security blanket.

"You don't have to tell me," he said as he lathered, "but it'll help if I know some details about you."

I bent, untied, and pulled off my Nikes while trying to maintain bal-ance. "I'm gay," I proclaimed, knowing this was what he wanted to hear. The pants slipped off, and as the doctor grabbed his gloves I whooshed off my Calvin Kleins (worn for special occasions) in one fluid pull.

"You understand this is confidential," he said with a snap of latex.

As he turned I nodded. There I stood in socks, shirt, and nothing else, butt barely visible under the hem of the shirt. I felt so stupid.

"On the table?" he said, as though I'd missed it the first time. I hopped up and sat there, wondering how to look both casual and helpful.

The examination was quick, confirming my theory that the critters were indeed crabs. We also checked for testicular cancer because men don't do it enough and finally for anything that shouldn't be there. Thank God, all was normal.

The exam having been painless and now over, I dressed as he wrote down what I needed to purchase to take care of the problem. I felt my confidence coming back. By the end of the day, I'd be cleaned up and on my way to continuing my new life. This was only a minor setback in my growth toward the new me, and now I was about to continue my journey.

He offered me condoms, lube, and a complimentary HIV test. Then, as a service to all the gay students who visited him, he asked me, "Are you aware of the gay outreach programs on campus?" This man held obvious care for his gay brothers.

At that moment I spoke without thinking, using the witty gay banter I'd grown accustomed to throwing out at parties. "Oh, sweetie, I *am* the gay outreach on campus."

I could have killed myself. At this point the doctor taught me the power of a wizened gay man. He looked at me over the top of his glasses, past the physical form that had gotten me so far in the gay world, and right into me. He looked at me with the eyes of a man who had seen too many students die of AIDS or have had the rest of their lives encumbered by genital warts and herpes. He was a man who had seen far too much and was one of the survivors whose job was to educate. And it wasn't an easy job.

For that instant I was naked again, because he didn't give a fuck who I was or who I pretended to be. I saw how I'd been acting since I'd come to college and made my big push. Only then did I see I loved telling my roommate all about my sexploits, giving him material he could use in his fantasies because in some odd way it made me feel like I'd lived something more exciting than normal people. It made me special.

But the doctor didn't care about any of the outside stuff. It didn't matter if I did or didn't get hard or if my dick was big or small. He knew me only as a student who stood there with an STD and was in need of his help. Without words his look simply said, *Yeah, and your outreach got you a crotch full of crustaceans. You're so cool!*

I was silent, and so was he. I let loose an uncomfortable laugh, and he looked back at his paperwork. Then I heard a chuckle, and he looked up at me, smiling. "That's a good one.... You've been out a while, huh?"

I smiled. The tension was relieved, but I was shaky and needed to leave the room quickly. "Well, call this number if you need anything." I took the number. "And Rick," he said as I was about to exit, "nice meeting you."

"Nice meeting you." I smiled and left. Out of the room my facade dropped, my hands shook, and I hurried away. After picking up my medicine and avoiding eye contact with everyone, I walked through the botanical gardens toward Hilgard Avenue where the Catholic Center was. The sun was shining and the weather beautiful. It was nice to be in the sunny warm winter of Los Angeles, and I hoped my worries were over.

But then I started shaking, as though a chilly wind had passed into and through my clothes. I needed to sit and rest, gather myself before heading into the house. And then they came. As I sat on a bench, tears rolled out of my eyes, burning with an intensity I hadn't felt since grade school. I wasn't ashamed, because anytime I play a game I have to consider the possible results. Thankfully, this was minor. But still I felt like an idiot. A foolish, young, immature, awkward idiot, just as I'd been at home in San Diego. I felt like a high school student again, unsure how to act or how to be cool.

My need for an image had required me to shed the brazen, inexperienced child I'd been, and while I could talk a good talk and I looked right for the game and the name "Rick" fit the picture, I was still a lost boy wondering who I was and what this was all about. I wasn't creating a new image so much as perfecting a fantasy I'd dreamed up when I was too young and scared to deal with my homosexuality. Only now, when I thought I had it all together, did I see I was nothing more than that same scared child, crying on a bench, alone in a park.

Gay and in Bible College

by Cory Liebmann

North Dakota

With a fervency to change the world, I left Milwaukee to attend a small Assembly of God Bible college so that God would prepare me to be a pastor. From childhood to young adulthood, I'd been the ultimate example of God's saving grace and power. As I'd been poverty-stricken and from a single-parent, inner-city home, every aspect of my life had pointed to a doomed future, according to most standards. The only things that defied my odds were a faith in God and a fundamentalist church that bore my burdens and built my expectations. I prayed and read the Bible with a passion, and I told others of my faith. I dedicated my life to converting the lost.

When I arrived at that small North Dakota prairie town to begin ministry training, I knew right away I was in a different world. The town had a population of only 2,000, and the students were a quarter of that. What a culture shock! I met no one my age who had come from where I had or struggled with what I had struggled. Few, it seemed, had a real passion for the things of God, but I had a passion to see people converted that others seemed to lack. As I grew more confident in my spiritual superiority, I was faced with a part of myself that I'd ignored and denied for many years: my sexuality.

Since I had lived only with my mother and was somewhat of a loner in high school, it was easy to ignore my homosexual feelings. But it was a different story when I moved into a dorm and was surrounded by other young men. My thoughts and feelings grew more intense. I could no longer hide my feelings because I was faced with them every waking moment, mostly because of Roger, my new roommate.

Roger accepted me as his friend from the start. We spent most of our time together and talked well into the mornings about anything and everything. Soon Roger started to be physical with me in a joking way when we were alone. Because Roger was a wrestler, we started wrestling together, just fooling around; Roger would pin me and not let go.

"I can feel you," he'd say with a gleam in his eyes.

I'd laugh. *He has to be joking,* I thought. *This can't be serious.*

Roger sometimes grabbed my butt, but I didn't take it seriously. I couldn't, though I never said anything to stop him.

Returning for our sophomore year, Roger and I chose to be roommates again, and my feelings for him grew stronger. As my relationship with him opened my eyes to my true feelings, I also faced a constant condemnation. At my college we were required to attend daily chapel services at which we would sing, pray, perform musical numbers, and then listen to people preach. I was convinced God was showing His displeasure with my new feelings when it seemed that every speaker was condemning homosexuals in his sermon. Whether talking about being "holy" or discussing politics, homosexuality always seemed to come up. In these sermons I heard of the dreaded homosexual agenda and their goal to convert us all. I heard that homosexuals were doomed to hell and that they were the worst kind of sinners. Most speakers seemed to be more preoccupied with homosexuality than I was.

So whenever Roger did anything physically suggestive, I didn't want to believe it was real. My confusion continued to grow. In chapel I took every chance I could to go up front at the preacher's invitation and pray silently for God to "fix" me.

"God, I've been trying to serve you all this time," I'd tell Him. "I haven't done what a lot of others did in high school. I've tried to live a holy life. Make it worth my while—get this thing out of me! Change me! I have these evil desires. Take them away from me! 'You won't be tempted beyond what you can handle' is what you tell us in the Bible. I can't handle this. I don't understand; I'm not supposed to be tempted beyond what I can take. I need you to help me."

Sometimes I cried. All I wanted was to serve God, to do what he wanted me to do, be who he wanted me to be. I knew if I let these feelings grow any more, I wouldn't be able to pursue my calling as a pastor.

The chapel wasn't the only place where I heard about the evils of homosexuality. At school I'd also hear students discussing the "homosexual agenda" and telling gay jokes. In classes homosexuality was called an "abomination" to God. I nearly developed a phobia of these situations, as each day I was more convinced of my gayness. I began to avoid certain professors who liked to get on their sodomite soapbox often. I missed classes more frequently, and in turn my grades declined. Every day I lived in fear of hearing people condemn or joke about "fags" or of someone finding out I was gay. It felt strange that the church had given me such horrible feelings. I also started to see the falsehood of the cliché "We love the sinner but hate the sin." I learned from observation that the church had only contempt for homosexuals; no separation was made between the person and his/her actions.

As I went through this persecution, my feelings continued to grow for my roommate Roger. I grew jealous when he did things with others. I became hysterical when he flirted with women. Even though he had a girlfriend back home, he started fooling around with girls on campus; I admonished him in righteous indignation for cheating on his girlfriend, but really I was jealous. Soon my jealousy had us fighting.

One evening Roger, our friend Pete, and I met up with Sharon and Jackie, two girls Roger and Pete liked, to play Monopoly. Roger and Sharon were openly flirting; her hand was getting closer and closer to Roger's butt. Distracted by anger I grabbed the wrong Monopoly game piece.

"Hey, put down my piece!" Pete said.

"I'm not the only one with my hands on things that don't belong to them," I said, looking at Sharon.

Roger got furious. "Cory, shut up and mind your own business!"

"I can't help it. It's right in front of me. At least have the decency to do it behind closed doors."

As jealous as I was over Roger's displays of affection with girls, I was much more consumed with jealousy over his apparent flirting with guys. Once in a while Roger, Pete, and another friend of ours, Tom, would joke around as if they were gay. All of them would actually hump each other, and sometimes they'd joke around verbally, insinuating they were having sexual relationships.

"Roger and I had sex last night, and God it was good," Pete said one time when we were horsing around. Whenever they said these things, I got real quiet and didn't say anything. But my jealously continued to grow.

One night Tom, Roger, and I went over to a girl's house to play games.

We had a curfew at our college, so I went home early; Roger and Tom stayed behind. Several hours later Tom and Roger showed up at our room, knocking on the window, joking around, silly grins on their faces. Roger had a nervous look; he giggled a lot, almost apprehensively, as if he knew I was going to be mad. With all of the joking about homosexuality, I was beginning to wonder if it was really a joke. When they came back so late with silly grins, I couldn't help but suspect they'd been having sex or something, and that infuriated me. The next day the three of us were supposed to go to Minneapolis to another Bible college to watch a basketball game, so Roger wanted Tom to sleep over.

"I don't want him sleeping in here," I said sharply to Roger.

"Why not? What's the problem?"

Tom sat quietly waiting it out.

"He's invading the very last space I have with you! I never get to do anything alone with you anymore. You're always doing things with other people now," I complained.

To my surprise Roger started crying. "I care about you, Cory. You're a good friend. But this is getting hard because you're jealous of everything I do with anyone else."

I felt bad that I had made Roger cry, so after we talked through things more, I apologized. We agreed to forget about it and go to bed.

That same semester in one of the chapel services we were asked to walk down a line of professors while each one prayed for us. I was grateful but not overly impressed with the general prayers from most professors, like "bless him" and "give him strength." Brother Green, however, prayed for me in such specific ways that I was convinced God had revealed to Him my secret.

"Lord, this young man is struggling so much and has called out to you for some time," he prayed. "Today I ask you to make that change he has been begging for. He feels isolated from his brothers in Christ and needs you to heal him." Although he did not name what my struggle was, he went on to describe accurately my spiritual and emotional state. I didn't have Brother Green for a class at that point, but I asked if I could talk with him sometime. He was more than happy to set an appointment.

When we met I confessed, after much hesitation, that I might be gay. Although he didn't feel that being a practicing homosexual was morally right, he demonstrated nothing but compassion. "Cory, you're not really gay if you haven't done anything, so the battle is not yet lost," he said. "You can still go into the ministry to which God has called you as long as you don't engage in homosexual acts."

I knew, however, that I was gay even if I hadn't done anything with another man. Nevertheless, Brother Green had given me some hope that I could return to my days of passion for reaching other people with Christ's message of salvation. Leaving his office, I believed I would not have to agonize over these feelings for the rest of my life.

With this new hope I went back to my dorm convinced my problems were over. But it took only a few more incidents with my roommate to bring me back to where I'd been. Since Brother Green had made me feel good and was so loving, I went to see him every time I felt major guilt or pain over my feelings for Roger. This was always a temporary fix, but the feelings and problems were always there.

For the second semester of our sophomore year, Roger said that all of us friends—Pete, Tom, Roger, and I—should share one bedroom together and use the other room assigned to us as a lounge. I rejected the idea for fear of giving up the last bit of privacy I had with Roger, but they all told me I either had to do it or they'd do it without me. So I agreed. The homosexual innuendoes—humping, wrestling, and explicit jokes—continued.

My jealousy consumed me. Often I'd come back from class early to check on Roger and make sure he wasn't doing anything with other people that I didn't want him to. One day I opened the door to our room to find Pete and Roger both in their underwear; Pete was standing up, and Roger was on his knees beside him, pretending he was straightening the throw rug. They looked at me with fear in their eyes.

"What are you guys doing?" I asked, shocked and angered.

"I was going to take a nap. You know I always sleep when I don't have class. We were wrestling, and I was straightening the rug," Roger said with an edge of fear still in his voice.

"Can't you see why I would find this a little strange?" I asked.

"What are you trying to say?" Pete asked.

"Well, it looks like you're actually acting out all of your joking around about being gay," I dared, looking straight into his eyes.

"I can't believe you're accusing us of that!" Pete lashed. "That's a serious thing to say to your friends. You're betraying us by accusing us of this. How could you say that about us? I thought you were our friend!"

"And you wonder why we don't do so many things together anymore. It's because you say things like this," Roger yelled. "I was just straightening the rug!"

I couldn't help noticing that Pete was semi-erect. With frustration and anger, I shook my head and walked out the door, slamming it. I didn't know what to do, so I decided to see Pastor Jones at the campus church. He liked me because we used to work together when I was a sponsor for the campus youth group.

"Pastor Jones, I'm concerned about some friends of mine in the dorm," I said.

"What's wrong?" My hall was known for being kind of crazy (well, crazy in Bible college terms), so he didn't sound surprised.

"Well, my friends have been acting like they're gay. They make jokes and little comments to each other about it. Lately some things have been happening that have been manifestations of these innuendoes. They say they're joking when they act things out, but it seems they aren't just acting. Recently something happened that was a bit more graphic." Had I said exactly what had happened with whom, Roger and Pete could have been kicked out of school. I feared losing Roger, so I talked about the incident in vague terms.

"It definitely sounds like what's going on is suspicious. Keep an eye on things, Cory. Try to stay away from them as much as possible if it continues. If they start to show a more definitive pattern, you'll need to confront them and tell them you'll have to talk with the hall director or the dean of students, OK?"

"Yes. Thank you, Pastor Jones."

As I walked to the dorm, I felt guilty I'd revealed something about Roger that could get him in a lot of trouble. Not to mention the hypocrisy that I felt, knowing of my own homosexuality. I never talked to Pastor Jones about the subject again, as all of the guys that Roger used to "joke" with, including Pete, transferred to other schools the following semester. It was back to just Roger and me, and I mistakenly thought my troubles were over.

It was just a matter of time before reality hit. I was starting to think God didn't want to take away these feelings, since I still had them after all my prayers and pleading. I decided to find something to take my mind off my feelings. So I joined the Army National Guard. After a summer of basic training, I knew I could overcome many things that had previously intimidated me. Still, I went to my monthly drills only to find myself a silent victim again; the military was as preoccupied with homosexuality as my fundamentalist college. In my unit I'd hear jokes, violent threats, and countless references to "Clinton's boys" from fellow guardsmen, including several students from my college. Not only did the military fail in helping me overcome my gayness but it also made it more visible to me. The conflict between what I was and what I wanted to be nearly devoured me.

After realizing the military couldn't change me, I decided to immerse myself in other projects to keep my mind off my sexuality. First semester of junior year, I flooded myself with responsibilities, taking on leadership roles. I served as an inner-city ministry leader, a youth sponsor in the campus youth group, and sports director for the campus radio station, and even went to Africa on a mission trip. Needless to say, I was overwhelmed with responsibilities. Spending so much time on activities, I rarely had time to think of my sexuality and was able to ignore it.

With my new leadership roles at school, I became quite visible to fellow students. One of the dorms even voted me the "most desirable to marry." Debbie, one of the prettiest girls on campus, started pursuing me, and although my only interest in her was to appear straight I decided to date her.

Soon after, Roger decided to transfer to another college. He said he needed a fresh start and wanted to go somewhere warmer. I was convinced, by the expression on his face and the awkwardness of the moment, that he was leaving partly because of me. I felt abandoned and heartbroken. It also wasn't long before Debbie told me that our relationship wasn't working, and we ended it.

After the pain of Roger's departure, I slowly came out of my social cocoon and started doing things with other guys again. Second semester of my junior year, I'd go to Minneapolis with friends to see Timberwolves games or other sports events or to gawk at gays outside of clubs. Because Minneapolis was a long drive, I often stayed overnight in hotel rooms with male friends.

These sleeping arrangements were not accidents but well-planned events for which I was responsible. In the hotel room I'd purposely take up a larger portion of the bed than was my share so there would be less room for the other guy sleeping with me. I wouldn't touch him, but still I lay there and hoped for affection or a passionate touch. The first time, my friend Philip rolled over and "accidentally" bumped up against me. When I didn't move away, he started grabbing and caressing me. I did this with six guys—several times with each of them. Although I always "set up" the other guy, I'd never make the first move.

During those nights I forgot every condemning word I heard in the chapel. I knew I wasn't the only one deprived of my feelings, yet we'd never say a word to each other the next day about it. If we didn't say anything, everything was OK. Although nothing serious ever happened during these encounters, I'm convinced it could have if those involved weren't so frightened about the other one breaking the silence. Not only would we have been ridiculed and condemned for our exploration, but also we would've been expelled from college. Fear silenced us all.

On one trip to Minneapolis, I went alone with my friend Rob, who was the most gorgeous guy I'd ever met, to see a Timberwolves game. After the game we talked about what to do next, though I already had my hopes.

"Are we gonna drive back tonight?" Rob asked.

"No," I said. "Not if I'm driving. I'm too tired."

"I don't have a license."

"Well, I already have a reservation at Super 8."

We drove to the hotel and entered our room. "There's only one bed," Rob said.

"If you're uncomfortable, I can sleep on the floor."

"No, no, no. I'm not worried about that," he said. "You can sleep up here with me."

We got into bed. We were watching some mob movie, and I couldn't believe I was in the same bed with such a cute guy. I fell asleep, but every once in a while I stirred and could see him looking down at me. When Rob was ready to go to sleep, we did some "unintentional" snuggling; like the others, we didn't speak about it afterward.

Right before winter break the next semester, Rob broke the silence. In a few days he would be transferring to a college closer to home, and we were hanging out in his room. In the middle of our innocuous conversation, he said, "I thought we were going to have sex before I leave here."

I must have looked like I'd seen a ghost. I did not—could not—reply.

At that moment how could I have known that all of my college struggles were not with God's will but with the fear others had put in me? How could I have known that two years later I would come to the honest conclusion that God does not condemn homosexuals, that God loves and accepts me for who he made me, a gay man who loves God with all of his heart? If only I'd known these things at the time of Rob's courageous statement.

"What?" I asked with a quiver in my voice.

"Nothing. Forget about it," he said quickly, then changed the subject.

Wait! I wanted to scream. I want to talk about it! Instead my fear took control again. I went along with the new topic of conversation. The fear that had been drilled into me at this college dealt the final blow. Faced with the situation I had prayed for, I let the moment pass and lost Rob forever.

After one more semester I graduated from Bible college still confused about my sexuality and my faith, but at least I was now free from the overwhelming fear I had experienced for 4 ½ years. Free to think for myself.

Cory Liebmann's ministry can be reached at Chapel of Hope, P.O. Box 05248, Milwaukee, WI 53205, phone (414) 297-9116, Web site www.chapelofhope.org, E-mail PastorCory@chapelofhope.org.

Finding My Place in the World, or Which Bathroom Should I Use Today?

by Taran Rabideau
University of Washington

It started innocently enough. I mean, it's common to go to college to escape. I was moving to Seattle to flee my family, my friends, my church, to break the Midwestern mold I'd been straining against for so long. I wanted to learn to live without being ashamed of part of who I am. I wanted to learn to live without the dishonesty of hiding something so important from people I cared about. I'd learned these things in Seattle, but it's what I didn't expect to learn that changed my life more than anything.

Upon my arrival on campus, I became an instant frequenter of the Gay, Bisexual, Lesbian, Transgender Commission (GBLTC). I attended meetings, held office hours, and went to social events. Although I felt I'd found an environment that was accepting of me, I began to feel like an outsider again. The butch/femme relationship I had with my girlfriend Erica was unique and even considered odd by our friends.

We'd only been together a month when we both went home for Christmas break. During the two weeks we were apart, we had long conversations every night on the Internet. One night after I'd had an argument with my mom, I tried to explain to Erica how trapped I felt at home. No matter what I did right or how many things I excelled at, my hair was always too short and my clothes were always too masculine for my mom's approval. I told Erica how I was always puzzled that as much as my mom hates that I'm gay, she hates the way I look even more.

"Every time my mom and I have this argument, she puts me down and puts me down, and then she always says, 'Don't you know you're a girl?' as if I'm going to come to my senses and put on a skirt and high heels," I typed to Erica in an instant message.

She tried to console me. "You don't have to prove to her you're a woman. Being a woman isn't about what you wear."

"That's not really what it's about. Just once I'd like to be able to answer her stupid question, but I don't know how. I mean, I know I'm a girl, but I don't feel like one. I wish I'd been born a boy." Erica cried while we were corresponding. She could tell how much I was hurting, but she had no idea I could actually do something about the pain I felt.

When we got back to school, we didn't talk much about that night. But one night at a GBLTC meeting, we watched a segment of a news show about Alex, a no-op, no-hormone, female-to-male (FTM) transgendered Harvard student. I watched in amazement as a guy my age talked on national TV about feelings I'd been too scared to discuss with anyone. When the tape ended Erica and I looked at each other with raised eyebrows, neither of us knowing what to say. This good-looking guy and his girlfriend weren't much older than us, and they seemed aware of a world of possibilities of which we were ignorant. Brett, the director of the GBLTC, tried to start a conversation about transgender issues.

"We have the word *transgender* in our title, but we aren't very good about including transgender themes in the things we do," he said. "So I'd like to try to change that. Does anyone have anything to say about the video?"

I was too nervous to say anything because I didn't know how people might respond, so I waited for someone else to speak up. No one seemed willing to offer a comment until one girl raised her hand and said, "Can we talk about something else now?" I felt deflated. I was about to stumble onto something important, then felt totally invalidated by her comment.

Erica and I had never talked about the possibility of my trying to pass as a man. I didn't know how to approach the subject, but Erica brought it up later that night.

"Is that how you feel? Like you're a boy trapped in the wrong body?" I felt my face get hot as I looked at my hands. I didn't know what to say. I was scared that she'd run away. I didn't answer her question out loud, but she knew. She could tell I couldn't talk about it yet, so she just held me and told me she loved me.

That quarter, Erica was taking a psychology class on human sexuality. I wasn't enrolled in the class, but I usually went to the lectures with her. Around the time I began to deal with these issues seriously, the class did a unit on transsexuals, transvestites, cross-dressers, and intersexuals as well as the proposed physical and psychological causes. One day they had a gender panel consisting of a drag queen, two cross-dressers, and a male-to-female (MTF) transsexual. People in the class asked questions about whether their families and people they dated knew and what their reactions were. Their questions were scary because for the first time I thought about how my choices would affect my relationships and not just how they would affect my body.

After class I went to the front. I wanted to talk to Diana, the transsexual, but I didn't know what I wanted to say or why I needed to talk to her at all. I waited until the crowd around her dispersed. I shyly introduced myself. She was beautiful and had so much dignity and confidence. My mind went blank.

"I didn't know what 'transgender' meant until a few weeks ago, and I thought I was a lesbian, but now I don't, and I don't know where I fit in," I stammered. My face was red, my heart pounded in my ears, and I was breathing so fast it was hard to talk.

She said, "So you're a guy?"

I nodded, still staring at my shoes.

"I thought so, but I didn't know if you knew yet."

When I looked up she had tears in her eyes. She hugged me, and I saw she wished all the pain she had gone through wasn't lying ahead of me.

A few weeks later the GBLTC held a discussion with two MTF transsexuals and one FTM transsexual, David. I was transfixed by how he appeared, with his goatee and low voice. If I'd seen him on the street, I wouldn't have had the slightest idea that he wasn't born male. I was naive but also excited and amazed that my future could be like that. I could actually do something to physically manifest the feelings I had.

After the meeting Erica went to coffee with friends, and I stayed and talked to David for nearly an hour. I didn't know what to ask, so he talked about anything he could think of. I was awed that someone who could've melted away into the straight world would choose to identify as something between male and female to reach people like me who are searching hard for an identity. I told him about Erica.

"One of the most important things about transitioning is not to be self-centered," he said. "It's so easy to get caught up in the stress and turmoil of transition that you forget she's also transitioning."

Erica and I talked that night. She curled into a ball, snuggled next to me, and cried. "I'm scared of the hormones. I don't want you to get crabby and get zits all over your beautiful face."

"You mean you won't love me if I'm a big mean zit-faced monster?"

"No, I'll still love you, but don't think I won't keep you in line. It's just hard to come to terms with the fact that you hate the body I love so much. I like that you're my girl, and I don't know if I can think of you as male or relate to you as a man or call you 'he.'"

"You don't have to be comfortable with everything tonight," I said. "I'm not comfortable with everything either. I don't know what changes I'll make or if I'll make any. But it's comforting to know there are possibilities out there if I decide to make physical changes. It feels so good to discover I fit in somewhere, that I'm not the only one who knows what it's like to feel trapped like this."

"I just feel alone," Erica said. "I know you need contact with other people you can relate to, and I know you need to talk honestly with them, and the only way you can do that is one-on-one. But I need some support too. Every time you need to talk, I have to leave. I don't mind doing that, but I have to try to explain to all our friends why you stayed behind. I don't feel I can share your secret, but I don't want to lie to our friends. It puts me in an awkward position because I don't want to tell anyone your personal business. But I need someone to talk to too."

"I'm so sorry. I guess I've been so nervous, I haven't thought about how hard it must be for you to leave whenever an important discussion takes place," I said. "I'm more comfortable with the whole issue now, and I'd like you to be there next time. I'm not ready for everyone to know yet, but if you need talk to someone about it, that's fine. I trust your judgment."

I was excited to discover something so new about myself. In some ways it was hard to enjoy fully because no one knew except Erica, so I felt like I had to come out all over again, and coming out was something I hadn't had much practice at. I look so dykish that I don't usually have to come out; people assume I'm gay. I knew that once I explained my feelings to someone other than Erica, it wouldn't be such a big deal. But I was having trouble with that first time. I didn't have to worry much about it, though, because Erica decided to take care of it for me.

April was BGLAD month at UW, and one of the programs was "A Night of Gender," sponsored by local transgender/transsexual education organizations. It differed from the regular GBLTC meetings because the audience consisted of a few of the regular members mixed with a lot of grad students and straight people taking notes for papers they were writing. The discussion stayed mostly on topics such as how professors can work transgender issues into their classes and how the world's perception of transgendered people has changed. Then the conversation turned to why people are scared of the words *transgender* and *transsexual*.

"Maybe the word *transgender* is scary because it doesn't only affect the person who uses that label," someone volunteered. "For example, if a butch dyke or a femme man decide they're transgendered and want to transition, does that say to other butch dykes or femme men that they must be transgendered also?"

Then Erica spoke. "It took me a long time to come to terms with the fact that I'm not straight. I'm finally in a relationship with an incredible woman, and then I find out that my girlfriend is really my boyfriend. It's hard to accept that I'll be seen as a straight girl with a boyfriend. I was finally OK with being in the minority, and I don't want to be perceived as 'normal' again. It's hard to figure out where I fit in now."

"I'm glad you brought that up," one of the panel members said. "We all need to remember we're a part of the same community, and we all need that community. You don't have to adopt a strict label. You were queer before, and you're queer now."

While Erica was talking I felt relieved and proud that she felt comfortable identifying us that way in front of everyone. Then I felt the eyes of all the people in the room boring holes in my back. I told her she could talk about it whenever she needed to, but I hadn't expected to be sitting there listening to her when she did. I hoped I'd be able to handle things as well as Erica was.

Later she told me that was the night she came to terms with the transition I was about to start. Spencer, one of the panel members, was the first FTM she had met whose personality was as attractive as mine in her eyes, which seemed to give her peace of mind. He told her that his wife of ten years identified as a lesbian when they met and had to go through the same identity crisis Erica was facing. His wife was also in charge of an FTM significant other E-mail listserv that he said he'd put Erica's name on. I got some information about a group of FTMs who met once a month at a coffee shop to talk about transitioning and living as a male, and the next week I started to attend. They talked about a lot of things I didn't have to deal with yet since I hadn't started my physical transition, but it was good to hear about their experiences and situations and feelings that I should look out for. The meetings became hard for me to go to, though, because I was envious of the guys who had completed their transitions.

Erica and I were still unsure about the decisions we had to make about the changes that would affect not only my body but also our relationship and Erica's view of me. We spent many hours on the Internet looking for any information we could get our hands on. Reading other men's stories about the joys and difficulties they'd experienced helped both of us. And it helped Erica to start seeing me as a man. She used the new name we had chosen more and more and often used male pronouns when we were alone. I, on the other hand, began to realize the gravity of my choices and started to think about how my new label would affect real-life situations such as employment.

One day at lunch Erica and I were talking about the GBLTC. I said I couldn't think of a job more fun than being director of a group like that. She told me to talk to Brett about how he got the job. The next time I was in the office, I met with him and jokingly said I was going to steal his job. He laughed, telling me he was leaving the country soon and that his position was open. So I turned in an application and set a time for an interview. Then the anxiety set in. I didn't know whether I should bring up my being transgendered. Most of the people on the interview board would be friends of mine or at least people I knew. Erica and I discussed it at length, and I thought about it night after night. Finally, I decided that if I couldn't be honest about myself in an interview for a position that had the word *transgender* in its title, then I would go through my whole life feeling ashamed; that's one of the things I promised myself I would overcome. After I made the decision, I felt proud of myself but was scared that when push came to shove during the interview, I would take the easy way out.

When the day of the interview rolled around, I was nervous, but still I sat before six people and told them who I was without being ashamed. The first question was, "Why did you apply for this job?"

I took a deep breath and answered truthfully. "This organization has done so much for me. I identify as transgendered and came to this realization as a result of the gender programming Brett has done this year. I want this job because I want to help someone the way the GBLTC has helped me."

Fears of discrimination also plagued me when competing for another job I had applied for. Before Christmas, Erica and I had both decided to apply to be resident advisers (RAs) in the residence halls. We both had to attend an intensive training course. At the beginning of the class, I was worried I might not get the job since I was so obviously gay. But by the end of the class, that was the least of my worries. I was surrounded by people who used the terms "gay, bisexual, lesbian, transgender" without having any idea what transgender meant. As the class started I was careful about what I said and how I portrayed myself, but over time my point of view changed. I realized this wasn't any normal job. I'd be living at work, and with the people I worked with and for. I decided I wouldn't be happy if I had to censor my personality and life all year long. I needed to educate others on the issues I was dealing with, and if the resident directors couldn't handle me and my life, then I wouldn't be able to work productively for them anyway. Erica and I became outspoken about GLB issues during discussions, and soon everyone knew we were together. When I became more comfortable with myself, I started to include transgender issues in some of my papers, but I never attempted to attack the subject in class.

At the end of the quarter, we filled out a dorm preference sheet. I ended up writing that I didn't want my ability to educate people and raise awareness to be smothered by someone who didn't feel comfortable with me. I wanted to work for someone who wouldn't ignore my diversity but let me use it as a tool. It was hard to be up-front like that, but I knew I'd thank myself when placed in an environment in which I'd feel comfortable. All the competition was over. The only thing left for us to do was wait.

Both Erica and I were hired as RAs and assigned to buildings across the street from each other. I was also hired as director of the GBLTC and will start that part-time position next semester in addition to being a full-time student. In his "passing the torch" E-mail, the GBLTC director introduced me and identified me as an FTM transgendered person. I didn't know at the time, but the E-mail went to all the Res Life people, so my resident director found out that I'm transgendered. We had a long talk, and she asked me many questions and has been supportive.

As far as my transition is concerned, changes are expensive, and I'm living on a student's salary, so I haven't made any progress with hormones or surgery. But I do plan to have surgery, take hormones, and fully pass as a man before I graduate. I'm taking little steps now. I've changed my name, and everyone I know in Seattle is good about using it.

Erica has already told her parents, who are quite religious. They treat me well, but I know they struggle with it. They still wonder why their daughter doesn't look for a "real man." They have trouble understanding the relationship, but I can see why. But they make sure Erica knows they love me because she loves me.

My family is a different story. My mom has always been controlling as well as fairly religious in a "family values" sort of way. She objects to my gayness on a moral level as well as on a what-will-my-friends-think level. She fancies herself a good mother, and my abnormality causes her to lose points in the Best Mom competition she seems to have with her church friends. I think she's a great person, a great friend, and a great mother except for the part of her that hates me because I'm gay. Most of the time she blocks it out and pretends it's not real, which has worked magnificently for both of us until now—our own little don't ask, don't tell policy.

In a year full of choices, my toughest one is this: Do I tell my mom and try to make her understand? Do I wait and try to explain things later when she asks why my voice is lower? Or do I take the traditional passive-child approach and sever all ties without giving her a chance? I don't need to decide right now; I can't decide right now. I'm only in college.

An Unsolid Matter

by Jennifer R. Mayer

Brown University, Rhode Island

"How would you feel if someone thought you were gay?"

The question floated through the hot auditorium on the third day of a three-day orientation session for counselors. It was fall of my sophomore year, and about 200 of us had volunteered to arrive on campus a week early for training (a small sacrifice), then spend the rest of the year in the dorms advising first-year students (a considerably larger sacrifice).

At a campus such as Brown, nicknamed "Diversity University," much of the counselor training focused on sensitivity to diverse groups. The morning had started out with role plays and discussions of racism. In the early afternoon we talked about sexism. Now we were rounding out the day with a conversation on homophobia, and the facilitator, a tall Asian man named Tim, again posed the question:

"How would you feel if someone thought you were gay?"

I fidgeted, crumpling the orientation agenda in my hands. I looked down, noticing my sweaty palms had dampened the colored paper. I kept looking down; suddenly there seemed no safe place to look. I drew my elbows closer to my body, to avoid touching either of the women next to me in the cramped uncomfortable wooden seats.

No one jumped to be the first on this one, but responses trickled in.

After a long silent moment, one guy cleared his throat and said, nervously, "I'm straight, but I wouldn't have a problem with it."

"I'm straight," chimed in a young woman, "but it would be all right if someone thought I wasn't."

"I'm straight, and I guess I'd wonder why somebody would think that of me," said the woman next to her.

As other students spoke I noticed that the first three words of every response were "I'm straight, but..." I mentally called it the "straightness disclaimer." Brown students might be progressive, but they weren't about to go out on a limb in public. Their responses made it clear that they thought dealing with homophobia meant talking about sensitivity to "them," not "us."

Some responses were blatantly offensive. "I would hope they'd think better of me," said one student.

"I can't imagine why anyone would think *that* about me," voiced another.

There must have been some positive responses, but none of them stick out in my mind like the negative ones do.

Still huddled in the wooden seat, my tension grew as images came unbidden to my mind: my fellow Girl Scouts whispering about my close friendship with our troop leader, a female army captain; the rumor spread by a high school boyfriend when I broke up with him after I caught him groping my best friend. People had sometimes thought I was a lesbian, even though I thought I was straight.

Finally, after the 12th or 13th "I'm straight, but..." response, I raised a trembling hand.

"People have said that about me before. I don't know." My voice quivered.

I didn't want to say the truth. I knew exactly how I felt about it: scared, uncomfortable, hurt. Of course no one had ever meant it as a compliment. Why would someone think I was a lesbian? Because I was ugly? Because I was overweight? Because they wanted to taunt me? From my experience it wasn't a positive thing.

Curious, the facilitator probed. "And how did you feel about that?"

"I didn't know what to think," I lied, flustered and eager to escape the 200 people staring at me, who were probably concluding I was gay because I failed to make a point of denying it. I hunched down in my seat, embarrassed that I wasn't able to be more honest but proud that at least I didn't include a straightness disclaimer.

Based on their responses, most if not all of my fellow counselors weren't any more comfortable about being thought gay. And prefacing their statements by assurances such as "Well, I feel that gays should have equal rights, but..." only made them more hypocritical.

By the end of the session, some in the audience started crying, as a kind of critical mass was reached. Slowly it dawned on me that there were gay and lesbian counselors with us in the audience. From the tone of the responses, we might've been talking about how to interact with some tribe in a faraway country, should we ever run across them. It didn't seem like information we'd need to use anytime soon. As each counselor asserted his or her straight credentials, the gulf between the straight counselors and the gay counselors widened. Finally Tim looked up at the audience, and I saw tears in the corners of his eyes.

"How do you feel when I tell you I'm a gay man?"

We all looked at each other in a shamed silence. We may have been going to a school that prided itself on being the most liberal in the Ivy League. We may have been self-selected as more sensitive and nurturing than our peers. But scratch the surface and it wasn't far to bigotry. It was like the feeling I'd had when I first learned in physics that matter we think of as solid is actually composed of a lot of spinning particles—a frightening concept. Things I had thought were solid weren't at all; beneath the surface, things could be whirling in directions I knew nothing about.

As the session broke up, I watched some of the gay counselors embracing each other in tears and frustration. I wish I'd said (and thought) the right thing, the courageous thing at that moment. Something like standing up and saying to the assembled counselors: "In two days, 1,600 freshmen will be arriving. Some of them will be gay. And I don't think any of you will be in a position to counsel them until you get over your own prejudices."

But I didn't, and oddly enough I don't remember how that session ended. I don't think the facilitator had time to do much more than reveal how hurt he had been by what some people had said. Perhaps more important is what didn't happen. We never, ever, revisited the topic in the counseling program. No one stood up and said, "Based on this maybe we should have extra training on homophobia." No one said, "There's a problem here." We left it hanging.

I didn't even go up to speak to any of the counselors who were crying, even the ones I knew. I filed away my discomfort and the whole session, under "Things to Think About Later." My convoluted logic went something like this: I knew that if I started to deal with it, a tide of emotions that I didn't want to handle would rise up. I was already struggling with a demanding academic and extracurricular schedule. I couldn't imagine taking on this burden too. That's how I saw questioning my sexuality: a burden, a hassle, and a lot of emotions I didn't need.

Besides, wouldn't it be selfish to stir up all of that trouble, to make myself (and everyone else) uncomfortable over something as frivolous as sex? I could picture myself crusading for civil rights or world peace, but sticking up for my right to explore my sexuality didn't fit with the person I thought I was. Maybe men were supposed to go after sexual pleasure aggressively, but it wasn't something women were supposed to seek actively. Women were supposed to take what they got, and as the Victorian mother said to the new bride, "Lie back and think of England."

Maybe my student counsels were more perceptive (or at least more honest) than I was. A few weeks after school started, I came home late one night to find that someone had scrawled YOU'RE QUEER in big, red letters on the message board on my door.

I can't deal with this right now, I thought, half fearful, half annoyed. I looked left, then right, down the empty hall. I wanted to erase it, but I stopped, realizing it had probably been there all day and that most of my 40-some students had seen it. I didn't want to broadcast that being called queer would bother me.

So I scrawled back QUEER? I DON'T KNOW ABOUT THAT. ODD, MAYBE, and left that message, and the original scrawled comment, on my board for two weeks, trying vainly to portray a cool unflappable equilibrium. But it was really an equilibrium as fragile as that of matter. Inside, things were whirling, and my outside wasn't acknowledging it yet.

As the year progressed I learned from one of my friends that my cocounselor, Marta, was living quietly with her girlfriend in the dorm. Before I learned this I had scarcely noticed the quiet intense woman with short dark hair or her girlfriend, Ella, whom I'd never even seen until a month after school started. After I found out I made a point of silently trying to demonstrate my acceptance of their relationship, though we never talked about it. I was amazed at their courage in living together in the dorm and at the lack of perceptiveness of some of the first-year students who didn't have a clue that Marta and Ella were involved.

Sometimes I'd stop by and chat at bedtime, leaning against one of the single beds in the room they shared, Ella's blond head on the left, Marta's black head to the right. We'd talk until late in the night, and when I closed the door behind me I imagined (with a secret thrill) that I could hear Ella climbing over to Marta's bed. And then...fade to black. I never envisioned anything beyond that, but even that little vision was compelling.

For some reason, we grew apart as the semester went on, and I didn't see much of Marta or Ella. Maybe they sensed my uncertainty and discomfort with my own sexuality. Maybe they avoided the dorm because it was dominated by several athletic recruits from the Midwest, whose attitudes about women (and virtually every group other than white males) were Neanderthal compared to the rest of the campus. The other counselors avoided these guys, but I took pride in being able to talk with them without being intimidated. Yet I suspected that the author of the memo board scrawl was Kevin, a particularly vocal basketball recruit from Michigan.

When the Brown University Lesbian, Gay, and Bisexual Alliance came to our dorm to do outreach seminars, Kevin and four other athletes huddled in the back of the room, a veritable phalanx of baseball caps and burly crossed arms. I heard them whispering behind me and felt their gaze like a prickly scarf on the back of my neck. I deliberately lingered after the presentation as the guys covered their discomfort with homophobic jokes.

"Man, we'd better get soap-on-a-rope in these showers," Kevin joked. Then he looked straight at me, with a knowing gleam in his eyes. "Yeah, and Jen, you better watch out for those dyke tennis players in the athletic center."

"Oh, yeah, like Billie Jean King and her gal pal," I said, chuckling uncomfortably. Although I didn't consciously identify myself as lesbian, I felt like the bear trapped in the sights of the rifle in the Gary Larson cartoon, pointing to the bear next to him, saying, "Please, shoot him, not me!"

I managed to avoid the issue for the remainder of my sophomore year, and my junior year, when I studied abroad. I did have a few disquieting episodes while I was abroad (once I complained to a friend in a letter about "another damn pass from a lesbian"). Even an unenthusiastic affair with a male Australian grad student didn't convince me I was playing in the wrong field.

But in the fall of my senior year, I began to look at women in a different way. I don't how it started, but I couldn't stop noticing women's bodies. The curve of their shoulders in their tank tops as they sunned on the campus green; the delicate collarbone of the woman who made omelets in the campus snack bar; the elegant bare feet peeking out of the sandals of my neighbor as she walked down the hall. The campus was one big connect-the-dots puzzle, and my brain kept seeing the shape of women's bodies outlined everywhere. For weeks, I walked around in a constant state of blush, a heightened sexual awareness I couldn't tone down or do anything about.

I couldn't get away from it. I started to notice the pink triangles that seemed endemic on backpacks and leather jackets, women with short wild haircuts that shouted "dyke," women couples holding hands defiantly. I averted my eyes every time I passed the graffiti on the sidewalk in front of the cafeteria, LEGALIZE CLIT-LICKING. What had begun as a whisper of thoughts started to accumulate until I consciously tried to stop thinking about it. Of course, I found that trying not to think about something is a surefire way to obsess about it.

At first I thought I could exorcise these feelings by reading about them. But I didn't even want to look in the card catalog in the library. I furtively looked over my shoulder, then flipped cards rapidly while looking behind me every few seconds, convinced someone would know why I was looking in the card file box between "Leprechaun" and "Lima Beans." Using the electronic card catalog was even worse. What if one of my dorm mates came up behind me just after I typed the word *lesbian* and I didn't have time to clear the screen? I picked the terminals farthest away from everyone else, ideally on Friday nights, when the library was nearly deserted.

When I finally mustered the courage to find the titles of the books, the next test came. Invariably the lesbian books were located within plain view of the reference desk. In my paranoia I was convinced the librarians had arranged the library so they could observe who was questioning their sexuality.

I'd snatch a book and scurry into one of the underground cubicles in the library. They were nicknamed the "catacombs," windowless bare rooms about the size of a phone booth but with worktables built into the wall. I'd always hold some innocuous title such as *The History of Needlepoint* in front of my book as I carried it to the monastic study cell. I spent Friday nights in the catacombs, reading *The Coming Out Stories* and trying to maintain scientific detachment. *No, I don't feel the way that woman does at all. Nah, that's not me,* I thought, finding some subtle point of difference between me and the women described in the books. But still each Friday night would find me furtively snatching lesbian books and reading them alone in a cubicle.

And then, checking books out. That was the next challenge. I'd try to pick out six or seven nonqueer books to check out at the same time. Infallibly the checkout clerk (who'd occasionally be a student I knew) would pull the queer book to the top of the pile and glance at the title. As the bar code was read, I envisioned an alarm going off. *Queer book...Queer book...Queer...*

As these thoughts rolled in my head, I transferred my energy into a frenzied extracurricular schedule, which I hoped would leave me no time to think. I volunteered to be the publicist for the film society, served as a writing tutor for two programs, and wrote for five campus publications. My GPA took a nosedive, but somehow I didn't care.

When I finally confided in two or three of my friends who were straight, they were supportive but perplexed at how timid I was about exploring my feelings outside the library or the Internet.

"Why don't you go to the lesbian-bi rap group at the women's center?" one suggested.

"Oh, I couldn't do that," I wailed. In my oversensitized state I could barely make eye contact with random women I saw on the street, much less an entire roomful of women openly interested in other women. Instead I continued my schizophrenic existence for the rest of the year...reading obsessively about gay and lesbian life and culture and participating actively in an on-line discussion group and anywhere I didn't have to confront a real-life lesbian.

In the spring of my senior year, a few months before I graduated, I found out about a new co-ed "Questioning and Coming Out" group, facilitated by Johnny, a gay sophomore I'd worked with in a tutoring program. I liked the "questioning" part of the group's name. Most of the coming-out books I'd read and groups I'd heard about seemed to regard questioning your sexuality as a foregone conclusion. If you even put the question to yourself, the answer had to be yes. I needed a window of uncertainty to feel safe exploring my feelings. The group's co-ed nature also appealed to me because the atmosphere would seem less charged.

Still I was so nervous that I got to the activities center a half hour early so I wouldn't have to walk up the stairwell the same time as everyone else and studied at the end of the hall until the appointed time. My legs shaking I walked into the room not looking up but stealing a sidelong glance that showed five men and two women already seated in a circle. Without looking up I planted myself between two guys, arms folded, hatches battened against danger.

Johnny, as facilitator, saw the signs of incipient panic and moved in. "So how's the writing center?"

"It's great, but it's thesis season. A lot of stressed-out grad students," I said, grateful to have something besides the main topic to talk about. I blathered for a bit longer until Johnny gently steered the discussion to the coming-out group's philosophy and rules for confidentiality. I finally looked up as he was talking and studied the other two women, Jill and Beth, both of whom were sophomores and seemed decades younger than I. They both had short haircuts with streaks of fluorescent color, leather jackets, and an air of complete self-assurance.

I hated them on sight. I felt a surge of tangled irrational resentment and envy as I looked at them. Why is it so easy for them and not for me? How did they come so nonchalantly to the realization that they might be gay after just their first year when I could barely get it together? I had liked to think of myself as stronger than everyone else, better able to control my feelings, but suddenly I felt like the dunce at the back of the classroom.

"Let's start by going around the room," Johnny said.

I was third, and when my time came I kept it short and vague. "I'm just here to explore some thoughts."

"I'm here to get some help dealing with my family. My parents are worried that lesbians lead lonely, unhappy lives, and I'm trying to convince them that this is the only way I can be happy," said Jill.

Beth was next. "I've only started exploring my feelings here, and I'm trying to think about what it's going to be like when I study abroad next year in Africa."

Despite their confident appearance, Jill and Beth's comments revealed some vulnerability, which made me warm up to them a bit more. We talked freely in the group. But I startled like a frightened deer when I ran into them on campus. Seeing either of them brought up a torrent of feelings: discomfort with the whole topic, envy that they seemed to be all right with who they were, attraction, and of course curiosity about whether they found me attractive. Once I passed Jill in a narrow passageway on the way to class and barely managed a choked "Hello" before half jogging away.

Beth worked at the campus coffee shop, which turned buying coffee into a highly charged emotional odyssey. First of all, I could barely look at her when I ordered, studying the menu above her head while she poured the coffee and handed it to me. Gingerly I'd take the cup and my change, trying to make sure our fingers didn't touch. Of course, half the time I'd either drop the change or lose my grip on the coffee, prolonging the agony of self-consciousness. And I could never figure out where I could sit and sip my coffee without wondering if she were looking in my direction. I took what I thought was the path of least resistance and quit drinking coffee for the rest of the semester.

Ultimately, I went to only three group meetings and stubbornly continued to resist the obvious conclusion that I was gay. Ironically, one of my rationalizations for not coming out on campus was avoiding the emotional hassle and the academic impact I knew would follow. By submerging these thoughts, however, I only delayed and intensified the effect when I finally did start to come out, which led to academic and emotional meltdown during the year most students pull themselves together.

After college I moved back to D.C., got a job, and dated a few men, putting all my thoughts about being gay on the shelf. It worked about as well as it had on campus; the more I tried to sweep back the tide of feelings, the stronger they grew. One of my female coworkers had been openly living with her partner for eight years, and her presence was one of many triggers that constantly brought lesbianism to the forefront of my thoughts, even while I dated a series of men.

Two years after I graduated, I was in the dwindling twilight of my last relationship with a man to whom I'd finally admitted having feelings for women. Then a few acquaintances from Brown announced they were coming to town for the 1993 March on Washington. With a mixture of thrill and trepidation, I agreed to go with them to the first dyke march.

With around 4,000 other women, we marched through the streets. At some point I looked back and saw a sea of women of all colors, which seemed to stretch for miles along Pennsylvania Avenue in front of the White House. I felt the energy of being in a large group of women who not only felt no shame calling themselves lesbian but who were even willing to be called "dykes." With women carrying torches and icons of goddesses, dressed and undressed in all sorts of ways, chanting and howling in the streets, it seemed more like an initiation rite than a political march. It made me ready to paint my face, beat the drum, carry the torch, and join the tribe of dykes.

After the dyke march I ran into five or six lesbian and bisexual women I recognized from Brown, including Jill and Beth. Seeing them I was transported back to that crazy senior year. Still exhilarated from the march, instead of running in the other direction I sat next to them. They looked at me in a knowing but not unfriendly way, as if I were a party guest they'd expected much earlier who'd finally arrived. All the feelings I had shelved were catalyzed into the open; all the thoughts spinning like particles in my mind were coalescing into a coherent idea: This is who I am, this is where I belong. Finally, I've come home.

You're Majoring in WHAT? Coming Out, Queerly Academic

by Terry Dublinski
University of Wisconsin-Madison

"After careful consideration of your records, we regret to inform you that we cannot admit you at this time...."

It was November 1994, and immediately upon reading the letter I knew my path would be an uphill battle. That first denial letter wasn't a surprise. Six years earlier I had flunked out of the University of Illinois, in part due to internalized homophobia and the severe depression that accompanied it. I knew my poor transcript might work against me, but I also had several things in my favor now: a new transcript with a straight-A average and a university that cannot by law discriminate on the basis of sexual orientation. After opening the denial letter, I sent a letter asking for reconsideration.

My life had changed immeasurably in the years after my first attempt at college. I returned home and entered the local community college, completing one year with a straight-A average. I knew, however, that I couldn't resolve my feelings toward my sexuality while in my home town, so I moved to Madison, Wis. Shortly after, I came out and made many friends on campus who were perfectly happy being gay. This helped my self-esteem immensely. I even spent time as a political activist on campus and briefly co-chaired the student queer political organization, but my life was still incomplete. I knew I'd never be happy until I returned to school and completed what I'd started.

I made the decision to return to school the spring of 1993, during the March for Lesbian, Gay, and Bisexual Rights in Washington, D.C. At Lambda Rising bookstore I happened upon a book called *Gay and Lesbian Studies* that contained an article on how to institute a program at a major public university. The book inspired me to complete all the required hoops and graduate from UW-Madison with a degree in LGB studies.

This is the story I wish to tell, the story of my battle and all the steps required; the reactions to, consequences of, and my personal feelings toward being the first lesbian, gay, bisexual—please, let's call it queer—studies major at the University of Wisconsin-Madison.

Being "academically out" wasn't an easy decision. The admission appeals committee that admitted me to the university knew I wanted to be a history major—this made sense because of my good record in history classes—but they didn't know the depths of my academic plans. I was tired of being left out. I was tired of not having information. I was tired of well-intentioned heterosexuals—who in actuality have no real understanding—writing about *us*. I wanted to make a change and felt that becoming the first graduate at UW-Madison in this emerging field might be a permanent way to do so. At the same time, however, I felt society would not look upon a queer studies major as being legitimate on its own since anything queer has historically been viewed by mainstream society as political and therefore marginal. Because of this I felt the need to overcompensate and triple major, with sociology as my main discipline, history for background, and queer studies as my focus, all with a certificate in women's studies for good measure. But would I be able to accomplish it?

In a university of more than 40,000, known for beer, bratwurst, and bureaucracy, creating a new and controversial program seemed impossible. Yet this same bureaucracy gave me an idea: How about sneaking in through the back door? The university has a little-used corner known as the Individual Majors Department. It's specifically designed for undergraduate students who wish to design their own "cohesive, interdisciplinary" major. This department facilitated my focus in queer studies: It sounded cohesive, was definitely interdisciplinary, and maybe it would work—but where to start?

I knew through the queer grapevine—how intertwined it is!—that there was an "out" gay professor of German named Jim Steakley. I'd read one of his articles (the subject matter was queer), and since I had a solid background in German from high school I figured his office would be a good place to start. My first full-time semester at the university was beginning, and I'd done some preliminary research on the red tape I needed to get around to construct an individual major, especially one that had never been done before.

His office was what I'd imagined the world of the "absent-minded professor" to be like. The entrance was a maze of floor-to-ceiling bookshelves, most with German titles but many containing obviously queer subject matter. What caught my eye most was his disheveled "organization system," a seemingly endless row of piles of papers, documents, slides, pictures, and other materials. But somehow I knew he would know just where everything was in the midst of this entropy.

With a full almost-gray beard and silver wire-rimmed glasses, Jim wasn't an imposing character. His entire demeanor fit in with his surroundings. Looking at him directly, I became captivated with his charming smile and a gleam in his eyes that made me feel welcome.

"How may I help you?" He made me feel at home immediately, and as I sat down my butterflies began to disappear—but not completely.

"I'm attempting to construct an individual major in lesbian, gay, and bisexual studies and need some help," I said. "I know your area of expertise is the German homosexual emancipation movement. But since my knowledge of the language is poor at best, I don't think I should specialize in German. Any advice you could give, though, would be helpful."

My statement instantly intrigued him, and we spent a few minutes discussing the preliminaries and my goals. The conversation quickly changed from me feeling him out for advice to him gauging my seriousness and resolve.

"Why don't you come back Thursday afternoon with all the necessary forms from the Dean of Students Office, and we'll go over it step-by-step to see what we can do," Jim said.

When I returned with the documents needed to construct an individual major, I soon realized I had stumbled, almost by accident, on the one person in the university who could probably help me most. It turned out that Jim was on an academic committee researching the long-range feasibility of instituting a new major in LGB Studies. Not only could he be of great service to me but I could also support the committee by proving a demand. That day we talked for two hours and went through every step: two applications, a letter from him, a letter from me, a supporting statement as to why each proposed class was applicable, and an explanation of how this major would affect my career goals—all in quintuplicate. Jim also offered to sponsor me and to be my "major adviser" for the duration of my undergraduate career, and he gave me a list of professors to contact. Some, including him, had taught classes with all or significant queer content, and others had classes in development. He pulled out the timetable and pointed out two classes offered the next semester to help give me an initial structure.

I was ecstatic. The most difficult task (or so I thought), that of finding an adviser who would see me through until the end, was completed. Now I needed to find 12 classes to fulfill the many requirements for "cohesion" and "progression from elementary to advanced." This would be more difficult than expected.

I became proficient at showing up unannounced during professors' office hours, like a door-to-door salesperson. "Hi, my name is Terry, and I'm designing an individual major in Lesbian, Gay, and Bisexual Studies. I'm wondering if..." Most professors I talked to had either taught a related class or were queer themselves, so it wasn't as intimidating as it might sound, but announcing that I wanted to be a queer studies major did catch some people off-guard, including myself.

After four months of footwork and interaction with more than 40 individual advisers and professors, I had formulated a cohesive 36-credit major in queer studies. The schedule included a patchwork of courses from ten departments, including human sexuality; a directed-study class on social movements through sociology, feminism, and social theory; Women in Literature; Education and Sex Role Socialization; Lesbian Culture; History of U.S. Sexual Identities; Comparative Literature of Alternative Sexualities; Homosexuality in German Literature and Culture; a directed study in queer themes in contemporary popular culture; and a six-credit senior thesis.

The last hurdle was the committee interview. To accomplish this final bureaucratic step, I needed to announce to a room full of academics my purpose and, by implication, my sexual orientation. Though I was nervous as hell, being "out in committee" was the least of my worries. What would this do to my college transcript? If this major were approved and the political climate changed, would I become a victim of the fundamentalist "recruitment theorists"? Could I ever hope to obtain a permanent job, or would I eventually be stuck in a "traditionally queer" occupational field?

Full of anxiety I entered the undergraduate Dean of Students Office the day of my committee interview. The secretary seated me outside the conference room in a hallway lined with bulletin boards and chairs. I felt like I'd been called to the principal's office, but I kept reminding myself not to stress out. Finally I was invited into the room and asked to sit at the conference table. At one end sat the dean of undergraduate students and three professors, all facing me.

I wasn't too worried about Martha Schmitt, the undergraduate dean, as it was her job to assess the major's bureaucratic structure and to make sure general education requirements were fulfilled; I'd already seen to that. I was more worried about the reactions of the three professors and their pointed questions. Having received their names ahead of time, I had snooped around for information on what their reactions might be. The chair of the committee was Joshua Blumfeld, my professor of Comparative Literature of Alternative Sexualities. I'd been a good student in his class, but since he was partially specializing in queer studies, the most academic and critical questions would probably come from him. The second professor was the assistant dean of the women's studies department, Jennifer Anderson, who also taught a feminist sociological theory class. I'd never met her, but word about her in the women's studies department was excellent. I believed my strongest support would come from her. The third professor was John Duncan, a medical sociologist. I knew little about the field or him, except that he received his medical sociology training during the 1940s, a time when the medical community had experimented with frontal lobotomies to "cure sexual deviants." This did nothing to placate my anxieties.

As I sat down at the large table, the dean of students introduced us. The committee spent the first five minutes reviewing my paperwork, which I'd impeccably completed, searching for possible loopholes with a fine-toothed comb, so as not to allow the university to nix my major because of a bureaucratic technicality. And then the questions began.

Dean Schmitt focused on general requirements of the major. "Terry, if you would, explain why you feel this individual major fulfills the requirement of elementary introductory courses which progress into more advanced, specialized subject matter."

"Well, when I decided on these courses, I began with human sexuality and literature so I could acquire a knowledge of the basic cultural and biological foundations of sexuality and sexual expression. From here, each of my more advanced classes are chosen from different academic departments where I can receive specialized training in issues and theories behind queer society from a broad range of viewpoints including social movements, history, and modern popular culture. My senior thesis will integrate these viewpoints and specialties into a cohesive project."

Professor Blumfeld asked the next question. "Why do you feel your academic goals cannot be fulfilled through a combination of existing majors or certificates?"

"The breadth of knowledge in this field requires an interdisciplinary focus as shown through my class choices, which are chosen from ten academic disciplines," I said. "It would not be possible, in my opinion, to acquire a proper foundation and focus without constructing an individual major."

"And what is that focus, specifically?" asked Professor Duncan.

"I want to investigate queer culture, how and why it has formed in the modern world, taking into consideration several theoretical viewpoints. From this foundation I want to learn how sexual minorities interact, are affected by, and change human society as a whole."

"Well, what *are* your end career goals?" he asked intently.

"After graduating I would like to work toward a Ph.D. in sociology, specializing in social movements and queer culture, and eventually teach university classes that would be cross-listed between LGB Studies and the social sciences." He seemed impressed.

Professor Blumfeld then piped in, "How would you respond if told that the university is not the place for purely political undertakings and that a gay and lesbian studies major can only have a political underpinning?"

"Well, that's one opinion made by certain people and groups, but my purpose is the pursuit of unbiased knowledge as to how sexual identity affects the social world," I said. "One aspect of this is the understanding of different viewpoints that question being one among many." He seemed to be attempting to be as critical as possible to get the dean of students to see that the time had come for an undergraduate to major in queer studies and that it wasn't being done for purely political reasons.

What amazed me was not their questions or even my answers, since I had come prepared for this kind of inquisition, but that at the start of the interview my anxiety immediately disappeared and I became completely focused on the task at hand. I understood by the middle of the interview that they had already made their decision; my job evolved into convincing them that I was prepared for the proposed undertaking.

Seemingly satisfied with my answers, Dean Schmitt addressed the structure of my major. "Jennifer, does it seem that all of these classes will be offered in the next three years?"

"I'm not sure," she said. "Most are offered fairly regularly, but Lesbian Culture hasn't been taught for four years because of funding limitations. But it looks like Terry has covered all the bases by including two alternate classes." She seemed to be making a statement about the university's commitment to queer studies while at the same time pushing for acceptance of my proposal.

Dean Schmitt said, "OK then, I move that Terry Dublinski's proposal be approved without changes." The three professors agreed and complimented me on my work. John Duncan even went so far as to call my undertaking "groundbreaking." My bureaucratic journey was over. I passed with flying colors and instantly became a unique individual within a university of 40,000 students. From that point on my academic life changed immeasurably.

When introducing myself as a student, one of the first questions asked is, "What's your major?" Do I explain it to them all the time? Honestly, no. I am a double major in sociology and history sometimes, sociology at other times, and sometimes cultural studies. Sometimes I identify myself as the only LGB Studies major on campus; it depends on the social scene, how much time I have, and my mood. This is a campus where many minority groups, excluding mine, have their own departments; they might not be well-funded, but at least they exist. Sometimes I get tired of explaining what I study. I'm constantly faced with quizzical looks: "So, you study sex?" My answer is yes and no. "So you study literature and history?" Again, yes and no. "Do you study AIDS?" "You study what?!" The list goes on....

In social settings people are either interested or think I'm strange. I don't know how many times men in gay bars have walked away from me because either they think I'm studying them or that I'm so "out" that the radical right must have me targeted as one of America's Most Dangerous Men. At a bar one time, a man that reminded me of the street men of my youth began to talk to me, and I felt the need to distract his advances. I'd had enough experience to understand that "talking shop" would turn down the heat, so I interpreted the "What do you do?" question as relating to what I did for a living, so I explained the fundamentals of my field.

He immediately left. Initially, I thought alcohol had clouded his ability to go beyond inane chatter, but the next time I saw him at the same establishment, the reason for his previous hasty departure became apparent. He must have thought I was straight—and studying *him*. In this second encounter he asked why I wasn't dancing. My answer—that I wasn't in the mood—didn't seem to satisfy him. "You can't just watch and study us," he responded. "You have to *be* us too." So much for "gaydar"—or at least his.

In the classroom I struggle to maintain a balance between academic respectability and disruptive political activism. I've found three basic types of professors, the first being like Jim Steakley, those who know, specialize in, and support queer studies. The second group consists of professors who support research and believe queer studies is a worthwhile undertaking but who have almost no knowledge of the field. Then there is a third type, those who believe in academic freedom but for whom the idea of queer studies is uncomfortable.

One example typifies professors such as this. I knew I was in trouble early in the first week of my History of the Social Sciences class when we began discussing "A Vindication of the Rights of Man" and Professor Walter Richards wouldn't accept the opinion that the writer didn't include women as equals. At the sheer mention of feminism, he closed down discussion, wherein I realized that if he couldn't accept feminism as a legitimate topic for discussion, queer issues would probably be even more problematic. He sat on his gigantic throne in front of the room, behind an immense oak desk, his yellowed lecture notes and weathered brown mottled leather briefcase on display. Obviously, the format of his class hadn't changed in years. Supporting this assumption, later on in the semester Professor Richards spent one day discussing Freud—and not discussing sexuality—in a lecture that seemed reminiscent of the early '60s. I was appalled.

The following week we were required to hand in written topics for our final research paper. Feeling I couldn't pursue my interests in classroom discussion, I decided to investigate an obscure branch of science around the turn of the century called sexology. Not only was this a critical juncture in the formation of Western queer identity and homosexual subculture but it was also completely relevant to the subject of the class. And on top of that, I knew it would make him uncomfortable.

Surprisingly, he approved my topic. I don't know if it was because of the controversial nature or because he was genuinely interested, but when it came time to present our papers I had my 15 minutes of fame. The class was captivated, but he shifted nervously on his throne, cringing each time sexuality came up. I received an A on the paper.

Another professor, Stacy Lin from Women's Studies, was so intrigued with my work that she restructured part of her class on education and sex role socialization to include more gay and lesbian information. I'm a firm believer that one cannot understand gender construction in the modern world without placing sexuality into the mix, but I noticed from the onset that the syllabus included little information on sexual identity and almost nothing about gays and lesbians. I politely and respectfully pointed this out, along with my professional interests, early on in the course.

She was impressed and worked with me to restructure the assignments. We broke into groups for the semester; our group's purpose was to attack sexuality head on. We assigned readings to the class that everyone, including the professor, thoroughly enjoyed. Over the course of the semester, the class went from about 5% queer content to almost a third, and everyone agreed that our understanding of issues surrounding sex role socialization became more intricate, intriguing, and complete because of it. I learned a tremendous amount about both the subject matter of the class and how to reach my goals without overstepping my bounds as a student. It felt exhilarating.

The reaction from students was mixed. I noticed that most men did not talk to me, either inside or outside of class, unless they were queer. In my first academic year, I gave up trying to make male friends in my classes; through necessity, I separated my academic and social lives. Luckily I had developed fully supportive friendships before returning to school, so any social limitations that occurred because of my academic interests were inconsequential and didn't affect me emotionally, at least not much. It seemed as if most straight undergraduate men were afraid of being labeled queer if they talked to me. Perhaps they were afraid I was interested in them—after all, all gay men *are* attracted to all straight men! Not all men are this aloof, and I believe most are good-hearted, but I don't have time to break down every barrier our society has created. One must choose one's battles carefully. Nevertheless, many students appreciated the issues I brought up, and I found that women particularly supported my work and were fascinated by our discussions.

My effect on other students wasn't initially obvious. I had little if any outside interaction with others in my classes and couldn't be sure whether my input served any real educational or social purpose. Then one summer evening I was out with friends having a beer in one of the local lefty student dive bars when a woman hesitantly approached during a break in the conversation at my table.

"Hi, Terry. Do you remember me? I'm Sharon. We had education class together last semester."

I didn't instantly remember her, but after staring at her for a second I placed her face. She had been a quiet student who rarely spoke in class.

"Oh, yes I remember now. How's your summer break going?" I could tell from her stance and look that she was nervous, and I wanted to make her feel comfortable. "Would you like to sit down?"

"No thanks," she said, then quietly added, "But I would like to speak with you a moment."

"Go ahead. How can I help you?" By this point her statements and demeanor had intrigued me so much that I was clinging to the edge of my seat.

She responded excitedly against the backdrop of cigarette smoke and Nirvana. "I've been hoping to run into you all summer so I could thank you. I've been struggling with my sexual identity ever since high school, but your additions to class changed my life. It became normal for me to come to class and discuss sexuality. I read about, thought about, and discussed it openly for the first time in our class last semester. I wanted to thank you because that class prepared me. I came out this summer, have a girlfriend, and am happier than ever. I don't know how long I would have struggled otherwise, but I'm forever thankful that you and that class were there when I needed it most." With that she gave me a heartfelt hug, then walked off into the darkness and mass of people.

My academic perspective is not just theory, stale studies, and endless discussions. I realized that these discussions helped someone become comfortable with herself. While Sharon was visibly shaken, she was also beaming with joy—this from a woman who had hardly said a word in class throughout the spring semester.

It makes me wonder: If I could have this impact on one person, how might I have affected others who never said a word? What effect, then, might a queer studies program at a university have on the entire student body? Or, in the long run, on our entire society?

Creating *Familia*

by Gabriela Rodriguez

Stanford University, California

"I know that guy," said Sam, my freshman roommate. We were in line to pay our tuition at the makeshift bursar's office the university had constructed in the student union. It was our first week at Stanford, and we were both first-year undergraduates. Surprised that she already knew someone at school, I looked to where she was pointing.

"Angel!" Sam called out. The guy turned around with a big smile on his face. He was a short Mexican with that humble self-consciousness a handsome man has when he doesn't know he's attractive. He was wearing shorts and a T-shirt displaying a beautiful golden tan that highlighted his Toltec features.

Eyes bright, he left his spot near the head of the line to stand in front of me, then hugged Sam. "Angel Fabian," he said, taking my hand.

After the introductions Angel and Sam chatted about their hometown and the friends they had in common. I listened, taking mental notes on Angel. He was from a single-parent home, pre-med, and had been raised in a small Central Valley farming town of mostly Mexican immigrants. Something about him, though, caused an alarm to go off in my head. I couldn't pinpoint it, so I listened without comment.

Finally Sam made it to one of the tellers, and Angel and I were alone together. He smiled, then turned to face the front of the line. I listened to the conversations around me. Sound bites of summer internships, European vacations, and the drag of being back in school. I sighed, feeling loneliness in my bones, and wondered what my classmates would say if I told them about my summer: three months filled with 40-hour weeks to raise money for college; Saturday nights in West Hollywood, hustling old dykes for drinks. No European trips, no one to complain to about being back in school. I turned back to Angel, a light suddenly going on in my head.

"Are you gay?" I whispered. I saw him stiffen and waited anxiously for his reply. He nodded through hunched shoulders. "Good, so am I," I said. His shoulders relaxed. "Wait for me outside."

An eternity later I paid my bill and rushed outside to see if Angel was waiting. He was sitting on one of the sofas, leafing through his calendar.

"Girl, you got some nerve," he squealed with joy as I approached. "I can't believe it. Do you always come out to people like that?"

"Not usually," I said, not wanting to admit I hadn't really come out to anyone before. "I was beginning to believe I was the only queer Latina here. I went to the Lesbian, Gay, Bisexual Community Center [LGBCC], and I got that look I used to get when I was in West Hollywood, you know..."

"The kind that makes you feel like a piece of meat," he finished. "Where are you from, girl?"

"Compton."

"Really?" Thanks to gangsta rap music and the evening news, the fame of my city had reached across the nation. It had even made it to Angel's small farming town. "So what's it like?"

"Not as bad as the news makes it sound, but bad enough," I said. "All you hear in rap songs is how bad it is to be a man of color in Compton. I guess no one ever thought about rapping about what it's like to be a woman, a gay woman at that, in Compton. You know, I was one of three gay people at my high school. The other two were guys...one got the crap beaten out of him; the other transferred. Anyway, what's the scene like here? Are there any clubs, any groups, any cute girls?"

"Boy, did you come to the wrong place," Angel said. "There's an 18-and-over club that's all the way up in Berkeley. As for groups there's Centro Chicano and the LGBCC. And as for cute girls, well, you're it."

"Shit! It's like high school all over again. But this time I'm not going to be closeted!" I exclaimed more to myself than to Angel.

"Calm down. People are staring. Look, I have to go. Give me your number and I'll call you later, OK?"

We exchanged numbers, and Angel left. I didn't see him again until the second month of the quarter, two days before one of the *Movimiento Estudiantil Chicano de Aztlan* (MEChA) meetings.

There was a knock on my door.

"Come in," I shouted from the comfort of my bed. I was lying on my stomach reading a book. I didn't bother to turn around, figuring it would be someone from the dorm looking for my roommate. Since I had come out to the dorm the month before, few people would even talk to me.

"*Hola, bella. No me das un abrazo?*"

I turned around, stunned. "Angel!" I rushed to hug him, crying.

"Hey, what's the matter? God, if I'd known you'd be this happy to see me, I would've come sooner." He let go when he heard me laugh. "What's going on?" I sat on the bed and waited for him to pull up a chair while he took off his backpack.

"Let's see. Since I saw you last I came out to my roommate, I came out to the dorm, and oh, I'm failing half my classes. Let's just say I'm not doing well."

"Whoa, girl! How did this happen?" he asked.

"Well, it started with that stupid game, Crossing the Line. You know, they bring in someone from Residential Education during one of the house meetings. About three weeks ago the game was held at our dorm."

✳   ✳   ✳

At the first house meeting, the residential assistants announced that we were scheduled for Crossing the Line in two weeks. They told us it would be one of the most significant experiences of our undergraduate lives, that many long-term friendships would be born during the game, and that we must not miss it. Everyone in the dorm attended the session.

The facilitator was a tiny red-haired woman with glasses too small for her face. "The rules are simple," she said, drawing an imaginary line across the middle of the lounge. "Everyone will stand at one side of the room. I'll ask a question, and if you answer yes, you cross the line. OK, who is a freshman?"

With the exception of the RAs, everyone crossed. The questions began easy enough but grew harder as the game progressed. For every question she asked, a number of people crossed, until she said, "Who is questioning their sexuality or is either gay or lesbian?"

She left out bisexual, but I crossed anyway. I looked to my left, then to my right. I was alone. No one else had crossed, and the room grew quiet.

I felt the hair at the back of my neck stand on edge. It felt like an eternity had passed before she asked her next question. The game went on with fewer people crossing the line.

When the game was over, the facilitator left. We all fiddled around not daring to look at each other. Not knowing what to do, I went to my room.

I was already in bed when Sam came in. Her hair was down, hiding her eyes. She went directly to open her closet door. When it became obvious she was looking for nothing in particular, I blurted, "In case you're wondering, I'm bisexual."

❋   ❋   ❋

"What did she say?" Angel prompted.

"She said it was OK with her, then darted out the door. We haven't talked much, partly because we haven't been in the same room long enough to say more than a few words to each other. I think she doesn't know how to deal, being Catholic and all."

"Give her time," he said, patting my hand. "What about the dorm?"

"Well, nobody said anything at first. And everything was fine...until I found this homophobic joke in the house log. And of course I responded, saying that not only was the joke tasteless but also that as a queer woman I found it offensive. That led to more responses. Some agreed with me; some didn't. After that I got fliers from the Campus Crusade for Christ stuffed under my door, encouraging me to find 'salvation through repentance.' And a girl down the hall invited me to one of her Bible study sessions to save my soul from my 'sinful lifestyle.' I kindly turned her down. Pretty much everyone ignores me, but I can feel their eyes on me as I walk down the hall...at least it feels that way.

"I thought it'd be different here, you know. But it's like high school. Except this time all the shitty things are happening to me." I sighed, remembering the night I had the conversation with my RA.

❋   ❋   ❋

The hall was empty, but I heard soft music coming from Kim's room. I stood outside her door for a while, staring at the name plate: KIM KAO, HONG KONG. Finally I knocked.

"Come in," came Kim's reply.

"Hi, can I talk to you?" I asked faintly. I tried swallowing, but my mouth was dry.

"Sure. Would you like to sit down?" She got up from her desk and moved toward the futon.

"Sure," I said, grateful that at least my knees weren't going to give out. "Listen, I won't take much of your time. I just, uh, oh boy. Here goes. Kim, it's no secret that I'm gay. And since that stupid game, things between Sam and me aren't great. So I was wondering if you could talk to her. Because as it is we can't be in the same room together because she immediately bolts out the door."

"So, you think that your being, uh, um, uh, gay bothers her?"

"Come on! After hanging out together at almost every orientation event and eating every meal together, she's suddenly shy around me?" Kim stared at me as I tried to calm myself down.

"What would you like me to do?"

"I don't know. Talk to her...try to make her understand...." I could hear how useless my words sounded.

"I don't know how. We weren't trained to deal with these issues. If you can think of—"

"Look, why don't we hold one of those LGBCC speakers panels here? In fact, I'm going to one tonight. I could get you contact information."

"That would be great. But if we do schedule one, it'll have to be next quarter. Residential Education has scheduled the events for this quarter, and since they're supposed to encourage dorm bonding, they can't—"

"I've had all the dorm bonding I can stand!" I said. "Do you have any idea what it feels like living with someone who can't stand being in the same room with you?"

"Please, calm down. I'll talk to Sam. If you like, I can come to this meeting you're going to tonight."

I took Kim up on her offer, and that night we made our way across campus trying to find answers to my problem. We arrived just as the panel was beginning. The dorm lounge was filled. Two white men and two white women sat on the panel. Each told their coming-out story and discussed how their friends and family had reacted. A couple of speakers had had positive reactions; the other two hadn't. Afterward the audience asked the usual questions: "When did you know?" "Have you ever been attracted to a member of the opposite sex?" I was getting bored until I heard someone ask, "Are there a large number of bisexuals in your community?"

"Well," began one of the guys, "I think we're all potentially bisexual. But mostly it's a stage people go through during the coming-out process."

"Like we said before, we *are* diverse," said one of the women before she was interrupted by the second woman.

"Of course there are a lot of people who are bi in theory," she said angrily, "people who think being bisexual is 'neat' and politically correct. Some even show up to events, but when it comes to getting political, all of a sudden they disappear. They just come to sleep with our women, but as soon as they get the chance, they run back to the protecting arms of heterosexuality."

"Of course, please keep in mind that these are our views and that we don't speak for the whole community," broke in the first woman.

I left feeling dejected. I'd been out to myself since I was 8, and didn't feel my bisexuality was a stage. The anti-bisexual sentiment and the hostile attitudes I would encounter later formed my decision to identify as a "queer woman of color."

＊　＊　＊

"I don't know what's worse, being afraid of being found out or dealing with being out. I can't wait for next quarter to 'open the lines of communication,'" I lamented to Angel, clawing the air with my fingers. "Especially with the tension between Sam and me. And to be honest I don't know if having the panel will help. Like I said, I didn't identify with the speakers."

"I'm so sorry, *mi hija.*"

Sam walked into the room. "Angel, what a surprise! It's so good to see you. What are you doing here?"

They chit-chatted about the quarter for a while. Then there was a bit of silence. "Sam, I have something to tell you," Angel said. "I'm gay. You'd probably find out soon enough, but I'd rather you hear it from me. I'd also like to ask you a favor. My family knows, but no one else at home knows. I'd like to keep this quiet for now. *Tu sabes como es la gente de chismosa.*"

"Of course, Angel, don't worry about it," Sam said, shocked. "I understand." Then she excused herself by heading toward the bathroom to get ready for bed. She had told me before that she respected and admired

Angel for holding onto his heritage. She'd also described how proud she felt when he became the first person from their town to attend a big-name university such as Stanford. Shyly, she'd admitted Angel had been one of the reasons she had applied to Stanford. I couldn't help wondering how his coming out would affect her.

"And you think I'm outrageous? She's going to think this room is cursed," I said turning to him.

"Well, she was going to find out in a couple of days anyway. Listen, I met these two grad students, and we got to talking. We want to start a queer Chicano group on campus. Are you interested?"

"Yeah, of course. What kind of group? Support? Social? Political?"

"Well, why don't we all meet so we can decide? How does tomorrow night at midnight sound? I know it's late, but it was the only time we were all free."

"Sure."

"Cool. Let's meet outside the bookstore. Now I have to run because I'm due at a study group."

"Study group? But it's nearly midnight!"

"Yeah, but I'm pre-med. You should try to find a study group too. See if that helps you with your grades," he said, heading out the door.

I would, Angel, but no one wants to hang out with a queer.

The next night we met as planned. After the meeting Angel asked for my opinion.

"To be honest I think they're too nationalist and too comfortable with their sexuality to care about dealing with people who are just coming out."

"I know," he said. "But we've got to start somewhere. Look, we'll make an announcement about the group tomorrow at MEChA and see if anyone's interested. We'll take it from there, OK?"

＊ ＊ ＊

"I'd like to welcome everyone to Centro and to the MEChA meeting," said Alex, the meeting facilitator and MEChA cochair. "I see we have some new faces in the crowd. Why don't we start by introducing ourselves, then we'll proceed to the business at hand. Don't forget that all announcements are made at the end of the meeting, followed by the study break. So let's start."

At announcement time Angel started. "Hi, for those of you who don't know me, I'm Angel." He was interrupted by applause and cat calls. "And this is Gaby. We're starting a group for queer Chicanos called *La Vida Loca Collectiva*, so if any of you are interested, we'll be hanging out for the study break, and you can get more information."

"Any more announcements?" asked Alex, piercing the silence.

At the study break no one approached us. I could see people looking at us out of the corners of their eyes. Whenever we approached anyone, their conversation died down, and they smiled at us politely until we walked away. I got so uncomfortable that I suggested we leave. "Now what?" I asked Angel.

"We outreach. We get the word out."

For the next two quarters, Angel and I did outreach. He signed me up for the LGBCC's speaker panel. When I asked why, he replied, "You said you couldn't relate to the speakers. Well, let's give the audience a new perspective. Besides, girl, as long as you're going to be stared at, you might as well stare back."

Before I knew it I was going all over campus talking about my experience as a queer Chicana at Stanford. Sometimes Angel would be on the panel with me when he wasn't at some other event advertising the group, which we were now calling *Familia*, due to a falling out with the grad students.

The rift occurred after the first meeting of *La Vida Loca Collectiva*, which was held at El Centro Chicano. We had requested the use of one of the rooms during a time slot in which the Centro was usually empty, to protect the privacy of those attending. Five people besides the four group organizers showed up. Several curious community members also marched in and out of the meeting to see who had showed. One of the new members mentioned that this made him feel uncomfortable.

"Look, you fucking faggot, no one is here to hold your hand," snapped a grad student. "So just deal with it!" We were stunned.

After the meeting, we confronted the grad student. "Why did you say that to John?" exclaimed Angel.

"Why, you bunch of *pendejos*! Who the hell do you think you are? No fucking sellout is going to tell me what to do. This was my idea, and I can do and say what I want!"

After this incident Angel and I knew we were alone, left to become our own family, our own support. So we created *Familia*, Spanish for *family*.

When I wasn't doing outreach, I was attending MEChA meetings, reintroducing myself every time I spoke, signing up for planning committees to whose meetings I never got called because someone conveniently forgot to call or E-mail me with the meeting times. There were times, however, when members of MEChA did remember my name.

"Hi, I'm Joey. I got your name and number from one of our lists," said the squeaky female voice on my answering machine. "I was calling because we're bringing Gloria Anzaldúa to speak on campus. We were wondering if you'd like to have lunch with us. There will be a group of us from El Centro Chicano, and you, of course. We thought it'd be great if we could show Gloria that we do have some queer Chicanas. You know, let her see how diverse we are. I think she'd enjoy having someone she could talk to."

I erased the message, not bothering to call back. But the work went on. And so did dorm life.

One day I was reading on the couch in the lobby, lying flat on my stomach, face buried in a book. I looked up when I heard someone coming down the steps. Then the footsteps stopped. One of the guys from the dorm, Jeff, was standing in front of the message board at the end of the stairs. He grabbed one of the fliers off the board and balled it up. "Burn in hell, fucking faggots," he muttered. He threw the flier into the trash, giving me a frightening look on his way out.

I got up and pulled the flier out of the trash. It was an announcement for a new queer Christian Bible-study group. "God Is Love. Come Join Us," read the flier. I was shocked and horrified at what Jeff had done. I walked to my dorm room with the flier in hand. Tears were streaming down my face, my heart pounding faster with every step.

"What's wrong?"

I heard Sam's question but couldn't speak. I kept remembering the gay boy in my high school, the one who'd gotten beaten up. He was found outside the public library with a broomstick up his butt, bleeding, begging for help. *What if this guy had the same intentions? What if one night while I was walking to my room...or what if I was alone in the room....?* With each thought, my heart pounded louder, my mouth drier and my throat tighter.

"Hey, Gaby, are you OK?" Sam repeated.

"No. I just…saw one of the Jeffs…he took this down…and…" I handed her the flier. She read it and went to get me some water.

"What happened?" she asked, handing me the glass. After I explained, she threw her long hair back in anger, took me by the hand and dragged me to my RA's door. We knocked, but no one answered.

"Look, Sam, it's not going to do any good. I've talked to the RAs already. It didn't help. They don't know what to do, so why don't we drop it?" I was scared and didn't want any trouble, especially if I might get hurt.

"OK," she said, dragging me downstairs toward the case where all of the dorm members' pictures were posted. "Which one is he?"

"What good is this going to do?" I asked angrily. "And since when did you become so concerned after ignoring me for the last quarter? If you want to help, why don't you speak to me when we're out on campus or at El Centro? Do something about your own homophobia!" I darted out the front door.

I came back to the dorm the next day. Sam wasn't in the room. On my bed I found a note that read, "I'm sorry. —Sam." After that she made it a point to speak to me every time she saw me on campus.

By spring quarter of my freshman year, *Familia* had a roster of 45 members. Some came to our political events; some showed up to the socials; and others attended support-group meetings. Similar groups were started by other people of color who felt their respective communities and the LGBCC weren't supportive. There were BlAQS (Black and Queer at Stanford) and Q&A (Queer and Asian). Things were starting to look promising. Before I knew it my freshman year was over. I packed my bags and went home for the summer, looking forward to the coming year and all its possibilities.

During the summer I received an invitation from the Dean of Students Office of Multicultural Education to speak at a freshman orientation program, Faces in the Community. I agreed and returned to campus a week early to prepare. Once on campus I stopped in at Centro, where a Chicano orientation meeting was taking place. As I walked by, all talking stopped. Nothing seemed to have changed; I was still someone to be ignored.

Three days later the orientation program Angel and I were invited to speak at began. When it was his turn to speak, he proudly told the entire freshman class and the VIPs how proud he was to be a Chicano gay man. *Familia* members cheered and whistled from the front rows. But I could also hear laughter in the audience and a few snide remarks made in the dark by Chicanos who weren't part of *Familia*. They too were seated toward the front of the stage hoping to show "support" and solidarity.

When it was my turn, I went on stage. I heard the audience moving expectantly in their seats. I held up my hand to shield my eyes from the almost blinding light pointed directly at me. For a second, I looked into the audience and spotted the only familiar face I knew. There in front of me, in a small TV reflecting what a camera was recording, I saw myself: black hair, black eyes full of fear. And I realized I was tired of being afraid of who I was, of what people thought. I put my hand down and balled up my meticulous, politically correct speech. I spoke about my experience at Stanford, about the homophobia in communities of color, and about the racism and bi-phobia in the white lesbian and gay community. As I spoke my fear disappeared. I told the freshmen the truth as I had lived it. I wanted them to understand that they had a choice. They could try to fit into the boxes their communities had built for them, or they could create their own space. After all, had we not created *Familia*?

I didn't stay to hear the audience's response. I jetted off the stage and headed to the waiting room, staying until the auditorium had cleared. When I finally stepped out, a group of people were waiting for me. They wanted to introduce themselves and thank me for my honesty. For those first few weeks after the event, I couldn't speak in public without being approached by people congratulating me on my honesty. Granted, not everyone responded as nicely. I did get hassled by some Chicanos for "embarrassing the community" and showing a "divided front to the administration" and a "lack of compassion toward our own." Nasty notes and messages were shoved under my door. But the response wasn't always bad, and eventually things died down. I became known as "The Angry Queer Chicana." And *Familia* continued to thrive.

Familia is now a solid group on the Stanford and UCLA campuses. In the fall of 1997, *Familia* made history by sponsoring the first Queer Latino/a Youth Conference, "Reflections of Leadership: We Are the Ones We've Been Waiting For." We are currently planning the second annual conference. For me, we evolved from a handful of scared kids to a group of daring community activists, carving a space not only for ourselves but also for those to follow.

Ending a Eulogy

by Jerome J. Graber

Loyola College, Maryland

I took the last stroke and held my oar steady at hands away. The green and gray blade drifted over the rushing water, and the four of us delicately balanced our boat with the weight of the extended oars. Our momentum cut the shell through the water until, at the last second before the boat succumbed to gravity and listed to one side, our coxswain, Jeff, called sharply, "Blades down!" We responded by loudly slapping our oars onto the water in perfect unison. Several other boats were finishing their pre-race drills nearby. As I was doing my last-minute stretches, a boat with four guys, the smallest of which dwarfed my teammates, pulled up next to us. As they drifted a couple of them yelled to us in mocking falsetto voices.

"Ooh, that one's cute!" a guy with a shaved head called out.

"Hey there, sweetie-pie!" another exclaimed.

My gut sank, and I hung my head. Did I look that gay when I rowed? I felt embarrassed that my teammates were seeing this. From the driver's seat, Jeff was looking at me, horrified, but no one was watching him. Everyone was looking at me and chuckling softly with expectation. The guys in my boat eagerly awaited my response, so I swallowed the knot in my throat and called back, "Hey! What's your number, hot stuff?"

My teammates laughed. They knew I hadn't had a date since coming to college the previous September. Spurred on, I gave a coquettish wave and an exaggerated wink, leaving the opposing rowers with troubled expressions. The six boats in our race lined up for the start, our oars frozen in position. When the marshal dropped the flag, my boat took off like a shot, pulling just ahead of the other boats. It was one of our hardest races of the season. The other boats were seconds behind us, and when one of the other teams began to pull up even, Jeff barked and growled at us from the coxswain's seat. Dave groaned from behind me with each stroke, and my lungs were burning before the race was even halfway over. Each time my oar dropped into the water, I was pulling with my entire body to push the boat ahead. After what seemed an eternity of ragged breaths and tortuous strokes, we crossed the finish line, and immediately we collapsed in exhaustion. After several painful breaths we all reached to clasp one another's numb bloody hands in congratulations. The team that had taunted us pulled in well behind, but now, at this end of the race course, they had nothing to say.

I had started cluing people in at Loyola since my second week there. I was completely open about being gay in high school, so it felt like no big deal. I had come from a small rural town and sat in my desk alongside the children of farmers. In Clinton, N.J., everyone knew everyone, and teachers in our school were sometimes educating a third generation of families. When I came out my sophomore year, it took place gradually, without any huge revelations, just the slow acknowledgment of something I'd been hinting at since eighth grade. When the whole school eventually knew, I wasn't just "that fag." I was someone with a name, a history, and a lot of good friends. Aside from odd looks and a couple of cold shoulders, I didn't have any problems with prejudice in high school.

When I announced senior year that I was planning to attend a small private Jesuit college, my friends thought I was nuts. After spending four years of high school knowing only one other gay person, didn't I want to go to a big school where there'd be more people like me? Not really. My need for friends didn't dictate that they be gay, and if they were it didn't mean I'd automatically get along with them. I had enjoyed the close atmosphere of my high school and had learned valuable lessons. Who'd have thought I'd be as accepted and happy there as I was? Why shouldn't it be the same at Loyola?

Within the first few weeks of college, any nagging doubts I'd had were allayed. When people I'd just met tried to set me up with girls, I had to gently explain that I didn't have anything against women, but.... And without exception, the people I met were interested, asked questions, seemed a bit nervous, and laughed when I made jokes about it, just like high school. As the semester passed, more and more people knew through word of mouth that I was gay. But there was one difference from high school. People I had casually met would send me an E-mail or call or make an excuse to drop by and talk. Lots of them wanted to talk about a friend who thought they might be gay. It was amazing how many of those "friends" turned out to be them.

Shortly after starting college I was also introduced to rowing, something I'd never done. I had run track and cross-country in high school for a couple of years but never thought of myself as an athlete. Most of the people joining the team had also never rowed. I talked to the coach at an activities fair, and he followed me halfway across campus trying to get me to join. So I did. The first time I stepped in a boat, I knew it would be worth it. I'd seen other people row, and it looked so graceful, so effortless. But when I was doing it myself, I prayed to every deity imaginable that the oar wouldn't leap up and crack me in the skull, leaving me looking like a deranged hockey goalie. Sweat poured down my brow and stung my eyes. I couldn't make my blade go into the water the same time as everyone else, and my arms felt like rubber all day long afterward. But I loved it. On the way back from practice, the 12 of us would laugh and talk in the van, all adjusting to college life. Getting up at 5 in the morning has a strange bonding effect on people that lasts throughout the sleep-deprived, zombie-stumbling, falling-asleep-in-lectures day. I knew soon I'd have to mention something to them about my being gay.

We practiced together every morning, went to races together most weekends, and slowly began to hang out more and more with one another outside of crew time. As I would with any group of people, I started making little jokes. My teammates weren't stupid, of course; a few of them had their suspicions, so they picked up pretty quickly. When we were ordering uniforms, I said, "Wait! Leave this to me! Fashion design is in my genes." Or I would pounce on one of the members of our women's team, tell her how she was gorgeous, I loved her, I couldn't live without her, then whisper in a sultry voice loud enough for everyone to hear, "Do you have a brother half as handsome for me?" Someone (I don't even remember who) casually asked me questions one day while a bunch of us were sitting around. They were the usual innocuous curiosities, anything from "Do your parents know?" ("Yes") to "What's it like to kiss a guy?" ("Great! Wanna try it?" or "Just like a girl, but with stubble.") Of course, the most frequently asked question would come up when a beautiful girl walked by, and my wide-eyed teammates would ask, "That does nothing for you?" I'd shrug, and they'd clasp their heads in exasperation. My homosexuality became another joke among the guys, like anything else we'd poke fun at one another about.

Every time we were all out together, George, the most outspoken and hilarious of my teammates, would make conspiratorial eyes at me and ask, "Hey, Jerome, is that guy gay? What do you think of him? Would you take him home?" Besides the stereotypical clues, the criteria that would elicit his line of questioning were the following: anyone wearing pastels, anyone not wearing something affiliated with sports or beer, anyone wearing black shoes, anyone not physically attached to a female, and anyone who glanced in my direction. At first I'd answer, annoyed, "How should I know?" But later I explained the quirks of "gaydar," about which he was greatly amused. Our game would begin when I'd say, "George, who in this room besides me is a homosexual?" He and the others would compete to see who could correctly identify as many people as possible (usually at a bar, party, or restaurant), with the ultimate judge being, of course, me, the only actual certified practicing (or trying to at a small Catholic college) homosexual in our circle.

Of course, the person in our group with the most keen interest in the topic of homosexuality was also the one who said the least about it. I had my suspicions about our coxswain Jeff, an upperclassman who acted as a kind of assistant coach. I didn't say anything, but the way he kept his distance while the rest of us bonded and laughed when we'd joke about my sexuality fit the pattern of people who'd been coming out to me.

One day at the end of fall semester, George, Jeff, two other teammates, and I had driven to Washington, D.C., for the day. On the way back George had begun another round of "Queer Q&A," asking questions more and more ridiculous to see how long I'd go on making up answers. As usual Jeff was silent when the topic came up. I'd been wondering if anyone else had noticed this pattern when George seemed to read my mind. With a sarcastic lilt in his voice, he turned around and looked Jeff straight in the eye. "Jeff, don't you have any questions for Jerome? You're awfully quiet back there."

Jeff looked back and forth suddenly, his eyes wide, and muttered defensively, "No, no." George started laughing, and Jeff told him to shut up. Had Jeff told George he was gay? Or did George suspect it like I did?

Over Christmas break, Jeff sent me a letter in which he made a couple of cryptic comments on how he "would like to get closer to me" and felt I was a "special friend." I called him, and we talked about it, and he finally admitted he was gay. He was a senior, and I was the first person he had ever told. He had never spoken about his feelings before, and they came out in a flood. Jeff's teenage experience had been more typical than mine. His classmates teased him, first for being quiet and shy amid the jocks and prepsters of his private high school. This turned to taunts and jeers of "Homo!" and "Queer!" as they grew older together. During his senior year FAG had been spray-painted on his car in the school parking lot, the same car with which he had once tried to kill himself. Many other terrible experiences surfaced as Jeff and I spoke more in private when we came back to school in January. Throughout high school and college and at home, always feeling isolated, Jeff had joined the crew team as a way to make friends and to make himself seem less gay. When he had told his parents he was joining the team, his mother warned him, "Don't run with the rest of the team, Jeff. Stay at the back of the pack. You run like a girl. Don't let them see." Mothers always seem to know, don't they?

The guys on the team did make fun of Jeff for the way he ran. His feet would circle beneath him, and his arms would flail wildly to each side. And it was funny precisely because he was so self-conscious about it and so many other things. But Jeff took ridicule much too seriously. I made fun of George for his "swarthy" Greek heritage, and George made fun of Mike for his Long Island accent, and Mike made fun of...and so on and so on, and someone would make fun of me for being gay. If I didn't get a joke, they'd all look at each other, and someone would start off, "It's a straight thing..." and the rest would finish, in unison, "...you wouldn't under-stand." But these jokes, ridiculing our differences, were just that: jokes. By making light of the differences between us, we eased tensions and made ourselves more comfortable with each other. Our jokes allowed us to sat-isfy our curiosities about each other in a good-natured way, getting our prejudices out in the open.

George, in a rare moment of sincerity, admitted to me that he felt bad for the abuse he and his friends had heaped on people in their high school who they had thought were gay. Of course, he had never actually known a gay person before, so how could he have known what he heard about them wasn't true? Our team had more than 50 people, and I was the first openly gay person any of them had known. Now that George knew me, he knew what gay people were like. Just like one of the guys.

Jeff wasn't just one of the guys. He was too afraid to be. We'd hang out with him and have a lot of fun with him, but he maintained a distance with his shyness and lack of trust. Even after he had talked with me and had seen how well I got along with the other guys, Jeff didn't want them to know. He refused to talk about it with them. He insisted that when I wasn't around, they made fun of me. I'm sure they did; we all made fun of each other. That's how I could be sure I was just like the rest of the team. But Jeff took it the opposite way, I think because that's what he had expected.

For over a month, Jeff would pull me aside and speak in a hushed tone, always about his past. He never wanted to talk about what would happen if he told our friends, and telling his family was unthinkable. Instead, it was a continuous loop of stories about how mean people had been to him in high school. He told me how he had no friends and how he thought people were evil. I started getting sick of it. I'd heard it all before, and fortunately for me I couldn't sympathize. I hadn't had these experiences, and I didn't see why what had happened in the past was more important than what was going on right now. Jeff was especially close with George and Mike, but when I suggested he try them out, he refused. "I can't, I can't…they would hate me" was his answer. Never mind that George and Mike and everyone else had no problem with my being gay. Jeff would turn white and stare blankly when I talked about being gay in front of our teammates, afraid I would mention him. He didn't seem to realize that, as bad as things had been for him, they could've been a lot worse. He wasn't dead, but the way he lived he might as well have been.

Other people besides Jeff came and talked to me. Some had told their close friends before, but no one I met my freshman year had told their family or was completely open about being gay. Most of the people who talked to me, however, eventually opened up more. As they've come out to more people, many of them have gained greater confidence and have started to see they are not and never were *just* homosexuals. People in the closet seem to define their whole lives on the basis of their sexuality. Everything they cherish is held in a delicate balance against the terror of others finding out they're gay. They could be brilliant, athletic, talented, etc., but they think it will all come crashing down if someone finds out.

I was getting sick of being the only openly gay person around. As much as I enjoyed the friendships I had among my teammates and class-mates, being the black sheep grew old. I got tired of making cracks about myself and feeling I had to explain the strange clips of men in drag and leather people on the 10 o'clock news. Because the only individuals most people identify as gay are those that fit their stereotypes, it was shocking to most people I met that I didn't conform to their preconceived notions, regardless of whether those prejudices were negative. *I* knew there were plenty of gay men who weren't Dorothy-worshipers and lesbians who shaved their legs and didn't wear combat boots. But none of the homo-sexuals I knew were willing to stand up and say so. It seemed as if, ironi-cally, that the straight people I knew appreciated my being out more than the gay people did. I felt as though the closeted people I met were using me as a sounding board for their problems, and I didn't feel like installing a psychiatrist's couch in my room. I had better things to do than listen to paranoid stories about mobs of people at the castle gates with firebrands. My gates were wide open, and the crowd was full of curious friends.

Two weeks before spring break my freshman year, I received a call that a friend from high school had been in a car accident. Four days later I was catching a bus home and then watching someone I'd grown up with deliv-er a eulogy for his best friend. Sean stood at the lectern, shoulders bowed but head up, and looked at each and every one of us, trying to sound happy as he reminded us of the times we'd enjoyed with Chris. Flowers and young people were everywhere. The incongruity of people my own age dressed in dark suits and shuffling about speaking quietly left me in a daze. I didn't even hear most of the service; it felt like déjà vu—all about the past, about things Chris had done in high school, the friends he'd had, the things he'd done and enjoyed. He looked so still lying there, and I wished he could sit up and talk with me as we had hundreds of times before. But that was all gone now. When I found his mother's face among the crowd, it was the first time I'd ever seen true despair. Every other sor-row anyone had revealed to me paled to the profound grief I saw with one glance. No longer crying for her only son, her face was drawn and dark, collapsed, while her eyes stared blankly into the space ahead. When Sean came out of the church where the body of his best friend lay still and white, there was a mob of people waiting to comfort him.

When I returned to school the next day, Jeff was one of the first people

I saw. He asked me no questions about the funeral but jumped right back to where we'd left off. He was telling me more and more details of teachers who'd been mean to him, classmates who didn't talk to him, how cruel his brothers were, etc. None of it even seemed directed at Jeff because he was gay. He was blaming every bad thing that had ever happened to him on his sexuality. I was lying on my stomach on the ugly uncomfortable dorm couch, no longer listening. I stared at the wall and thought about how I didn't want to get up for practice the next morning and wondered how I'd done on the organic chemistry test I took the morning I left. I must have lain there awhile without responding before Jeff noticed I had stopped paying attention. I bowed off that I was tired and wanted to get some sleep. The next day life was back to my routine of practice with ergs and running and lifting and stairs, class all day, a second workout, dinner, some schoolwork, and then a visit upstairs with George, Mike, and Jeff.

I'd been pushing Jeff recently to come out to George and Mike and was hardly able to hide my frustration over it. I started making excuses for not visiting him in his room, knowing he would never dare talk to me in my room, where privacy was nonexistent. Jeff finally relented and told me he'd spoken with George first, then Mike. But he asked me not to discuss the topic with them. Jeff wanted to keep things private, worrying that if we all talked about it, we might slip up and say something in front of our other teammates.

Two weeks later we were all getting ready to leave for Florida for spring break. No more dank weight room at 6 A.M. We'd be back on the water in the sun, and by the time we were back in Baltimore, it would be warm enough to row on the water again. I was talking to Mike and flippantly made some crack about how tired I was of listening to Jeff whine about being gay. I was halfway into my next comment before I realized Mike was just sitting on his bed, staring at me and looking dumb. Well, dumber than usual.

"What?" I asked casually.

"Jeff who?" he asked, crumbs of a tuna fish sandwich falling down his chin.

"Your roommate, Jeff, of course."

"Jeff admitted to you that he's gay?"

Now it was my turn to be surprised. Some chaos ensued, but we soon sorted out that Jeff had never talked to Mike about being gay as he had told me. We waited until George got home, because I was sure Jeff had told him, but he laughed when we asked him about it, thinking it was a prank. I was so embarrassed. My first thoughts were of what Mike and George would think of gay people now. Would this be the basis on which they'd view me from now on? How could they trust gay people at all?

When Jeff finally walked in to see us sitting around the table, he could tell something was up. I wasn't angry by then; I was just tired and wanted to get this over with and go to bed. I took him alone in the back room and started out by asking him again how George and Mike had reacted when he'd told them he was gay. He repeated what he had said earlier. I asked if I should bring George or Mike into the room to verify that and then asked him why he had lied. For once, Jeff had nothing to say. George, Mike, and I were up for hours, trying to reassure Jeff it was fine that he was gay but not fine he had lied to us. After talking with Mike and George, Jeff finally started to look relieved.

After that, things were awkward among all of us. No one knew what to think. No one trusted anything Jeff told us anymore, least of all me. He still never talked about being gay, which made it even worse. And when I made jokes the laughter was hollow, and people nervously looked at Jeff to check his reaction. The few times I talked to him, we argued. We didn't understand each other's views. On spring break everyone had a great time, but I couldn't hide my anger at Jeff. Most of our team didn't understand why I was suddenly so mean to him. I was short with him in practice, and the friendly atmosphere of our boat changed irreparably. We were still doing well, winning every race of our spring season, but it was now a quieter celebration. Jeff tried apologizing for what he'd done, but I felt it was perfunctory, since he hadn't changed his behavior at all. I constantly felt I had to be on my best behavior, like I had to prove that not all gay people were like Jeff. I couldn't trust that they still thought the same way they had before. Jeff and another teammate graduated in May, my freshman year was over, and I was relieved. I had no idea what Jeff was going on to do, and I didn't care.

I've rowed for three years now, and I'm training for next year. I've been in conference and regional championship boats more than once. I'll be the team captain my third time next year. My scars and medals prove I try as hard as anyone else. But it isn't a daily concern. In the fall I orient our novices. They show up nervous for practice, acting tough, trying to impress each other, their coach, and me. They call each other "fag" and "homo," and I just smile. Soon enough I let them know I'm gay the same way I tell everyone else.

Occasionally, the new people come to me and apologize for slanders I never even noticed but that they remember and feel guilty about. One day I was talking to Rich. I'd been his team captain his freshman year and lived with him the following summer. He looked sheepish as he hung his head and said to me, "Jerome, I'm sorry about using the word *fag* that time."

"What are you talking about?" I'd never even heard Rich swear.

"You know..." His eyes were firmly on the ground. "I couldn't tell at first. I'd never met a gay person, but I didn't mean it if I hurt your feelings. I felt like such an ass."

"When was this?"

"It was early last fall, and we were all standing around, and I called someone a fag, and you were standing there. Jon hit me on the arm and hissed at me to be quiet, then explained later. I had no idea." I still couldn't remember this. I'm sure I didn't even notice it. I usually didn't. But he looked so guilty that I accepted his apology and blew it off. Then I thought about Jeff for a moment and added, "But you know, Rich, you could've hurt someone's feelings like that and not even known it. That's why so many gay people are afraid to tell anyone the truth. You never know who might be listening when you say something like that—or how they'll take it."

Periodically someone would mention Jeff to me. They heard he was in New York doing research or at school in Boston. One day sophomore year, Mike came up to me and asked, "Did you hear Jeff is gonna be on campus next week?"

"Really? What for?"

"He's giving a speech." Mike paused for effect, grinning from ear to ear in expectation.

I had to bite the hook. "On what?"

"Being gay at Loyola."

The lecture room was packed that night, but Jeff didn't look nervous at all. He jumped onto the stage and sat there, swinging his legs, speaking in an unfamiliar voice loud enough for everyone to hear. He talked about his experiences in high school and at Loyola, lightening up the depressing past with jokes and funny observations. He had a strong rapport with the audience, who responded well and asked a lot of questions. Someone asked him what had made him finally decide to come out, and he didn't look at me at all, even though he had seen me in the audience.

"My senior year I met someone...." My roommate and teammate, Brian, was sitting beside me, and he began elbowing me in the ribs.

Jeff talked a little bit about this person, a freshman who had been so different and completely open, and about how it changed how he saw things. When Jeff began to talk about how the real problem had been his own perceptions and not the prejudice of the people around him, I couldn't help smiling. He talked about some of the friends he'd made on the crew team and how well they'd dealt with his being gay. Jeff mentioned his best friend, George, who was straight, and how they wanted to write a book together about how gay and straight men can be friends. I think they could call it *Men Are From Mars and Some Men Are From Venus*.

I listened to Jeff discuss the things he was doing now and how being gay had nothing to do with most of them. Jeff wasn't talking about the past anymore, and he sounded happy with his new life. While he talked I thought about the times I look at pictures of our team, all of us smiling for whoever won the race that day. I also thought about when I drive the van early in the morning on the way to a race, when the sun is just rising, and I look in the rearview mirror and see all my teammates, my friends, collapsed in the back, sound asleep, some snoring gently. I thought about the parties we have, when some people (novices) drink too much, so we walk them home and put them to bed. I thought about all the people who have come and gone from the team but are still my friends. I thought about how, when I walk across campus, there are at least 40 people to stop and talk to, to commiserate with in my sleep deprivation. I thought about the beautiful orange morning on the water, with the *schluck...schluck...schluck* of my boat's oars slicing the water in unison as the shell glides swiftly over the lapping waves. I thought about every medal we'd ever won and how my teammates would stand on the dock in a crowd to greet us.

When Jeff finished speaking that night, the audience immediately rose to their feet and applauded. Some knew him, but most did not. I saw him look around the room and catch the eyes of everyone he recognized, and when he caught mine I was smiling so hard my cheeks hurt. Afterward a crowd was waiting to see him. And he was smiling with them.

Babel

by David P. Vintinner

Duke University, North Carolina

My back to the Greek and Chinese Bibles, I sat in Duke Chapel's nether regions, a basement lounge under the crossing where cathedral wings meet center aisle. My soft red chair was the focus of a semicircle of 20 others. Those seats were all filled, as were the chairs of the second ring, brought in from the kitchen. The last people entered, whispering their hallway conversations, and took their places in back or on the floor. I closed my eyes and mimed prayer to avoid looking at the pained expressions of the freshmen who had just joined the group or the heavy-shouldered slouches of older members. I writhed with guilt for shaking their faith, for rocking the boat.

I'd been a member of the Baptist Student Union since my first week at Duke. Until recently I'd been on the BSU Council, coordinating the group's community-service activities. Almost every Friday night, rather than visit frat parties or bars, I would dine, worship, and play games with these 20 or so other Baptists. But this first Friday of November in my junior year posed a different agenda: We were there to discuss the continued membership of an admitted homosexual. Me.

Our minister waved his arms to gather attention. "My name is Ted Purcell. Since we have a number of guests this evening, I'd like to emphasize that this is a meeting for the community of the Baptist Student Union." Ted was ducking his head slightly, the way we all tended to in the basement. He lowered his eyes tiredly as he set forth his definition of a Christian community. "We are a community of sinners," he said. This was how he spoke whenever the subject of my sexuality came before the group over the past month. He understood my coming-out to be a challenge to the whole Baptist Student Union, one we had to respond to as a single community or else fracture. He could not avert the inevitable clash of beliefs; the pressure in the group to "have it out" had grown. But I couldn't bear for the issue to be dragged out any longer.

I wasn't the only one tired of Ted's community speech. Michael Weiss sat to my left, fidgeting, looking at the audience. Of those in the BSU who disapproved of calling my alternative lifestyle Christian, he was the most outspoken. He had graduated two years before but returned in time to become inextricably involved in my story. He was hosting a separate Baptist Bible study on Wednesday nights about how wrong Ted and I both were. To him I was the worst of heretics: I'd done nothing yet was unrepentant about what I wanted to do. He was more than ready to be my prosecutor that evening. John David White, my defender, sat to my right, watching Michael with concern.

Ted introduced the three of us and described the plan for the evening. After I gave my testimony, opening statements would be made, pro and con, followed by rebuttals and discussion, and the Baptist Student Union would decide, Baptist-like, democratically, what if anything should be done. As Ted prepared to hand the floor to me, a youth minister visiting from a nearby church interrupted, raising his hand as he spoke, "I think we should open with prayer." The first blow.

"Of course," Ted replied. Did he even see how he had been undercut?

The prayer was of the "popcorn" variety: Everyone could speak as they were moved. Most Fridays, when the Baptist Student Union barely filled the lounge seats, popcorn prayers were erratic and pausy but bearable. That evening, silences lingered as a mob of friends and strangers reluctantly asked things of God. Ted prayed for wisdom for us all. The visiting youth minister prayed for guidance to the Truth. John David prayed for strength. I had the honor of closing the prayer with a demand that God fulfill His promise to make all things work for good. Smiling at my irony I left out the end of that verse, "for those that believe in God."

Somewhere in the past month, I'd come to the decision that I might not believe in God anymore. Faith had become irrational. I understood the divine imperatives to throw myself in front of a train to save a stranger's life or to renounce everything I owned and help the poor. And I'd always believed in the ideals of service, humility, integrity, and honesty. But I had tested the divine imperative of honesty, telling my Truth, and now Christians were turning on Christians. The loving God of my youth had fooled me into

tearing apart my closest group of friends. That wasn't what Truth was supposed to do. If that was God's will, I thought, then God had made a holy mess.
It was easier to believe in no God than a stupid one, so I forced myself to
swallow the possibility that I was alone. I surely felt alone as my parents
voiced their despair about me and as turmoil brewed in the BSU. Since God
was either powerless or out of the picture, I saw it as my job to fix the dis-
cord he and I had made. Honesty had gotten me into this mess, and honesty
alone could breach the gaps that partial truth had formed.

It was time to give my testimony, to explain the theology I had developed through years of journaling, soul searching, and praying. I had to
give my best answer to their unvoiced question: "How is it possible to be
gay *and* Christian?" I began, of course, with a Bible story, the common
language of everyone in the room.

Once upon a time, when Israel conquered Canaan, two-and-a-half of
the 12 tribes sent a request to Joshua: They did not want to live in the
Promised Land. Moses had promised them another territory on the other
side of the Jordan. Joshua released them with a blessing.

The two-and-a-half tribes left Israel and returned to Gilead. Finding
themselves separate from the Ark of the Covenant, they erected a new altar
at Geliloth on the Jordan. When word spread to the rest of Israel, they were
horrified. "Idolatry! Already!" they cried. They remembered how harshly God
had punished the whole nation when individuals broke the covenant in the
desert, and here were a great number suddenly flouting God. Israel gathered
to make war on the two-and-a-half tribes, a war of holy self-defense.

Joshua intervened, sending Eleazer the priest to warn the heretics. The
two-and-a-half tribes responded as one, appealing to God. "He knows!"
they said. "And let Israel know: If we have raised up another god, we
deserve to die. This monument is not an altar. It is a witness between you
and us that in generations to come, though we do not live in the Promised
Land, we worship the same God." Eleazer was pleased by this and
returned to Israel with their explanation. The Israelites gladly put down
their weapons and prepared for war no more.

My story finished, I leapt into my testimony full steam. "I'm gay," I said,
"and have probably been since before my first male crush in the third grade.
But I was never willing to be gay if it meant turning my back on God."

I saw faces change in the audience. Carol nodded as if she understood. She had been my prayer partner the year before and was supportive though still unsure about homosexuality. Behind her, two visitors from Inter-Varsity Christian Fellowship exchanged glances. I knew what they were thinking. Their eyes said, *See? He already admitted he gave up on God and decided to be gay.*

I focused for a moment on them and explained how I'd kept a journal for years that was filled with attempts to find "healing" and pleadings to God for release into straight love and marriage, the procreative promised land. I described how, one night a year and a half before, I had prayed for a dream of guidance and woke to a dream of gay love, good gay love. "I was confused," I said. "I tried to ignore it, but you know what happens when you try to ignore God. He starts popping up everywhere." Nods and chuckles confirmed my delivery was working. I suddenly felt it important to keep them entertained while I spoke. I had to be charming. I took a moment to amuse them with some of God's signs to me: the statewide BSU slogan that year of "Telling Your Story" and a typhoon named Gay hitting Guam, where I once lived. "God continued after me, guiding me to believe that loving men is not a mortal sin. Gay love is not the promised land of straight love, but it still can be a good thing, another lifestyle, on the other side of the Jordan. By claiming to be a gay Christian, I'm not rebelling but affirming that I too, as a gay man, still worship the same God."

Those words rang a little empty in my ears, so I changed the subject. I decided to delve into the meat of my new theology, honed by months of debate with my disapproving minister father. I wanted to direct it to Charles or Susan, who would have been open to it, but they were both conspicuously absent from the room. I paused a moment too long looking for them, wondering why they would have chosen to be absent. I caught a reassuring smile from John David and barreled forward again. My theology went like this:

1. God created me. My body, mind, and certain animal instincts are all of His creation. They make me finite. As a finite creature I'm dependent on food, water, and God for continued survival.

2. As the Psalmist wrote, God will satisfy my desires with good things. Jesus preached neither the suppression of desire nor the reckless gratification of it. Thus desire isn't forbidden by some holy Law. I'm not under a

Law by words of St. Paul: "All things are permissible to me, but not all things are beneficial. All things are permissible, but I will not allow myself to be enslaved by anything."

3. I'm commanded to love God with all my heart, soul, strength, and mind—entirely all of me. Anything left out becomes a barrier between my hot-burning Baptist soul and my God. Anything, including my desires, including my yearning for a man to love and be loved by. Therefore, I had to bring my longing for a man to God, with hope and faith that my desires would be filled, exalted by God.

This said, I sat back, aware of omitting my agnosticism and doubts. But I'd done what I'd promised; now the ball was in their court.

John David's hands trembled as he began my defense. He calmed them by scratching at the beard he'd acquired during his semester in Germany. His outward anxiety somehow enabled me to be calmer. His voice was soothing as he read from the Bible in his lap. "'And now these three remain: faith, hope, and love. But the greatest of these is love.' Love is more important to God than condemnation. All of us are sinners; none of us can judge. Which of us can cast the first stone?"

I thought this an unfortunate beginning considering he and I were wearing matching Celtic crosses. I wondered if we looked like boyfriends. He sensed my discomfort and leaned forward in his chair to try harder.

"David is struggling to live a Christian life, and that's all we can ask. As a church, we should welcome each other and try to live as God would want, even though we often make mistakes." He referred to the story of the Apostle Peter and the first Gentile Christian, where God changed the rules and said, "Do not call anything impure that God has made clean." I looked to Danny and Jessica, second only to Michael in their disapproval of me, and saw their scowls. I agreed with them: All in all, John David's argument could be pigeonholed as liberal Christianity.

Next came Michael. Sullen anger flashed behind his glasses as he addressed the room. His expression showed that he had been gracious to wait so long to speak. I felt my pulse in my skull. "The Bible is infallible," he began, then read the half dozen anti-gay passages. He accused John David and me of muddying the issue with other references. "This is clearly what the Bible says. If we question it, what are we left with that is more certain?"

I looked at him and smiled; he had used my father's arguments exactly.

I was numb to them now. I ignored the nods around the room as I felt a rush of adrenaline. Michael was no longer a threat. I felt cocky. He hadn't even said the words *family values,* nor had he developed what I thought would be his strongest argument: Romans 1, where Paul explains how homosexuality and idolatry are intertwined. If he had used that, I may have been forced to admit my agnosticism. If he had questioned my faith, I might have confessed I no longer had it, that I was alone and fighting to defend myself. But he had used only Righteous Interpretation of the Law. I could steal that thunder.

Ted motioned for me to respond. Sitting between a progressive and a fundamentalist who used to simply be friends, I decided to distance myself from both. A high school debate tactic: The moderate is harder to topple; call everyone else extreme and you'll seem more reasonable. "I don't fully agree with either of you," I said. As I slapped down my own defender, he looked at me with shock. "John David, I can't dismiss the importance of the Bible's words as easily as you. I can't bracket off verses and ignore them. And Michael, of course, I can't agree with your interpretation, but…" And then I discussed those verses, how I considered Romans 1 to be my greatest obstacle, how I had to look at other verses. I explained that I focused on what I did understand—service, humility, honesty, selflessness—rather than what I didn't.

I confessed that, for a time, I'd followed the Old Testament Law to the best of my ability: I'd traveled to Israel, eaten kosher, tithed, and wore only pure cloths. I explained how I thought the Law was a beautiful thing to obey, a gift to God when it can be done. But sometimes one is commanded into uncleanliness, like the prophet Hosea, who was commanded to wed a whore. I, like Hosea, was being called into a questionable lifestyle.

Neither my tone nor my face showed I had lost track of my argument. I meant to come around and end on a positive note, with the words "Christian life" or some such. Instead, my closing words had been "questionable lifestyle." As people tried to figure out what I'd meant, I looked to Ted, who stood again to take charge.

Ted tried to give John David and Michael the opportunity to respond to my criticisms, but the room soon spun out of his control. Michael appealed to one of the visiting youth ministers, who stood in the back and said, "I want to tell you all a story." He began to describe a gay man who had been saved and had come back to God. "We are here to discuss our own stories," Ted reminded the visitor, an indirect method of asking him to remain quiet.

Another visiting minister then launched into a story about his own college roommate who had decided he was gay later in life and left his family. Carol interjected from her seat, "Even straight people leave their families."

"Only those that don't listen to God and don't work out their problems in faith," Danny snapped.

The second minister nodded, looking at me, "Are you sure you trusted God to heal you? Did you wait for Him to act on His time, not yours?"

John David raised his voice, "You think God should *heal* homosexuality?"

A debate ensued. Michael, Danny, and the two ministers continued to paint the homosexual act as an avoidable sin while John David, Carol, and I made occasional outbursts that egged on the conservatives. Most of the crowd remained silent. With a sinking feeling I dropped out of the debate and tried to resume my above-it-all demeanor, restating how I'd prayed four long years for healing. John David and Carol drew Ted into the debate for support. I watched painfully as he tried to control the discussion, as he failed to remain above it, and finally called the conversation to a halt.

Ted split everyone into small groups and gave each group a couple of articles by modern theologians, one pro-homosexuality, one con. He and I then went to his office to wait while the members deliberated. He asked how I was doing. "Fine," I said, though "numb" would have been a truer answer. "And how are you holding up, Ted?"

"Do you want to pray together?" he asked.

"Silently."

Am I really calm? I asked myself in the voice I'd once reserved for conversations with a God I trusted. I hadn't been calm the night before. Alone in my dorm room, amid candles that failed to soothe, I had curled up in bed, crying silently not only because I was to be tried by my friends but also because I was alone and would never again believe in the safety of a community of faith. I cried because it was painful to learn not to trust. Comfort came unbidden through Betsy, my former and final girlfriend. She knew this trial was coming and what it meant. She found me and held me and let me use her lap like a mother's to cry loudly, unrestrained. She urged me to sleep, then left. I rose from my bed with a numb determination hours before the trial. I didn't have any more energy to be afraid.

Ted studied my expression and held my hands. "Thank you for doing this. I consider you a great gift to the Baptist Student Union. We're lucky to have you, and I for one am learning much from your example."

I nodded my thanks but thought, *Learning what? How to crucify yourself for no reason?* He didn't suspect my cynicism. Why was I consenting to this trial? I reminded myself it was the only way. Truth was an end in itself. Believing that Truth could never be corrupted, I hadn't hesitated to admit my homosexuality once I'd accepted it. I was as sure of my homosexuality as I was sure of God. After I had worked it out slowly and carefully—reinterpreting the Bible and rebuilding my theology from scratch—it never occurred to me that others might not be open to my new belief. I hadn't guessed that people prefer old truths. Everything crumbled in the face of their rejection and denial. Truth became useless, God became a hollow idea, and my virgin homosexuality became the focus of too much attention.

"This is what we need to do," I assured. "It's the only way to move the group past this difficult time. If anything will end the closed-door theologizing and polarizing arguments, it's this. Nothing else will allow everyone to voice their beliefs and discuss them." I was sure that only I could bring it all to a final grueling resolution by putting myself on trial, by making myself vulnerable. The decision to excommunicate me or accept me would be theirs. And everyone wanted a decision to be made, especially me. I loved my friends. If I had to leave for the integrity of the group, then so be it. I didn't admit to myself that I was saving my skin the only way I knew how.

"Our 15 minutes are more than up," Ted said. "Are you ready?"

We returned to a cross-examination by a jury of my peers. Ted's role diminished as I began to handle it like a press conference. I sat facing everyone else in the room; my defender and prosecutor had retired to the back of the crowd. The questions were all the things no one had asked me in the past month:

"Are you dating anyone?" asked Teresa. ("No.") "Do you hope to?" ("Yes.")

"Do you believe it is possible to have a faithful gay relationship?" asked Jennifer, the BSU president, who was engaged. ("Yes.")

"Are you a virgin?" demanded Danny. ("Um, yes." *Technically*, I added to myself.)

"Is it environmental or biological?" (Jessica)

"Do you think it was your parents' fault?" (Ned)

"How are your parents dealing with it?" (Carol)

"What if you are wrong?" (Michael)

"When did you know?" (Chris, I think)

"Are you sure you can't love a woman?" (Some freshman)

"Are there really 10% of you?" (Who was that?)

"Do you think gays should adopt?" (I don't know these people.)

Patiently I fielded all questions, encouraging them. To do otherwise at that point would have shown weakness. I had to see it through to the end, barely noticing that the meeting had degenerated into a freak show. By then it was almost an out-of-body experience for me. I responded automatically until questions slowed. As the evening drew to a close, I asked a question in return, "Now that this is finished, should I continue in the Baptist Student Union, or should I move on?"

Blank looks, first at me, then at each other. *Oh, yeah,* I saw them thinking, *we've got to decide something here. This isn't a free show.* The eye contact between them grew more deliberate, decisions silently made. Some looked at each other and knew it would be them or me. Others looked at each other and knew they couldn't throw stones. Still others looked away. Finally Jennifer, the president who would be an officer's wife in a matter of months, cleared her throat. "Well, if you say you want to still be a Christian, we can't very well ask you to leave, now can we?"

Another silence, and I said, "Thank you."

And with that, half the Baptist Student Union decided they wouldn't return. The crowd broke, then mingled. John David hugged me. I walked up to Michael for a handshake. I thanked him for voicing his beliefs publicly. He looked smaller, helpless. I held his hand firmly and realized this was victory.

After John David graduated the next semester, I realized it hadn't been a victory. It was a moment like Babel. Everyone present was faced with the horror that there is no common language and there is no common faith. The group quickly dwindled to only a dozen. Michael departed for divinity school. Those left behind still didn't agree, but they were the ones who could handle it. "The whole evening was wrong," Michael later said to someone, "We should never have done something so adversarial in the church."

I wondered about his words as the averted gazes continued. Despite the decision of that night, I no longer felt like a member of BSU and was never comfortable with them as a group again. I drifted away. And as I grew apart from them, I saw more of them as enemies. How could they be friends if they still believed the rules and taboos that condemned me?

Then I realized my maze of Christian rules and ethics was artificial. I pushed my way through the walls and discovered that open space outside called promiscuity. I stopped attending church. My agnosticism eventually cooled to belief, but I couldn't forget how alone I felt that November evening when I had needed God most. I wouldn't trust Him, the church, or the virtue of honesty for a long long time.

Teamwork

by Lisa Walter

Harvey Mudd College, California

We were ahead by more than 15 points in the middle of the second quarter, ahead so much that we sat eagerly on the bench, waiting to be put into the game. As freshmen, we knew we were about to get some playing time. While the starting five continued to cream our opponents, Julie and her girlfriend entered the gym holding hands. The pair walked along the sideline and up several rows of bleachers to find some seats. Kammi, one of our freshman guards, was sitting next to me on the bench. I saw her eyes follow the couple from the moment they entered the doorway. She leaned toward me and whispered, "Hey, Lisa, look at those two girls over there." She motioned to Julie, unaware I knew her, let alone lived with her. "I can't believe they're doing that in public! Hey, Kelly, look!"

Everyone on the bench turned their heads one by one to look at Julie as the message was passed from one player to the next. A minute later our entire row of women in white and maroon were all blatantly staring at Julie and her girlfriend. I glanced up to see her expression. I think she noticed my team staring, but it didn't seem to bother her. She kept watching the game and talking with her girlfriend. I meekly smiled at my teammates, pretended to laugh it off, and tried to focus on the game.

After we won we all headed into the locker room for the five minutes we were allotted to change before our team meeting.

"Ugh! That's so disgusting!" Kammi said as soon as she was in the door. "I can't believe those two girls came to our game. That's so gross!" Our freshman point guard, Kelly, nodded her head and made a face as if she had just seen someone eat feces.

Stacy, our freshman three-point shooter, said with a provoking smile on her face, "There are lesbians in our gym, Kammi! Lesbians! Lesbians!"

"Well, don't let them in here! I'd die if someone on our team was gay, changing in the same locker room as us. They'd be checking us out," Kammi said with a fierce smirk.

"Luckily, we don't have that problem on this team," Stacy added.

"Yeah, thank God nobody here is like that," Kammi continued. "Damn dykes. They shouldn't even be allowed in the gym. We shouldn't have to deal with that when we're playing."

I dressed as quickly as possible. I was nervous someone on my team would wonder why I didn't join in the conversation and suspect me of watching them change or shower. I was sure one of them would be able to figure out sooner or later that I dated women as well as men. I was also sure that if they knew Julie was my suitemate, it would cause more problems than I was ready to deal with.

Julie was a huge role model for me during my freshman year. Like me, she was half Asian and half white. Like me, she played a varsity sport. And like me, she led an alternative lifestyle. She was a senior and had survived the rigorous academic program at our small technical school.

Our school is unusual in that it sits on the same campus as four other small private colleges. Only 650 students are enrolled at my school. Combined with the other colleges, the five student bodies form the student-run organizations, such as the LGB Student Union and the intercollegiate sports programs. Our varsity women's NCAA Division III basketball team consists of students from three of the five colleges, but I'm the only player from my school.

From the start I was open about my sexuality at my college, just as I'd been in high school. My college has provided an open and supportive atmosphere, but I quickly learned that this wasn't the case at the other schools. Conversations with upperclassmen during freshman orientation and at parties I attended at the other colleges made it clear that gay jokes and homophobic attitudes were prevalent and seemingly acceptable there. I didn't feel safe in this respect when I spent time with students from other colleges—including my teammates—which made being on the team a challenge. During our five-month season of six-day-a-week, two-to-three-hours-a-day practice and game schedules, my teammates and I spent more time with each other than with anyone else.

Julie and her girlfriend attended all our home games that first month my freshman season. And after a month of listening to remarks about them from my teammates, I'd had enough. I finally told them Julie was one of my suitemates, hoping they might stop criticizing her. Instead, it provoked a range of responses.

"How can you live with something like that?" Kammi asked. "I'd move out if I were you. It's not fair that you're stuck living with a lesbian. You should complain because the college shouldn't do that unless you specifically request it."

Kelly, on the other hand, became curious about Julie. "What do they do for sex?" she asked, wanting to know all the details.

"Ask them yourself," I said, feeling annoyed.

By the end of the season my freshman year, no one on my team had figured out my sexuality. None of my teammates knew anyone at my school, so it was easy for me not to disclose anything to them. I was tired, however, of not being able to be myself when hanging out with them. We were spending more and more time together outside of basketball, so things like dating and friends came up in our conversations all the time. I talked only about the men I was dating and left the women out of it.

I came out to two of the more open-minded players on our team at the end of the school year: another post player, Anna, and one of our guards, Christina. They were pretty indifferent about it, and neither brought it up again. I thought that if these two didn't care, maybe the rest of the team wouldn't find it so bad either.

Around the same time, I also started attending LGBSU meetings, where I found support when discussing my team. I was the only Asian person there and one of the slim minority who considered themselves bisexual. I'd hoped to find other Asian students and more bisexuals. I identified strongly with the other ethnic minority students in the LGBSU and the issues they faced: the strong stigmas in their cultures against being anything but straight and the difficulties of finding others with whom to identify. Though no other students in the LGBSU identified as Asian and though I was one of few who identified as bisexual, I found a great deal of support through the other members. I listened to several students from each of the five colleges tell their coming-out tales, and the majority of their stories had happy endings. This shed a bit of hope on my situation, so I considered doing what I wanted most, letting my team know who I really am.

During preseason my sophomore year, our college hosted a basketball tournament over Thanksgiving weekend. On the second night of the tournament, Kelly, by then my closest friend, invited one of the men's teams from Virginia to her apartment along with our women's team. The players trickled into her living room in small groups that Saturday evening, and we had a few conversations about our team records and coaches, interspersed with shots of hard alcohol. Everyone had arrived by a quarter to 11, and all of us, slightly intoxicated, crowded around a coffee table. We had two large bottles of vodka and several liters of Kool-Aid to share among the 20 of us, and we decided to play the drinking game "I Never."

"I Never" goes like this: One person starts out saying, "I never... smoked pot," for example. Everyone who has done what the person said takes a drink, while everyone else watches.

My palms were sweating, and I quickly downed a half-and-half vodka and strawberry Kool-Aid and poured another.

The point guard of the men's team from Virginia went first. He paused for a minute to think of something good, something maybe someone in the room had done but that he had never tried. He looked around the room at each of us. "I never...kissed someone of the same sex."

No one in the room budged. My eyes passed from one person to the next. This seemed to be a good opportunity to come out, and I could always say later that I was drunk and didn't mean it. I grabbed my Kool-Aid and vodka from the table and took a sip.

Everyone stared. My teammates dropped their jaws. But by then I was so drunk, I didn't care what they thought. The next player said, "I've never slept with someone of the same sex." I took another sip, and on it went until people ran out of things to say or I passed out; I don't remember which came first.

The next day my teammates acted as if they had forgotten about the night before, as did I. It wasn't until three days later on a van ride back from a game that one of them got up the courage to ask, "So, do you consider yourself bi?" I nodded, and for the rest of the ride, there was dead silence.

A week later our dorm hosted a party open to students of all five colleges. I volunteered to check IDs and stamp hands during the 11-to-1 shift. Many of my teammates were at the party, and drunk. As things were wrapping up, Stacy, physically supported by two of her friends, came by.

"Lisa, how's it going?" she loudly slurred, tripping over her own foot. I smiled. She looked in the general direction of her friends. "Hey, guys, I'm going to say bye to Lisa." She took a step toward me and landed with her arms flung around my shoulders, simultaneously planting a kiss on my cheek. I braced my arms around her to keep her from falling over. Then she kissed me again on the cheek, this time closer to my mouth.

I looked at her friends, who were intoxicated too, and said, "I'll see you tomorrow, Stacy." She jerked her head from where it was resting on my shoulder and brought her lips close to mine. What the hell was she doing? Images of her telling people how I came on to her when she was drunk at this party flew through my head, and I turned away. She proceeded to kiss my neck as I brought her a step closer to her friends. "Make sure she makes it back to her dorm, OK?" I smiled and handed her over. My shift had just ended, and I went to my dorm room. I never brought it up with her or anyone else on the team.

My teammates began to refer to me as a lesbian, and I found myself correcting them constantly. Anna, Kelly, Janelle, and a few freshmen on the team approached me once and asked, "Does being bi mean that you have an equal preference for both men and women?"

I told them, "For me, it's more like 60-40 in the direction of women."

I tried to be open about my sexuality and told my teammates I'd answer any questions they had. Some of them started asking in confidentiality what it was like to be with a woman, and many told me they had thought about it a lot.

Kelly, in particular, was curious, and her questions were the most explicit. Once she said, "So, you don't have to answer this if you don't want to, but I'm curious...does a man's or a woman's cum taste better?" She turned bright red and smiled nervously.

I laughed, drawing a blank. This was a question I hadn't expected anyone to ask. "Well, they're kind of different, you know. I mean, you can't compare them. I guess they're both kind of good." My complexion quickly matched hers.

Questions from teammates became easier to answer, and the context in which they asked them became more and more casual. Frequently we'd be sitting in the locker room and they'd ask me whether certain phrases offended me and about my dating life. Janelle asked me once, in front of our team, "Does it bother the guys you go out with that you've dated women?"

"No, not really. It's fine with them," I said.

Anna followed up with, "Does it bother the women you date that you would still go out with a man?"

"Yeah, most of the lesbians I date have a problem with it, but with bi women it doesn't matter, of course."

The more questions they asked and the more questions I answered honestly, the more comfortable everyone was becoming with my being bisexual.

During winter break my sophomore year, Christina, our starting guard, and I became close. We went out to get frozen yogurt several times and sneaked into the college pool in the middle of the night once. I stayed with her at her apartment for most of the break, since my campus was completely empty and we still had daily practices.

Every time I spent the night at her apartment, we shared a bed in the room of one of her roommates. One night as we lay in bed in the dark, I asked, "Have you ever had sex with a guy?"

"Yes," she hesitantly responded. I was surprised. The other players viewed her as one of the most conservative people on the team, and everyone thought she was still a virgin.

"Have you ever had sex with a woman?"

"Yes, in high school. My best friends found out my senior year and told everyone. I lost all my close friends. It sucked. I didn't tell anyone except my roommate when I got here. That's why I never talk about high school."

"Christina, I can't believe you dealt with all that when you were in high school. You're an incredibly strong person."

I continued to spend the night at her apartment, and we ended up talking more and more the following nights. I told her about my ideas on relationships, how I was going to date whomever I wanted whenever I wanted, regardless of gender, and she liked that image of freedom. She said she wanted to have a relationship with a woman again, that she wanted to be free to live her dating life as she pleased, that she was in love with her best friend who happened to be a woman, that she hated that she couldn't do any of these things because of the conservative attitudes at her school. Christina even told me she didn't really like her boyfriend and went out with him only because he pursued her.

One night I asked her, "Why do you sleep in here?" I was wondering why we'd been sleeping in her roommate's room instead of her room this whole time.

She must have thought I was asking her why she'd been sleeping in the same bed as me instead of her own, because she stuttered and said, "I'm attracted to you, Lisa. I've been attracted to you for a long time. Last school year I told my best friend and asked her if she thought you might feel the same way."

I was speechless. "Wow. That's flattering. Thanks for your honesty. It means a lot. You know I think you're beautiful, Christina."

She laughed in disbelief. We lay silent for half an hour, trying to fall asleep. I laid my hand on her shoulder. Then she reluctantly said, "Do you think it would be bad if…we just lie close?"

"I don't think it would be bad, but I'm not sure what you mean by 'bad.'" We pressed our bodies together, her silhouette fitting snugly against mine, and lay without moving, without breathing. I stroked her shoulder, arm, leg, stomach, and back, and she stroked mine. We stayed up most of the night, still as statues, stomachs churning, minds racing.

The next morning I came back into the room after dressing and apologized for keeping her up. She said, "That's OK. I wanted you to." I lay next to her again and caressed her body. She returned my advances, first touching my shoulder, then arm, then left breast as I slid my hand across her chest.…

Christina and I were secretive about the time we spent together those few weeks. Although we never talked about it, I could tell she didn't want anyone on the team to know. The day before everyone returned to campus from winter break, we woke up and lay in bed together as usual before it was time to go to practice. I asked, "So when are you getting back tonight?"

She turned her head away. "Lisa, you can't spend the night here anymore. We can't keep seeing each other like this. My roommates are coming back, and my boyfriend is going to be back soon, and everyone will be around."

I was stunned, but looking back on it I can't say I didn't see it coming. Christina wanted a relationship when her peers weren't around. I was enraged, but I'm not one to argue much or drag things out. I gave her a confused look, glared at her, and said, "All right." I grabbed my stuff and walked out the door.

I dropped by Christina's apartment a few times to say hi, but she didn't seem to want me there, so I reluctantly stopped visiting and calling and eventually stopped telling friends about my wonderful teammate. I resented that she had let us become so close and then cut me off, that she stayed with the boyfriend she didn't like for so long and didn't make an attempt to talk to someone she was interested in.

Practices were weird for the rest of the season. Every time Christina and I had to guard each other, she became nervous and lost the ball. One of the assistant coaches noticed this and asked me what the hell had gotten into her; I shrugged. I was unable to get much support from anyone, unable to channel my thoughts, feelings, and anxieties about the situation. By that time I was actively involved in LGBSU but couldn't get support there because I promised Christina I wouldn't tell anyone about her personal life. I spent every practice the rest of that season trying to ignore her ignoring me.

The team dynamics had become uncomfortable in a number of other ways. In addition to Stacy making a pass at me earlier in the year, Kelly was coming on to me every time she got drunk. Soon I felt like the team's token lesbian. It seemed that everyone on our team who wanted to experiment with a woman tried to do so with me. I guess it was flattering, but when you're looking for a relationship, you don't want to be someone else's science project.

Though some of my teammates were making my life uncomfortable, others were doing the opposite. Teammates who felt close to me began to actively reprimand and correct anyone on the team who dared to make a homophobic comment, whether I was around or not. Anna and Janelle approached me in the locker room before practice one day to tell me about such an incident.

"Lisa, we were hanging out with Heidi yesterday, talking about our team, and then the subject of gay people came up," Anna said in a low voice. "Heidi said she was glad there wasn't anyone on our team who liked women, and I was like, 'What about Lisa?'"

Janelle continued, "So then Heidi said, 'What *about* Lisa?' And we told her you date women. We thought she already knew."

"I thought so too. Maybe it slipped her mind," I said with interest.

"Anyway, she was really homophobic about it. She said she didn't feel comfortable changing in the same room with you anymore and also mentioned that you were still dating men, so according to her you're just experimenting. I got pissed off and told her she needed to be more open-minded or quit the team. After all, she's only a freshman," Janelle said.

Although this sounded harsh, I realized that some individuals on my team respected me and were going to stand by me. I was glad to hear that my lifestyle wasn't only tolerated but also accepted in an environment where this was important to me.

Kammi and Stacy still kept up with their homophobic remarks whenever they saw Julie and her girlfriend and other same-sex couples at our games, regardless of the admonishments they received. Whenever they talked to me about who I was dating, they were interested in hearing only about the men. Some of my teammates tried to avoid the subject of sexuality altogether. I felt like I was in the middle of much of this, so I was happy when the season ended. Stacy, Kammi, and Heidi didn't return to the team the following season for unrelated reasons, and I was relieved to know I'd no longer have to hear their comments.

Just after basketball season started my junior year, a formal dance was held at one of the colleges. My teammates were planning on attending in a group with their dates, and I was dating a woman at the time. They automatically assumed I would bring her with me, and it was no big deal.

The morning after the dance, I showed up to practice bright and early along with the rest of my teammates, all of us feeling a little out of it from drinking the night before. I changed from my sweats into practice gear. As I walked by the full-length mirror in the locker room on the way out, I glanced at my reflection. "Holy shit!" My neck was covered in hickeys of various shades of red and purple. I didn't have any cover-up with me, and practice was starting in two minutes.

Everyone noticed the hickeys the moment they saw me. "Lisa got lucky last night!" one of my teammates called out. Our coaches came into the gym about a minute later. The head coach approached and said, "Hey Lisa, what guy gave you those hickeys?"

"Oh, nobody, Coach," I smiled. Everyone looked at one another and laughed. After practice we went to the locker room to change before going back to our rooms.

Anna said, "Did you hear what Coach said? I can't believe she actually asked you that!" Everyone giggled. Although my coach was clueless about whom I was dating, it was clear that me being bi was no longer a big deal to my teammates.

The following week our team took a day trip to a mall in a neighboring city. Anna and I were supposed to drive. Six of us met in the parking lot, and Christina and I arrived last. The other four had already piled into Anna's car, leaving Christina and me alone. We looked at each other. "Ready to go?" I asked. She nodded and reluctantly got into my car. We hadn't been alone since our last morning together a year prior. I was so nervous that I stalled the car on the way out of the parking lot.

The ride was two hours long, and for the first hour or so we talked about basketball. Then out of nowhere Christina said, "Lisa, I think you're a cool person. And I want you to know I'm sorry about that whole thing last year. I was weirded out by the situation and didn't know what to do. I know I acted strange, and I'm sorry." My stomach cramped. I had come to terms with what had happened between us a year ago and wanted just to be able to talk with her. I was a bit startled she brought it up.

"Don't worry about it," I said. "I didn't know what to do either. I thought you didn't want to talk to me anymore, so I left you alone."

"That wasn't it at all. I think you're an incredible person. I can't be strong like you and do things however I want. You can."

I was amazed at how one awkward moment had evolved into an overwhelming atmosphere of relief. We talked for the rest of the ride and caught up on thoughts and feelings that had stemmed from the previous winter. After that day we were able to talk again. Finally after an entire year, it was no longer awkward to guard her during practice or talk with her alone. She still chose to confide in me about her feelings for other people, and she told me she was still in love with her best friend.

I have one year of college left. Though it's been difficult because I haven't found many other Asian bisexuals, I realize that the experiences accompanying this unique identity have made me stronger. Also, coming out to my basketball team has made a huge difference in the atmosphere on the court and off—from homophobia to tolerance to acceptance to appreciation of our differences. I'm looking forward to our next season.

It's a Long Journey, So Bring an Extra Set of Clothes

by Ian Fried

Ohio

I looked up from behind the podium. Forty eyes were staring back. Sweating, I took a deep breath and began.

"Transgender identity is about rewriting gender; it's about questioning the cultural imperatives that assign us a sex and make us live our lives as that sex." A few members of the graduate-student audience nodded, and I returned to my notes.

"Transgender identity draws upon humankind's history of gender-bending to show the limits of binary sex and gender and to suggest that gender nonconformity is not a sign of deviance but conclusive proof that not all pegs fit neatly into the holes created by sex and gender...."

And from there it just seemed to flow. My voice grew stronger and my hands less shaky. For 30 minutes, I explained in academic language what I'd spent the past few years discovering through my own life. That although most can live with the label *boy* or *girl,* not everyone fits into such distinct shades of blue and pink. That growing up as a boy who wants to be a girl is normal, at least for a segment of the population. That *man* and *woman* are oversimplified terms we use to explain a combination of biology, socialization, and sexuality.

To my surprise no one looked puzzled or confused. Instead of having to clarify myself, I was challenged to take my ideas further. My speech ended, and I spent the next hour leading a group discussion.

"You imply that gender is something we perform, but isn't our identity crystallized long before we're able to choose?" asked a graduate assistant from Minnesota.

"So what's next?" asked another from the University of Chicago. "Will transgendered people be able to move beyond the medical institutions that have regulated them, or will they always be influenced by the scientific establishment?"

I felt myself beaming. For the first time, I was able to share my ideas with others who had been exploring similar issues with similar passion. And our talk was just one of many queer discussions going on within walls unaccustomed to housing such ideas. My small conservative Midwestern university, usually hidden by endless rows of cornfields, was hosting the national conference of gay, lesbian, bisexual, and transgendered graduate students, an event that turned the university on its ear for one glorious weekend. For a brief time, my college town of 14,000 served as the center of queer thought and life.

The night before, about 80 of the conference-goers took over the town's nightlife in a massive pub crawl. We headed up the town's main street and one by one turned the hangouts of frat boys and sorority chicks into giant queer bars.

In one bar a burly linebacker eyed someone from our group. He started to make a joke, "Hey look at the..."

But as he turned to find someone to share his insight with, he realized it was he who was out of place. He shook his head and walked off.

It was a personal triumph nearly three years in the making.

Rewind 2 ½ years....

In the dorm room of a gay male friend, I was reading his copy of *When Someone You Know Is Gay*. I picked up the book to learn more about him, but as I started reading the chapter on drag queens, transvestites, and transsexuals, a pink light bulb flickered above my head. When I got to the part about a male professor who likes to wear women's clothes, it hit me like a ton of bricks. That thing I've always done but never talked about. Why I always wanted to play house—and play mom. Why I went to bed hoping that overnight God would see fit to make me a girl. Finally words appeared to explain a part of my life about which no words had ever been spoken.

The next morning I rushed to the library, which apparently stopped acquiring books after 1950. A few relevant books were sandwiched on a shelf between *homosexuality* and *pedophilia*. The titles sounded daunting: *Transsexuality in the Male: The Spectrum of Gender Dysphoria* and *Sexual Varieties: Fetishism, Sadomasochism, and Transvestism*. But my curiosity outweighed my fear—barely. After making sure no one was watching me,

I grabbed all the books in the section and headed toward another part of the library. Although most were rather clinical, one book, simply titled *Transformations*, was a collection of stories and pictures of cross-dressers. Before I knew it two hours had passed and I had read the life stories of half the 20 or so people that were profiled.

I went back to the library a few days later. To my dismay the books I had removed hadn't been reshelved, so I decided to give the magazine database a try. Among the few articles I discovered and printed out was an article from the 1980s suggesting humiliation therapy as treatment for transvestism. I read how a doctor tried to "cure" his patient by making him dress up in his favorite outfit, then sending him into a room full of people who laughed at him. I could hardly believe what I was reading. Whatever I felt about my newly discovered gender identity, I knew this wasn't the answer. But for the first time since I had read the chapter in my friend's book, I felt like a freak. I took the rest of the printouts, stuffed them in my bag, and ran out of the library to my dorm. I shut my door, flopped on the bed, and cried.

Return trips proved somewhat more fruitful. I found more recent articles that described a budding transgender movement. But the people they were talking about were nowhere near rural Ohio. One article did mention an online discussion group, alt.transgendered. So, my search for other gender-benders led me to a deep dark place: the computer lab. There in the basement of our science building, I read for the first time what it meant to be transgendered.

There was "Susan," a transsexual computer worker who had told her bosses that he was becoming she. "Diane" told of hours spent getting ready to go clubbing and the wild nights that ensued. Others told their fantasies or how to make fake boobs or their latest experiences shopping for clothes.

While I still wasn't sure where I fit in, ideas like these made me nod, smile, and feel less alone. More than anything what hit home was the way people described themselves. One idea that stuck was the idea of a tomgirl—like a tomboy, only the other way around.

I began spending a fair amount of time online, which meant making up stories to my girlfriend, Michelle, about where I was all the time. Never one to hide things from her, I knew I was going to have to explain.

After one of the longest and most terror-filled Fridays of my life, we went to her dorm room, and I tried my best to share something I was just beginning to understand. Taking a deep breath I pulled out the chapter I'd read a few weeks earlier.

"Here, read this, please," I said stiffly.

She read, and I nervously waited, sweat dripping. I felt my body tensing and saw hers tightening as well.

She looked up when she was done. *So?* her eyes said.

"I kind of feel like the professor," I tried to explain. "I like to wear women's clothes."

There was a pause. It may have lasted only a moment, but it seemed painful and interminable.

"I'm not gay," I added.

That seemed to help. Michelle's body untensed a notch. Mine followed. "So...why do you like to do that?" she asked.

"I guess it's just the way I feel inside. I don't feel like I'm a woman. But I feel there's a part of me I can't express as a guy. I guess maybe I feel somewhere in between."

"How long have you felt this way?"

"Ever since I can remember."

Another pause. "Well, I love you. *All* of you."

We both cried. She hugged me. "You're so wet, honey," she said, feeling my sweat-soaked shirt. We both laughed. She wanted me to stay, but I felt I needed some time alone to recover a bit.

The next night we looked through the picture book that showed different transvestites. It was a bit scary for both of us. She wasn't ready to see her boyfriend looking like one of the "girls" in the pictures. I wasn't ready for that either. I wasn't even sure it was something I wanted. Her questions got a bit harder, and not all my answers were comforting.

"Do you wish you had breasts?"

"Sometimes."

"Is it a turn-on for you?"

No response, but I think my red face was enough of an answer.

I also made the mistake of wearing the only piece of women's clothing I owned at that point, a pair of bright pink tights concealed underneath my jeans. When I showed her she burst out laughing.

I felt embarrassed, and Michelle was clearly a bit taken aback. I tried to explain that it wasn't the color I liked, but the damage was already done. Still, the evening ended with lots of hugs and reassurances and another round of "I love you." We talked a lot over the next few nights and things settled down, even if it was still a bit confusing.

Feeling somewhat reassured I began to let myself indulge a bit. Sometimes after class I'd drive 20 miles to the nearest outlet department store. The trips were both exhilarating and terrifying. Every time I heard a call over the PA system, such as "Security, dial 304," I was sure that was the code for "My God, this boy is trying on dresses."

I was thrilled to finally be shopping in the right section, but I was also obsessed with what those around me might be thinking. I heard voices in my head that never came.

"Young MAN, can I help you?"

"Sir, do you realize you're in the women's department?"

Often I'd grab a pair of jeans or something from the men's section before heading to the dressing room. Sometimes I ended up buying the jeans, because I couldn't get up the nerve to buy what I really wanted. Slowly I realized no one cared what I bought.

After a couple of months, I had quite a collection. But I was still afraid to wear any of it beyond the confines of my dorm room. I engaged in the age-old transgender tradition of "underdressing." Longing to make some statement of my newfound identity but fearful of doing anything that would be noticed, I'd wear a pair of tights under my pants or a body suit under a button-down shirt. Finally I built up enough confidence and began to display a glimmer of the trans-girl within.

It began in ways hardly noticeable to the rest of the world, but to me it was as if I were bearing my soul. When I went around campus with a pair of tights barely showing through ripped jeans, I thought I was wearing a sign that said, HEY, I'M A CROSS-DRESSER. Michelle was very supportive at this stage.

"Are you *sure* I can wear this?" I'd ask.

"Honey, no one's going to notice."

These ventures out, however, only intensified my curiosity. Who were these other transgendered people? And *where* were they? I sure didn't see them anywhere.

While scrolling through an Internet mailing list, however, I noticed a posting from a student at my university. I sent an E-mail and got a response back from Bob, a cross-dresser. After a few letters back and forth, we decided to meet in person for lunch at his apartment.

He looked like any other guy on campus, as did I. At first we were both nervous and defensive.

"I'm not a transsexual," he said.

"Nope," I agreed.

"Just like to wear women's clothes."

"Yeah."

It was our way of rationalizing the situation, a little internalized transphobia. Sure we were cross-dressers, but at least we weren't transsexuals. In our minds at that time, transsexual was one step further removed from "normal."

Bob and I talked about sports for a while, still trying to reassure each other and ourselves. Finally we got back to the whole transgender thing. We found we had a lot in common, particularly our experiences as children. Both of us recalled wishing we had a sister in whom to confide our feelings. We both remembered nearly getting caught dressed in a female friend's clothes. But as we talked more, it became clear that we were at different places. I was just becoming aware of all the unanswered questions in my life. Bob felt he had things worked out. He liked to wear women's clothes but only by himself or with his girlfriend. He had found his comfort level, while I had yet to try out my wings.

Realizing I had much to discover and explore—and that the rural Midwest wasn't the place for such discovery—I began looking for a way to get some space. One of the hardest parts of coming out was allowing myself to appear in a new way to people I knew. I was balancing what I wanted to do and my fear of what others might think.

That's when the study-abroad catalogs caught my eye. It was something I'd always considered, but suddenly it seemed an obvious choice. Eventually I settled on Amsterdam. I didn't know much about it, but I knew it was a big open-minded city. Besides, the University of Amsterdam catalog mentioned classes such as "Social Theories of Sexuality."

I carried the course catalog in my backpack at all times. As my professors lectured I pulled out the dog-eared pages and tried to imagine my life in Amsterdam. My mind was spinning with possibilities. What did I want to try? Who did I want to become? Michelle was supportive of my decision and eventually decided to spend a semester abroad herself, studying in another part of Holland.

From the beginning Amsterdam proved to be the free space I needed. My first class was European Sexual Cultures. There were about 40 students, and we went around the room with each of us introducing ourselves—who we were, where we were from, and what area of study we were interested in. I felt my temperature rise. I knew this was an important test. Do I say what I'm really doing there or pretend I'm taking this class because there was no room in "18th-Century Dutch Literature"? When my turn came I took a deep breath and said:

"I'm interested in transgender studies—transvestites, transsexuals, that sort of thing."

Unbelievable. I had told the world what was on my mind. No one else, however, seemed to share my sense of the situation's gravity. There was a nod, maybe a "Hmm, that's interesting," and then it was on to the next person.

For the first few weeks, I pondered how to "out" myself to the 80 other foreign students with whom I lived. I knew I wasn't going to be able to sneak around, and yet I dreaded the thought of explaining myself 80 times. With the language barriers, I knew I couldn't explain it in abstract terms. So when it came time for the first party, I decided to show up in a skirt, a recent purchase from one of Amsterdam's open markets. I sat in my room for an hour getting ready, terrified of venturing outside. I wasn't wearing makeup or anything, just a T-shirt and a long flowing skirt. But like the other steps, it felt immense.

When I came to the party, everyone looked my way. A gaze became a glare.

"Why are you wearing a skirt?" asked Lola, a woman from Spain and one of my closest friends.

"I wanted to."

"Whose skirt is it?"

"Mine."

She burst out laughing and ran out of the room.

The party went on. Needing to recuperate I sat in the hallway. After a short while someone approached and said, "I think it's a nice skirt." With that my temperature lowered a couple of degrees. As other people asked questions, I tried my best to answer.

"Do you do this often?" asked Beth, an American girl from two floors above me.

"Every now and then," I said, knowing this was the first time I'd done so in public and having no idea when the next time would be. By the time I had a chance to look for Lola, she had already gone to bed.

The next morning I knew I had to try to explain things to her. I tried to say something about how I understood it could be funny for her to see me in a skirt but that I was expressing what came naturally. But I guess another friend had already talked with Lola, because she seemed to understand already.

What was shocking one week became commonplace the next. Soon no one thought twice when I put my laundry out to dry—jeans here, a skirt there. I became another colorful part of Amsterdam for those around me. My confidence grew, as did my hair, which I hadn't cut since arriving in the Netherlands. By December, with my pony-tail length hair, I ventured out for the first time in a dress wearing makeup.

I developed my own style. I tried things out. I learned what I liked— long flowing skirts, playing with gender, being seen as not quite a man and not really a woman. I also learned what I didn't like—wearing any outfit I couldn't wear while riding my bicycle, walking long distances in heels, and trying to be a "real" man or a "real" woman instead of being me.

Not everyone knew what to make of me. At one party I was hit on by a gay man, a straight man, and a woman, presumably straight. At times *I* wasn't sure what to make of me. But I loved having the space to try to figure it out. And when late in spring I arrived at a party in a shirt and tie, everyone thought that was a laugh.

I also gained a sense of community in Amsterdam. In the windows of the red-light district, I saw transsexuals from South America who found the sex trade an escape from countries where they faced death or imprisonment just for being who they were. I talked with professors who studied the classic thinkers of gender identity: Hirschfeld, Foucault, and Kraft-Ebbing. I also attended a meeting of cross-dressers.

I had no idea what to expect when I arrived. The door simply said NVSH (a Dutch agency originally brought about for gay rights, later expanded to include other sexual minorities). Mustering courage I opened the door. Inside was a little bar with a couch, a couple of dressing rooms, and some of the tallest people in heels I'd ever seen. Since I was only 5 foot 6, I think everyone in the room had eight inches on me.

"*Spreekt uw Engels*?" I asked the person at the door, who appeared to be a rather ordinary-looking woman in her 50s.

"Yes," ze said, then explained a bit about the group and its history as the longest-running transvestite organization in Holland. (I use *ze* and *hir* as gender neutral pronouns.) But quickly ze got caught up in another conversation and walked away. I could only imagine what everyone was excitedly chatting about. With my minimal Dutch I could make myself understood but couldn't find a way to join any of the conversations. So mostly I just sat and watched.

Seeing a 6-foot-tall "lady" with a 5 o'clock shadow and a wedding dress also rattled my confidence. No matter how I dressed, when I looked in the mirror there was a reassuring face. Even with a little makeup, the familiar contours told me things were as they should be. I guess I saw in these people what I imagined the world saw in me, which wasn't comforting.

Still, as I left the meeting I was on a high, like when I'd bought my first outfit or went around campus for the first time with tights peeking through my jeans. Eager to share with someone who understood, I went to a pay phone and called Michelle.

"I went to a Dutch cross-dressers meeting."

"How was it?"

"Great," I said, skipping over the isolation and fear and focusing on the accomplishment of having gone there.

As I biked home after our conversation, my thoughts returned home. I thought of what it had been like on those first shopping trips, of hiding the purchases underneath "boy" clothes and feeling some measure of freedom. And I thought of where I was and how much freer I felt. Could I be this free at home?

This concerned me almost daily. I didn't want to give up the freedom I felt by being out, but I also didn't want to give up the prominence I'd had on campus. When I returned for my senior year, I'd be close to entering the real world. I'd need recommendations from my professors. There would be job interviews. And what would my friends think of the new me?

Could I afford to be out? Could I afford *not* to?

To my new friends it was a no-brainer. Amsterdam was, for all of us, a yearlong party, but they thought it was time for me to face reality. And their idea of reality was boys in pants, girls in skirts (even if I did have more skirts than most of the girls there).

I returned home without deciding anything but with all these ideas still dancing in my head. Luckily it turned out to be too late to turn back. I wouldn't allow myself to take a giant painful leap backward. Determined to make the most of what little might be available, I got more than I bargained for. In being comfortable with myself I found most people incredibly supportive. I learned an important lesson: Just because people don't understand something doesn't mean they won't be understanding when given the chance.

The first thing I decided upon returning home was to get a single dorm room. Now I can't imagine a better investment. I needed a space to be as transgendered as I wanted to be. And from that shoe box of a room, I plotted my way *out*.

I looked around, trying to figure out where I might find an accepting community. We certainly didn't have a transgendered student group, and our gay/lesbian/bisexual organization didn't include the *t* that was just starting to be added on a few campuses. But I decided that was probably as good a place as any to start. As a freshman I'd been active in my school's GLB student group but just as one of many straight supporters.

Early in the year the group was having its annual literary reading. I decided to read something from Kate Bornstein, one of several transgender authors I discovered over the summer. Choosing the book was the easy part, but choosing what to wear was a nightmare. I was more nervous than I can ever remember being.

"Should I wear this?" I asked Michelle, pointing to a long flowing tie-dyed skirt.

"Or what about this?" I said, pointing to another long skirt. "Or..." I said, looking for something that would somehow convey the totality of my gender.

"How about this?" Michelle suggested, pulling out a short skirt and a pair of leggings.

"Isn't that a little short?" I asked, picturing myself running into someone I knew. All of a sudden my fears came crashing down, and I started to cry. "Maybe I won't go at all."

Luckily Michelle again comforted me and gave me the kick in the butt I needed.

"Oh, no. You're going," she said.

I settled on the short skirt and leggings but grabbed a full-length overcoat to wear until I'd be safely inside the room where the reading was taking place.

"How do I look?" I asked, my eyes begging for approval.

"You look *fine*."

As usual, Michelle was right. Everything went great. Two professors even read a scene by a transgendered playwright.

I took a more public step out at my dorm's Halloween masquerade dance. Again it was a day filled with a lot of preparation but somewhat less trepidation. After all, what better day is there for a coming-out party? Besides, I realized that when I wanted to pass as a woman, I could do so fairly easily, thanks to my slight build, short stature, and fair features, not to mention the long hair and pierced ears. The week before, I had calmly and coolly walked into the outlet department store and purchased a pair of pumps.

I slipped into a smashing velvet gown. One of the women in my dorm put my hair in an elaborate braid, and my girlfriend made sure the make-up was elegant but not over the top. With everything set I made my way into the dining hall-turned-ballroom.

"Who's that cute girl?" one of my friends asked loudly. His jaw dropped as he realized the answer. "Wow" was all he could muster as I said, "Hi." Many others gave an admiring glance before realizing it was the "guy" down the hall. In addition to taking first place in the "cross-gender" category, I'd also put the image I wanted to present in everyone's mind.

Some people may have thought I was just trying to wear a great costume, but anyone who asked got the truth. At first I tried to explain in a theoretical way: "Well, our society makes a lot of assumptions about what it means to be a man or woman, but for some people it's not as simple...."

But most people didn't understand until I got more practical. "For me, it means dressing in a way that better represents the gender I feel—a skirt one day, my hockey jersey the next...." And since I was still wearing dresses by late November, I think it was clear to most people that it was more than an act.

Having to explain myself all the time was tough, but it was also an opportunity. Most people have preconceived notions about homosexuality. With transgender, at least for now, there's the mixed blessing of being nearly invisible. When you say you're gay, it's pretty clear what you mean. Most people, however, have never even heard the word *transgendered*, nor have they met someone who identifies as such. My coming out was a continual challenge, but even my conservative school turned out to be a pretty open place. In a sense everyone was "coming out," trying to figure out who they were and what they wanted to become.

Reaction wasn't all positive. When I wore a dress instead of a suit to the formal of my improvisational comedy troupe, a couple of members felt I was mocking the event. "Why do you have to do that *here*?" asked one person, who perhaps thought I was just a comedian taking things too far. But several others came up to me and said that whatever my reasons they admired my courage. I also had a refreshing chat with one of our troupe's former members, a lovely small-framed woman who confided that she had to pad her strapless gown to keep it from falling off. We both understood gender was something you perform.

Also I wasn't out to everyone, which complicated matters. In my dorm everyone knew, but outside I had friends who knew and those who didn't. In some places, I knew I'd never find acceptance—the guys I went to the hockey games with, the guys I played hockey with. Each time I went out, I worried I'd see friends who didn't know. Or what if my professors saw me? Such was the price of not being totally out.

As I did come out at school as transgendered, the heavens didn't open up, music didn't begin to play, but I did find there were new conversations I could enter, points of view I could express that I couldn't have without identifying myself. It meant I didn't have to sit quietly when someone made a joke about the transsexuals on *Jerry Springer*. It meant that when I took a class in lesbian fiction, I brought an entirely new perspective on topics such as "butch" and "femme." It meant that when I heard about the queer conference that was coming, I got to be on the organizing committee.

Even though the conference included *transgender* in its title, I was the only transgendered person at the committee meetings. On more than one occasion, I asked, "But what about transgender?" As a result, the conference featured several transgender-themed papers, and the second evening a drag ball was held in the student center—definitely the first in my school's 150-plus years. And when it came time to walk across campus in a skirt to deliver my thesis, I was ready.

In the Closet With the Door Wide Open
by Jared S. Scherer
Brandeis University, Massachusetts

"**Y**ou have 30 seconds to strip to your underwear. Do it now!"

"Yes, sir!" replied ten trembling voices in unison, as if all of us really, really wanted to get naked. Nervously excited, I did exactly as Steve, our pledge master, instructed. Out of the corner of my eye, I saw two of my pledge brothers, Jeff to my left and Kevin to my right, slowly take off their clothes, one article at a time. As we were standing there, nearly naked and completely vulnerable, I couldn't help stealing a brief glimpse of them, with their smooth chests and bulging packages right next to me.

"Stand against the wall!" Steve barked.

"Turn around!" yelled Brian, another brother in the house.

"Get on your knees!" said Tony, with a cool humble tone surrounding the command—obviously something he felt comfortable demanding of ten naked young men.

"Do it now!" Steve said, once again making his presence known.

Dozens of commands were shouted at once. It was cold and dark, and we were confused.

"Time for fun and games," Steve uttered in a snide domineering voice. This wasn't going to be fun. Amid the snickers from the rest of the brothers, I could almost hear my pledge brothers' collective thought: *Oh, shit.*

"Close your eyes," said cool Tony.

A few moments passed while we kneeled in nervous anticipation. *Splat*, the unmistakable sound of an egg being split open. *Crack*. There's another. *Crunch*. When it was my turn, an egg was broken over my head. And the slimy icy yolk dripped down my chest. I was one of the luckier ones. Out of the corner of my eye, I saw fellow pledge Kevin with raw egg in his...let's just say, in and on other places of his body. *Oh, great, this is really going to smell in a few hours,* I thought.

As I attempted to process what was going on and what I was getting myself into, I should have been asking myself, *Is this hazing or another fantasy of mine coming true?* Actually, all I could think was, *Don't get a boner, don't get a boner...not now, Jared....* Here I was kneeling in line with nine other naked, young, and virile pledges, and I was trying hard (excuse the pun) not to get physically excited. With the stench of raw egg everywhere and with people yelling at us, there was little time to process everything intellectually and emotionally. That was the spring semester of my freshman year of college, when I was just beginning to understand what being gay was about.

Ironically I'd decided to join the most popular fraternity house at Brandeis as a way to hide in the closet. I'd thought that if I were in a fraternity no one would ever suspect I was gay. I'd even convinced myself I could pretend I was straight. Who would know? Obscuring the real me amid a sea of 50 men was the perfect front. These were guys who liked girls. They were athletic, the epitome of masculinity, and I pretended to fit in with everyone quite well. I wore flannel shirts, khaki pants, and baseball caps like everyone else. No one would find out about me. I wouldn't allow that to happen. "Jared can't be gay," they'd say. "He's in a fraternity."

On the flip side, how could I not join a fraternity? Think about it. I'd be surrounded by 50 of the most athletic and best-looking men on campus. The homoeroticism of joining a same-sex organization is inevitable, and I think I initially immersed myself in the group to test out my urges and emotions. Could I control them? Would I need to suppress them? Would I have no other choice but to act on them?

By the time I reached college, I'd already come to terms with being gay but wasn't ready to tell anyone. Besides, whose business was it? Coming out was way too risky. The thought of placing that information into the open and allowing people to judge, ridicule, and realize my vulnerability made me sick to my stomach. By not telling anyone, I was building and maintaining a wall, creating a safe way to be two people at once. I found this to be a challenge when I decided to rush my fraternity.

During rush (which, by the way, is much like "cruising" in the gay community), current brothers in the house checked me out to see if I was a good fit: athletic, a good drinker, and savvy with women. I wasn't athletic, but I could usually drink anyone under the table. I binged, did keg stands, and passed out, all to fit in.

As for women, if you were good with the girls, you were good for the guys. The prettier the women, the more popular our fraternity. So during the two weeks of rush, when the importance to impress was at its peak, my next step was to find women to invite to the festivities, and I did just that. Luring women to these events was easy; they were also trying to fit in. They wanted to be seen at parties and events as much as I wanted to be seen with them.

I began dating college women and brought three different ones to the various rush events and parties. This went over well with the brothers, who were still checking me out to see if they liked me.

Though I passed two of the three superficial "social litmus tests," I think what won them over was that I was a genuinely nice guy. I had a personality and could join any conversation and even crack a good joke. This was the real me. I wasn't "gay Jared" or "straight Jared." I was a regular guy looking to join an organization that would accept me for who I was, not what I was.

Ultimately I played the game correctly. I could drink with the best of them, party with the rest of them, and as a result I was invited to join the sacred order of Phi Epsilon Zeta, thus beginning my ten-week pledge period and my double life.

I embarked on what was to become one of my best acting stints. The "scripts" in my fraternity usually revolved around sports or women, and since I wasn't an athlete and had no interest in sports, during the next ten weeks I talked about women.

I was already engaging in what I considered stereotypical conversations with my pledge brothers and the brothers in the house:

"So did you get her in bed?"

"Did you see the tits on her?"

"I wish I could fuck her."

I also continued dating women and had my share of relationships. I always had a good-looking woman on my arm at our events that semester. I'd even take them home and sleep with them. Some of these relationships lasted a few days and others little more than a few weeks. For the most part, I found them somewhat empty and meaningless.

I was dating women only to test my homosexuality and almost convinced myself I could be bisexual. I wanted to believe I could be physically attracted to women, but I realized I couldn't fight my true feelings. I was gay through and through. I thought, however, that by convincing myself I was bisexual, I could make a smooth transition into the gay community.

I began exploring the gay community by hopping on the Internet almost nightly. I could delve into an unknown world and be who I really was. Since my pledge brothers and I had a curfew of midnight, my computer became my escape. I found support and a forum to answer my questions from dozens of faceless guys in Cyberland.

In chat rooms I met many gay fraternity members at other schools who were also trying to figure this whole thing out. I had common experiences with many of them and found that the anonymity of talking via computer was quite fulfilling—and safe. The computer also became an avenue for me to meet some of these men in person. So when I wasn't dating women, I was tricking with men. I drove into Boston to meet most of them, away from campus so I wouldn't get caught. I talked to no one about it and made sure no one saw me "being gay."

During my computer exploration I was constantly interrupted with mindless pledge rituals. I was called at all hours to perform stupid tasks, and in general told to be ready to do anything at a brother's whim. Taking trips to the supermarket, returning books to the library, engaging in scavenger hunts, cleaning brothers' houses—it never ended. One night, however, about two weeks before the end of spring semester was much different....

The call came at 12:03 A.M.

"Jared," my pledge master Steve sternly began, "you have 15 minutes to get dressed in 100 articles of clothing, grab your books for the week, grab your keys, and get down to the house!"

This was it, the beginning of Hell Week, the final stretch before initiation. We went through intense hazing and were put to every possible test of wills the brothers could conjure up.

"I'll be right there," I said.

You know how difficult it is for many people to get dressed even in the morning. Try putting on 100 articles of clothing at midnight. It's not easy, and by the time I had squeezed into the tenth T-shirt and had put on the eighth pair of socks, I was sweating like a Dutch oven about to explode. And it was 15 minutes past the time I had to be at the fraternity house. *Oh, shit. I'm dead,* I thought.

I waddled to the house, bundled in every piece of clothing I could put my hands on, only to be greeted by roaring laughter. I felt humiliated. Mince, Snoopy, and Tony were all snickering at the other pledges and me. I couldn't stand them.

"Why the hell are you assholes so late?" Steve snapped as he herded us into the cold, musty, beer-smelling basement.

"Sorry, sir. We tried to get here as fast as we could," David, our pledge class president and makeshift spokesperson, quickly responded, as was standard protocol for situations such as this. But Steve rarely accepted excuses. Thus began the longest night (and week) of my life.

"Strip down and count out loud each article of clothing as you take it off!" shouted cool Tony. It wasn't in our best interests to pause or ask any questions, so we did as we'd been told. We all started to count out loud, "One, two, three…" I had only 57. Not bad. Kevin had 43. *Oh shit, we're dead,* I thought again—a recurring theme during these ten weeks. At this point no one was laughing.

As we stood naked, shoulder to shoulder, Steve shrieked, "Each of you stick your hand in this bag and take one out. Don't ask questions. Do it now!"

What at first seemed a phallic object turned out to be a magic marker (and just what was I thinking?). "Take your magic marker and turn to the pledge brother on your right. Draw a picture of a naked man on his back, and don't leave out any details." We weren't allowed to shower during Hell Week, so if the drawings weren't still on our bodies at the end of the week, we'd be caught and wouldn't be allowed into the fraternity. Jeff's drawing a naked man on my back in red ink and my drawing on Chris's back in green ink was both humiliating and intensely erotic—the former being the purpose of the exercise and the latter being the inevitable consequence for me.

I couldn't stop the trembling fear that crept up my legs and into my stomach and up my spine to the nape of my neck, the type of fear you can't do anything about. I started to quiver and felt like vomiting. I was trying hard not to get aroused but couldn't help it. My dick slowly began to rise as Jeff was drawing a man's groin on my back (who seemingly was nicely endowed). Somehow I willed my penis not to become fully erect. If it did, I'd surely be labeled "fag" and be outed immediately.

Distressed and sickened, we heard a beacon of relief as we were finishing the drawings. "Get dressed. Go to bed. You're going to need as much sleep as possible," Steve advised. I was safe, for now.

After the event I crept into a dark corner of the basement where we were required to live for the next seven days. I dragged with me the humiliation, fear, and confusion surrounding what had happened. No one could hear me or see me as I cried. I felt as though I were melting into my surroundings. I cried because I realized how difficult it was to be gay where no one understood what that meant. *How can I continue this?* I thought. *Am I going to make it? Can I pretend any longer?* The answers were not cut and dried. I struggled with the hunger to belong and the desire to be free, with my emotions *and* who I was.

Even after what I'd been through, I valued what fraternity life had to offer. I felt a sense of camaraderie not found elsewhere. I found a community of people who were there when I needed them. I discovered leadership opportunities, philanthropic activities, and community service projects in which I could participate and excel. This reasoning allowed me to feel comfortable joining my fraternity.

By the start of my sophomore year, I decided I would remain closeted until further notice and resolved to make the best of my experience. I even came to appreciate my two worlds, feeling like a voyeur looking at each life through different glasses. And I began exploring gay life a bit more vigorously. Even though I was terrified to be seen going out, I needed to find a community with which I could connect. So I started taking risks and going to gay bars. This gave me an adrenaline rush I'd never felt before (and it felt good!). *So what if someone catches me*, I thought. After all, Boston has one of the best gay scenes in the country, and I was determined to take advantage of it. I almost found it humorous seeing some of the guys at gay dance clubs proudly wearing their fraternity letters, "advertising" in a defiant sort of way. (I now know this is a popular and easy way to get dates with those looking for athletic frat-boy types).

Eventually people in my life outside of my fraternal circle noticed I was distancing myself from my fraternity. Although I'd never had any sort of homophobia directed at me in my house, I knew it was rampant. I heard the constant comments and jokes. It was cool to hate fags. Subtle comments such as "Don't touch me, you fag" or "Josh is such a homo" were uttered all the time. If you didn't joke about fags, then maybe you were one. Even though I believe my fraternity brothers had no idea what they were really saying, I tried to avoid the topic altogether.

I'd also hear about the hatred in other houses when someone either came out or was outed by his brothers. In one fraternity a brother came out and was forced to become inactive. In another a brother who had transferred to our school was shunned. He had joined the same fraternity at his old school but wasn't welcomed at the Brandeis chapter because he was gay.

Since I didn't want to be outed or treated as these two brothers had been, I avoided befriending "fags" at school. I was a visible and involved student—active with student government, volunteering for the admissions office, and working in the alumni office—who never risked being associated with the gay community or with someone gay. Being so visible as a student leader on campus, I had a heightened sense of fear of being found out. I refused to acknowledge those at school whom I knew to be gay; I wouldn't look them in the eye, or I'd walk the other way.

The only exception I allowed myself and the closest link I forged with the gay community was my friend Jennifer, who was an out lesbian on my campus and was a close and "comfortable" friend. I use the term "comfortable" because my connection to her was through student government and not through the gay community, so I knew it was safe to be seen with her. I would justify similar friendships any way I knew how.

Once when I knew the campus GLB group was throwing a party, I sheepishly walked by, attempting to steal a glance of the goings-on, desperately wanting to be there. I wanted to meet guys, dance, have fun, and be myself. But I didn't go in. My "guilt by association" mentality pervaded my life until my first experience with Billy, one of the most out and proud members of our campus community.

Billy lived in my dorm and would often notice me looking at him. I thought he was attractive but was too afraid to act on my emotions for fear he would out me. My impulses, however, were strong, and I couldn't avoid them or him any longer. I went to his room one night and relentlessly flirted, gazing into his dark blue eyes. Without saying it outright I was almost begging him to do something with me. Here I was, this "straight" fraternity boy wanting him to touch me. And indeed, he did more than that. He grabbed me, kissed me, and held me close, and after that one passionate night I pleaded, "Please don't tell anyone about this, *please!*"

I never talked to him again. I shut him out of my life as a way of denying anything had happened. I didn't know how else to deal with my intense fear. If I said hello to him on campus, it would surely tip someone off that I was gay.

A few weeks passed, and rumors started to fly. "Jared," Jennifer was nice enough to inform me, "I've heard some things about you and Billy. He said that you and he...well, you know...is it true?" I avoided answering the question, knowing I'd be outing myself if I told her the truth. What I did find out was that Billy had reacted as I thought he would, resentful and pained for the way I'd treated him. But I deserved it. He told all of his friends, most of whom were gay, about that night, and I thought they'd keep the rumors to themselves. I was wrong.

Several months after my secret night with Billy, Jennifer summoned me up to her room during a party at her house and closed the door.

Jennifer told me she was concerned I wasn't being true to myself and reminded me how I hadn't answered her questions about Billy and me. *How the hell did she remember that? Oh, shit...I'm caught,* I thought, avoiding her stare. Then she dropped the bomb.

"Jared, are you gay?"

Who the hell did she think she was? How dare she ask such a question! No one had ever confronted me before like that. Of course I was gay, but I'd sworn I'd deny it forever. But if I told her no, she'd know I was lying. If I told her yes, I'd be out of the closet. What the fuck was I to do? Diplomatically, I answered, "No, not really." Then I explained why I had just said no, and then I told her the truth. I was outing myself because I was ready to tell someone.

A few weeks after that conversation, I shacked with Jason, a guy from another fraternity on campus to whom Jennifer had introduced me. Jennifer was definitely a closet-case magnet. She knew almost every gay person on campus, both in the closet and out, and had a great way of putting us in touch with one another. Yes, I was fearful of being discovered, but these fears subsided when I realized I wasn't the only Greek fag at school and that there were many other people, even on my own campus, who were trapped in the same world I was. My relationship with Jason, however, was much easier to contain considering we were both in the closet and wished to keep it that way.

I was so excited about my new relationship, I had to call Jennifer right away. "I'm coming over. It's important."

I told Jennifer what had happened between Jason and me. She sat quietly and after a long pause said in a quiet caring tone, "Jared, you are lying. You're lying to yourself and every other person who thinks you like women. You're lying to the women who think you like them. By not telling them who you are, you're lying. You're leading a life of hypocrisy by being part of an organization that perpetuates homophobia. Be true to yourself and know who you are, and if nothing else, stop lying to everyone."

Jennifer's words hurt, and I started to cry because I realized she was telling the truth. But she only wanted me to be happy and be who I really was.

"I don't know how to keep this going. I don't know how to pretend to be straight and in a fraternity." I had so much bottled up inside, and I let it out with each sob. She hugged me and without saying a word told me she'd be there to help. At this moment I realized each half of my double life was finally colliding. I had known it would only be a matter of time before my straight fraternity life and my gay closeted life would shake each other's hands and never let go. This was the time.

From that point forward I remained mostly in the closet, but this time the door was wide open. I was no longer afraid to venture into the Boston gay community for fear of being caught. I no longer felt it necessary to avoid being seen with other gay people on campus (for crying out loud, I was one of them!). I was comfortable enough to be who I was. I did, however, make the conscious decision not to be completely out on campus. I came out to just a few close friends and finally stopped my charade for the GLB community, and it felt good.

I didn't disclose my sexuality to everyone because I didn't think it would make such a difference. I felt I'd been leading a life in which people knew me as Jared; I in no way wanted to be seen as "gay Jared." People heard the rumors and believed what they wanted to believe. I even wished to keep many of them guessing, mostly my fraternity brothers. It became a game, helping me to cope with the rumors. Eventually people questioned me; I artfully dodged the real answers.

"Jared, are you gay?" my pledge brother Kevin once asked.

"Why, do *you* want to fuck me?" (my customary witty response)

I'm a proud member of my fraternity and have had many valuable experiences. The word "fraternity" means many things to me. I'm a leader in my house, I find their camaraderie to be quite fulfilling, and the social aspect is for the most part one great big party. I'm many things to many people, but being gay is a small part of who I am. Indeed it is an important part of who I am, but I want people to know me and see me as a person, not just as a gay man.

Ultimately, I think there's something to be said for not disclosing your sexuality. It may not be the right thing for some people to do, and for myself, I feel it's nobody's business who shares my bed, unless *I* want them to know. I'm not sure I'll ever come out of the closet completely, but for now I'm taking it nice and slow, telling people close to me only when it feels right.

There's a right time for everyone to take the nails out of their closet door, even if it's one at a time.

Taking Away the Invisibility

by Ruth Hackford-Peer

Utah State University

Sophomore Year: Winter Quarter

Alie arrived home that night and announced that she owed us ice cream. We all knew what that meant. Alie was playing a game that had been played among Mormon roommates for years. She'd been kissed, so she owed her roommates ice cream and a juicy story.

There were six of us, and I was the only one who wasn't Mormon. We were living in the residence halls at Utah State University. I dished out the ice cream as the others showered Alie with questions. Did you like it? Was he a gentleman? How did it happen? Did he have a certain look in his eye? Alie enjoyed the spotlight. She took her time and relished in the details: what Dave had worn, what the moon looked like, and how good he smelled.

I cut her off. "Come on Alie, get to the good stuff. You guys have dated exclusively all quarter. It's about time he kissed you."

"Fine, fine. We were holding hands, walking up Old Main hill when he lifted my chin with his hand and told me he had a wonderful night. Then he—"

"Did you like the tongue part?" I asked, knowing I'd get a rise out of her.

"Ruth, you know I'm not going to *French kiss* until I'm married."

"What's the big deal about your first kiss then? You've kissed your mother the same way you kissed Dave." My question was immediately dismissed when Kris suddenly realized this was Alie's first kiss. Not just her first kiss with Dave but her first kiss period.

Finally the ice cream was gone, the kiss was analyzed and reanalyzed, and everyone except Cyndi and me went to bed.

"I want to be kissed too, Ruth," she said, crawling to the edge of the bed near me.

I served as her expert on anything to do with men. Once Cyndi made me count the men I'd kissed and was horrified that it was over two dozen. But I didn't tell her I kissed so many guys in hopes that the next time would be better than the last. I didn't tell her I had sex just to prove to myself that I was "normal."

Cyndi stretched out next to me. We leaned on our sides facing each other. "It's highly overrated," I said. I also didn't tell her I'd often thought of kissing *her*.

Soon the conversation switched to marriage, and I told her I would never marry. She admitted she often thought the same way, but inside she knew Heavenly Father had planned for her to get married. I tried to convince her I *knew* I'd never marry, but I couldn't tell her the reason. I wasn't sure she was ready to hear it or that I was ready to admit it.

"What if I were gay, Cyndi? Don't worry, I'm not, but what if I were? Would we still be this close?"

"Well, I wouldn't be lying next to you, that's for sure! But I would help you overcome it. We could still be friends."

I had my answer. She would help me overcome it.

Sophomore Year: Spring Quarter

I sat in the auditorium during a campus-wide program called a "Religious Smorgasbord," where representatives from ten churches were speaking. Each spoke for three minutes on the basic premise of his or her church; then the audience got to ask questions. To screen the questions, each audience member was given a pencil and a 3-by-5 card as he or she entered. If we chose, we could write a question, fold it, and pass it to the aisle. I listened intently to the representatives, but no one mentioned *it*. Since I could be anonymous, I decided to write my question, "What is your church's view on homosexuality?" I folded it, then glanced at Pam, my roommate's friend who was sitting next to me. She was scribbling on her card too.

She looked at me. "Can I read your question?"

"Can I read yours?"

"Yeah, if I can read yours."

"Sure," I said. I suspected she too was gay, and was hoping she'd read my card and that we could talk to each other about it later.

She read my card as I opened hers, which said, "What is the response of your church toward homosexuality?"

I folded the card and passed it to the aisle. I glanced at her.

"Why did you write that?" Pam asked.

I chickened out. "Um, I have an uncle who's gay."

She looked down. "I have a, uh, friend who is."

Junior Year: Fall Quarter

A bunch of us were drinking, most of us underage. But we weren't driving anywhere, and I was with friends I trusted. Jess, my best friend from high school, had just transferred to USU. She and I hadn't hung out much after graduating. We were playing a twisted version of Truth or Dare—without the dare. When someone told the truth, anyone who had committed a similar truth had to take off a layer of clothing.

I decided to work my way down. Eventually I was topless but still had on my socks. All of a sudden I started to feel dizzy and needed to lie down. I was feeling sick, but also the questions were getting racy. I knew they could turn to homosexuality at any time, and although I'd never even kissed a female, I was afraid the others would find out what was on my mind.

I apologized and made my way to the bed and closed my eyes. A short while later I opened them to Jess sitting next to me. "I came to check on you," she said.

She was rubbing my neck and shoulders, and I was keenly aware I was still topless. I was feeling much better and knew I could return to the party, but I wanted to stay with Jess. She caressed my belly, moving her way up my chest. I reached for her, and suddenly we were kissing.

I was kissing my best friend! The kiss made me feel whole for the first time. This was what I'd always wanted but feared. Loving her felt so natural. I whispered, "I love you," then louder, "Jess, I love you. I love you."

She pulled back. "Don't freak out on me. It was only a kiss. Don't get all lovey. Besides, I only came to say bye. Roger just got here, and we're going to his place."

She left me alone. More alone than I was yesterday. More alone than I'd ever felt.

Junior Year: Winter Quarter

"Bishop Ross, I really don't know why I'm here. I haven't been to church in years, and frankly I don't miss it. My old roommate Cyndi, she set this up for me. She knows something has been bothering me lately, and she's worried."

I was in the Mormon Institute building across from the student center. The institute belongs to the Mormon Church, and you probably won't find a similar phenomenon on any other state land-grant school, but Utah tends to be unique. Mormons are encouraged to take religion classes at the institute each quarter. It's a beautiful building with study lounges, classrooms, and bishops' offices.

I told the bishop what was on my mind. I knew the Mormon Church condemned homosexuality, and perhaps that's why I promised Cyndi I'd meet with him. Besides, I wanted to see what the bishop could do for me. I thought that if I could have Jess, then being gay would be worth it, but it didn't look like I could have her. So I hoped he could promise a quick fix.

But I didn't like what he had to say. He started by discussing how hedonistic our society is and how we must avoid sin that seems or feels right. He said I'd confused my feelings for women with my inability to develop intimacy with men and that I was unable to develop intimacy with men because I based my relationships with women on sexual feelings instead of higher ideals. He commented on my short hair and asked why I didn't like being a girl. He asked when I last wore a skirt.

I wanted to argue, to fight back. I wanted him to know who he was describing wasn't me. But instead I sat looking down and listening. He kept talking about my sexual thoughts toward women and Jess in particular. I needed him to see I was in love with her. I wanted him to explain the love. But he pretended it didn't exist. Instead he found my weak spots and drilled them. He asked about my family, how much they meant to me, how disappointed they'd be. He asked me if I wanted to be a mother. He told me it wasn't too late to turn back. He admitted he couldn't take away my feelings for women but said he could help me train myself. He advised me to think "pure" thoughts or recite a biblical scripture whenever I felt tempted to sin. He counseled me to leave all my friends and start over with a new group of better influences.

I refused to cry in front of him, but I knew I had to leave the room or I would. I thanked him for his time, got up, and started to the door. He left me with, "You say you want a stable relationship. Well, then, get married, Ruth. Stable homosexual relationships don't exist. You're strong enough to leave this behind. Get married. That's God's plan for you."

I left the institute in tears. That man didn't understand me. He offered nothing but guilt for the way I felt about Jess. He called me a sinner. He called my love a sin. I didn't understand myself either. I went to the bishop knowing he would condemn me, and when he did I wanted to fight back. I'd heard his arguments before, but this had been the first time I wanted to stand up and argue that love could not be a sin.

Junior Year: Winter Quarter

I was eating lunch at the student center when Pam joined me. We hadn't seen each other in a while, and although she was more my roommate's friend than mine, I still liked her. We'd been talking about our classes when suddenly I felt compelled to bring up the Religious Smorgasbord we'd gone to the year before.

"Pam, you probably don't remember this, but last year we were at a program about religion, and we asked questions on index cards. Remember, we both asked a question about homosexuality, and you asked why I did? I told you I had an uncle who was gay. Well, I want you to know that was a lie. Actually, I think I'm gay, and I was too afraid to tell you."

"I wondered if you were," Pam said. "I was having a hard time last year, wondering if I was and stuff. In fact, I'd never do it again, but I dated a girl in high school. I'm glad that's all behind me. I have a boyfriend now."

"I guess that's the difference between you and me."

"What's that?"

"It's not all behind me. I'm finally OK with it. Well, kinda, but please don't tell anyone."

Junior Year: Spring Quarter

I'd been in the spring training class to be a resident assistant (RA) for more than a month before we discussed diversity. That day, we spent the first half of class discussing racism, sexism, homophobia, and ableism. We took a break, then started the second half with an experiential exercise called a crossover. We were supposed to cross a line of tape whenever a statement applied to us. We were told the exercise would be confidential and that its sole purpose was to make us aware of and value the differences among us. The first statement was, "Cross over if you self-identify as female."

I stepped across the line and faced the men on the other side. I broke into a sweat, knowing they would ask about being gay. I didn't know what to do. I wasn't ready for everyone to know, but I was also sick and tired of lying. I was ashamed of my silence.

"Cross over if you self-identify as having a learning disorder." I knew it was coming.

"Cross over if your parents are divorced." I tensed up.

"Cross over if you have served a Latter-day Saints mission."

"Cross over if you self-identify as being gay, lesbian, or bisexual."

Go.

Stay.

Ruth, just do it! Stop lying.

I walked across the line and turned around to stunned faces on the other side. I was in tears.

Senior Year: Fall Quarter

My openly gay friend Jeff came up for the night. We were supposed to go to a bar, but he wanted his friend Ben to go too, and he was only 20. USU is a dry campus, and I was working for housing, so I told them we couldn't drink in my room. We ended up buying some beer and Boones Farm wine and headed up the canyon. Our friend Am came with us, and my roommate Michelle went along to drive us home. I was out to Jeff and Ben, who are both gay, but I wasn't out to Michelle and Am. Michelle had been my roommate for months, but we were just starting to get close. She was Mormon but was testing her wings a bit. She had tried alcohol, and we regularly went out for coffee. Practicing Mormons are supposed to avoid both.

Jeff and I had just finished off the wine when Ben grabbed the beer from the car. He set down the sack and pulled out two bottles. He then danced over to Jeff with the beer bottles poking out of his chest like two giant nipples.

Jeff laughed. "You dumb ass. The beer is going to be shaken up for a week."

"Take me, sweetie, I'm yours," he lisped.

"I don't want your tits. Give them to Ruth. She's the one who's into breasts."

Silence. Am and Michelle looked at me as if seeking confirmation.

I was scared, angry, and confused. I had no idea why Jeff would out me.

He knew I was terrified of anyone finding out, and he had just announced it to two people I cared about a lot.

I grabbed a bottle from Ben and held it to my waist. "I do not like breasts. I hate breasts. They are ugly saggy bags of fat." Suddenly I was in tears. "I like penises. I like dick!"

I fell to the ground and curled into a ball. Jeff held me. "Ruth, I'm so sorry. I didn't even think. It was an accident. I promise. I'm sorry. I am. It's OK. Come on, let's go home."

The entire drive home I drunkenly tried to persuade Michelle and Am that I didn't know what Jeff was talking about. "He's the one who's gay. He's just mad because I get the guys he wants."

I rolled out of bed the next day embarrassed and ashamed. I was afraid to go into the common room because I didn't think I could face Michelle. For once, I was more embarrassed about my behavior than I was about her finding out I was gay. I opened the door and saw a letter from Michelle on the floor. I grabbed it and went back inside to read it. All it said was, "I love you more today than I did yesterday because I'm finally getting to know the *real* you."

Senior Year: Winter Quarter

I went from an honor society meeting to class to the RA in-service without a moment to eat dinner. I called Jess. We were still best friends, and even though we refused to admit we were dating, there was obviously something strong between us.

"Could you bring me something to eat?" I asked. "I'm starving, and this meeting is going to last at least two hours."

"Sure, where are you?"

"In the Mountain View Tower basement. Thanks, babe; I owe you one."

Thirty minutes later Jess sneaked in. We were watching a video on elevator safety. She brought me dinner, leaned down, and whispered, "If I'd known what you were doing, I would have brought you coffee too."

I smiled and looked up. "Thanks." She brought her lips softly to mine for a split second, then grinned. "Anytime, sweetie." I ate my meal, keenly aware of the reaction of those around me. Many people in the room already knew because of the crossover exercise, but that was just admitting it; kissing Jess was flaunting it.

Late that night I received a phone call. "Hello," I muttered, my voice heavy with sleep. A female voice on the other end responded, "Hello, dyke! Live however you choose, but don't shove it down my throat. You shouldn't even be an RA!"

Surprisingly, I hung up the phone angry at Jess. I wanted her to be there and help me deal with the call. But she wasn't there and wouldn't be. The call, however, helped me put closure on what I had only deemed a relationship with Jess. Somehow I had wrapped up being a lesbian with being in love with Jess. I could finally admit to myself that Jess and I weren't dating and that we would never date. Somehow I was a lesbian and it had nothing to do with her. I was able to accept my adoration of her and start to get over it. I knew I could still be a lesbian without her.

Senior Year: Spring Quarter

I enrolled in a poetry class. I'd always wanted to but feared I'd be forced into sharing my writing with the class. My fears were well-founded. A few weeks into the quarter, I had to read in front of everyone. I picked out the poem I would read, a light-hearted humorous piece I'd written without much feeling. I felt comfortable sharing it. Then minutes before approaching the front of the room, I decided to read a real poem. A poem I'd written about being gay.

"Um, my poem is called 'Red Cedar Guilt,' and it's about a young gay woman who is afraid to tell anyone she's...that way. I guess I'll start reading now," I stammered. I began:

You promised a gift
everyone my age would be pleased to have.
(You didn't say "every girl.")
I wanted oak,
thought it would be a desk,
perhaps roll-top.
(Everyone my age needs a desk.)
Instead, a red cedar
hope chest
invaded the corner of the room.

I sucked in the aroma of disappointment,
exhaled guilt.

That cedar chest will never
honestly contain
what are most young women's dreams.
Never will it hold the
elements of marriage and (traditional) family.

I cannot tell you this.
Instead I thank you for the gift,
and deceitfully store
the homemade quilt
(I made it myself in 4-H),
the baby clothes, the shelf paper,
the dishes
(hand painted with a delicate flowery rim),
and all other domestic lies,
inside my red cedar hope chest
(Inside my closet).

This was the first time I had shared anything that personal with a group, and it felt good. My classmates' overwhelmingly positive responses amazed me. No one even responded negatively to the poem's topic. In fact, few negative comments were voiced at all. Mostly they shared support of my writing style and commitment to the topic. I stood at the front of the classroom nodding my head and shaking uncontrollably.

I couldn't wait until I got home so I could tell Michelle I read the poem. I knew she'd be proud, and I knew she'd love the poem. The next week I received several pages of comments about the poem from my professor in my weekly journal. The paragraph that struck me was, "Ruth, I don't want to make assumptions about you because of your poetry, but I want you to know that if you ever want to talk, about anything, I'd love to be there for you. You have an amazing, personable writing style. You invite the reader into the poem, and that is a talent. You're a good writer, Ruth, and you have my support."

I began to realize I had a lot of support but knew I wasn't going to find it everywhere. For years, I waited for USU to be more inclusive, for my teachers to mention that some of the authors we were studying were gay, for the housing office to allow same-gender couples to live in family housing, and for friends not to assume I was straight. But I could no longer remain invisible. I had to step up. I had to lead. If I didn't trust and risk and come out, I wouldn't find the support I needed.

Graduation

I grabbed a hamburger at my graduation party. I could hardly believe four years had passed since my arrival at USU. I mingled from one group to another, making small talk, answering the same questions again and again, until I finally walked off to be alone.

I thought back over the last four years. I never fully came out while there. Some people knew; some didn't. Mostly, no one discussed it. I did, however, progress from self-denial to self-acceptance, and I went from walking into a room and counting the people who knew I was gay to simply, comfortably, and confidently walking into a room.

Jeff bought me pride rings for graduation. I carried them in my pocket for weeks, knowing someday I'd wear them around my neck with pride. I also knew I'd come out to my parents that summer. And I knew I wanted to tell my friends—all of them. I wanted people to know the real me. I wanted things at USU and everywhere to change, and I was excited about my part in creating that change.

Out & About

by Suman Chakraborty

Princeton University, New Jersey

I still don't know his name. I knew him only as the guy who had gym class the period before me in ninth grade. Gym was right after lunch, and my early arrival in the locker room to change into my gym clothes always seemed to coincide with his changing out of his.

I watched him covertly those Tuesday and Thursday afternoons, trying to appear nonchalant as I looked around the locker room until my eyes rested momentarily on his body. It wasn't too difficult; I always picked the locker a few feet away from his. I never saw him naked and honestly never really wanted to. The sight of him in low-cut briefs was more than enough. Besides, my attraction wasn't about sex. I don't remember wanting to have sex with him (my deeply closeted mind couldn't yet accept the image of my having sex with a man). I just wanted to look at him. I wanted to take in the snug way his briefs clung to his body. I wanted to stare at the smoothness of his chest, the sexiness of his smile, the ease with which he carried himself, completely comfortable in his near nudity.

I came to cherish those moments, looking forward to them every week. In them I found the briefest tastes of freedom, buried amid the enormity of shame and confusion. Freedom to desire another man, even though it was covert. Freedom to feel attraction, though having no idea what to do with it. And even though that freedom was confined to the walls of that small locker room and ended when I stepped out, I found comfort in those confines. I was satisfied to keep my private world enclosed, cut off from everyone else.

I don't know how long I would have remained in the closet if I hadn't left home to attend college. Growing up in a solidly middle-class suburb of Montreal, Quebec, I could easily shut out any thought of a "gay lifestyle." That wasn't for me, I'd decided, and the constant reminders of marriage and grandchildren from my parents, who were still so entrenched in an Indian social mind-set, reassured me I was destined for a life with a wife and children. I don't know if I could have followed through with my parents' wishes, but living at home, surrounded by the people and places that reminded me of my family obligations, certainly made any thought of coming out almost laughable. That's if I had stayed home. I didn't.

When I first arrived at Princeton, I was content to keep the confusing array of thoughts and emotions buried deep within me. I'd managed to navigate through my high school years without having to confront my confusion in the open. It rested comfortably away from public discussion. I had never resolved what my feelings for the boy in the locker room meant to my sexuality (it was too overwhelming even to consider the word *gay*), and I would have been glad to go through college without ever talking about homosexuality with anyone.

Jason changed that.

The university had organized a night called "Reflections on Diversity," a mandatory meeting for all first-year students during orientation week. The night consisted of a few students and a faculty member talking about their experiences with diversity. My new friends and I laughed when we read about it. Diversity at Princeton? *Great, a few token minorities to tell us how wonderful things are at Princeton for us*, I thought.

"So what do you think it'll be like?" I asked Peter, a friend from international student orientation. "One black person, one Asian, and maybe a Latino?"

He smiled. "One will have to be a woman."

I snickered in agreement.

Though we were tempted to skip the meeting, our residential adviser had been well-prepared to deal with stragglers. Reluctantly 1,100 freshmen filed into monstrous Richardson Hall, ready for a short nap. I took a seat next to Peter in the balcony, carefully watching my new classmates take their seats. Glancing toward the large stage, I saw four students looking intently at pieces of paper in their hands. My racial forecast had been almost dead on: one black woman, one Asian woman, and a Latino man. The fourth student seemed strangely out of place.

"What's up with the white guy on stage?" I whispered. Peter shrugged.

I didn't spend much time thinking about it and slid lower into my chair.

I made a half-hearted effort to listen to the first two speakers but found my attention quickly wandering. When the white guy went on, I looked at him only because I was still curious why he was there. It didn't take long to find out.

It had never crossed my mind that anyone gay would speak. But Jason did. In front of the entire freshman class, he talked openly—almost casually—about being gay at Princeton. I only remember bits and pieces of what he said. I was too stunned, blown away that up there on stage, in front of more than a thousand strangers, this person was talking about being gay. It was almost too much for my closeted mind to handle. Years of walls and barriers came tumbling down, destroyed by Jason's presence. Only the thunderous applause he received jarred me out of my shock.

Looking back, the walls I had created must have been tenuous at best. Jason's speech unleashed everything I had kept hidden and pushed me to let my feelings escape the confines of my high school locker room. Scared and confused, I was ready to confide in someone. But how would I bring it up? What would I say?

My chance came a couple of weeks later. Peter, with whom I was becoming good friends, had a prospective student staying with him one weekend. Chris was a year younger than us and wanted very much to get into Princeton. He sat in on some of my classes, and we talked about what high school was like for him. The more we talked, the more I felt attracted to him. And while I was certainly nowhere near ready to tell Chris that, I saw a chance to tell Peter.

The night Chris left, I was sitting in the small bedroom Peter shared with his roommate Greg. I had already told him I wanted to talk to him about something important.

"So what's up?" he asked. "You sounded so serious."

I was amazed that I got right to the point. "Um, Chris was a nice guy. I liked him lot."

"Yeah, I liked him too. I hope he gets in."

"No," I said slowly, "I mean, I liked him a lot." Peter must have understood what I meant, and before I could gauge a reaction, I let it all out: Jason, Chris, what I'd been feeling, all of it. At one point Greg walked in without knocking, and Peter turned to him and, in a tone that left little room for inquiry, said, "Get out!"

It's a blessing that Peter was more supportive than I ever imagined someone could be. We talked for a long time, and I quickly realized I'd found a safe haven for my tumultuous emotions.

With Peter as my sounding board, I carefully began to explore the feelings I'd kept hidden for so long. I went to the library and found Joseph Steffan's *Honor Bound*, the first gay book I ever read. I pored over the pages, reading and rereading his coming-out story. I found the list of officers for Princeton's gay and lesbian student group and looked up their pictures in the campus facebook. Every Monday night at 7:30, I walked by Murray-Dodge Hall, where I knew the gay men's group met weekly, but I couldn't go in.

Armed with these new experiences, I slowly confided in a few other people, including Jeff, my resident adviser. He was, on the outside, a prime candidate for a raging homophobe: a big rugby-playing ROTC cadet from rural Washington state. Jeff seemed like one of the worst people to tell, since the campus was also abuzz with the efforts to end Princeton's association with ROTC because of the army's policy on sexual orientation. But still there was something about him I trusted, and one night I walked into his room and, without saying a single world, handed him a flier I had picked up from the health center. Written on the front in bold letters was: WHAT YOU NEED TO KNOW ABOUT SEXUAL ORIENTATION.

Jeff looked at me, looked at the flyer, and laughed. After giving me a hug, he and I talked for hours. He shared with me the story of a close female friend who had come out to him the summer before. I listened intently, finding in his recounting of her coming-out story many similarities to my own.

Not long after I came out to Jeff, my roommate Marc and I were talking late at night in our bedroom of the Holder Hall suite we shared with two other roommates. The campus was still talking about the ROTC issue, and he and I were arguing about whether openly gay men and women should be allowed in the military. It was 3 in the morning, and though the conversation began as idle banter while we had tried to fall asleep in our bunk beds, it quickly turned heated. Since Marc was black, I tried to draw parallels between the experiences of gays and lesbians and those of African-Americans.

"I can't understand how you can be so adamant," I said. "The military is using the same reasons to keep gays and lesbians from serving in the military as they did to keep black people in segregated units. How can you buy into their 'morale' bullshit?"

I realized I had touched a nerve. Marc leapt out of bed, turned on the lights, and yelled at me, "Don't you ever say that again. That's a totally different thing. How can you trivialize what black people have gone through in this country? Were gays ever enslaved? Did they ever go through what black people did here?"

As I lay there, stunned by his anger, I thought to myself, *Suman, this is a big strong football player* (future captain of the football team, it would turn out) *who's really angry at 3 in the morning. Take it easy.* So I calmed him down and told him we'd talk more the next day. He agreed and went back to bed.

A few moments later, I heard him say, "Suman, can I ask you something?"

"Sure."

"You're not gay, are you?"

I forced a laugh and said the only thing I could. "Gay? Are you kidding? I'm just pretty liberal about these things."

"Good, 'cause I could never live with a gay roommate; I'd be afraid he was lusting after me and undressing me with his eyes. I'd feel so uncomfortable."

What an ego! I thought. *He isn't even that good-looking.* More importantly, I thought, here's someone I could never come out to. I couldn't help thinking that most people would react as he did. We didn't say anything else to each other that night, and I didn't bring it up the next morning.

Not even my roommate's late-night outburst could stop my uncontrollable spiral toward the most hidden parts of me. I came out to a few other people, and each time I found a supportive ally, I felt more and more free. It was almost as if a wave were building inside me, gathering strength over the course of the following weeks. While I continued to worry about how some people might react (notably my parents and my less-than-supportive roommate), coming out to everyone was growing inevitable. The fear and shame I carried paled in comparison to the anxiety I was feeling over this unresolved part of my life.

I kept thinking back to a story I'd heard at international student orientation when I first arrived at Princeton. The dean of admissions spoke of a girl who had applied to Princeton years before. Her required essay was a response to the question, "What do you hope to get out of your years at Princeton?" She answered in one sentence: "I want to leave knowing more about myself than when I arrived."

"I admitted her," the dean said with a smile.

On November 22 the campus debate society hosted a debate on gays in the military. Since I was a member of the club, I knew I could attend without raising suspicions. When I walked into the senate chamber where the debate was being held, I recognized some of the audience members. They were the people from the gay student group whom I had looked up in the campus facebook. Sitting in the front row was Jason. The room was packed, and I wished I had brought someone with me. A bit daunted I took my seat near the front with other members of the debate society. I tried not to look like I cared too much, even though I was hanging onto every word.

The debate itself was relatively docile, except for the rantings of one of the conservative speakers. I listened to him with growing anger as he went on and on about how he didn't see what the big deal was with forcing gays and lesbians in the military to stay in the closet. Having struggled with the confines of the closet myself, I saw he had no idea what he was talking about.

When the four speakers were done, the moderator opened the floor to the audience. He alternated between the conflicting sides.

"It's about human rights."

"They're trying to get special rights."

"Gays and lesbians are seeking equality."

"They're trying to infiltrate our communities."

I'm not sure exactly when I decided to go up and speak, but when the moderator asked for one more voice in favor of gays in the military, my hand went up, along with nearly a dozen others. For a moment, I wasn't sure who the moderator was going to choose, but my status as a member of the debate society clearly weighed in my favor. He pointed at me.

The room grew quiet as I stepped to the podium, and I suddenly realized I had no idea what I was going to say. Retreat was out of the question. My voice trembling, I started to speak.

"I've been listening to everyone talk for the last hour, and I don't think I can let this night end without sharing with you what I've been thinking." I turned to the one who had said that staying closeted wasn't a big deal. "I have to tell you that you don't know what you're talking about. I know it is a big deal. That's what I've been struggling with since I got here."

Over the next few minutes, I came out to a room full of people I didn't know. I barely remember the words I used. I do remember talking about what the past few months had been like. I do remember fighting back tears when I called myself a gay man. And I remember, ironically, that right before I started speaking, Jason got up and left.

People came up and congratulated me after the debate, many from the gay and lesbian student group. I had apparently stolen the show but was still in a daze. I could only smile sheepishly. That night I met many of my gay and lesbian classmates who I would soon call friends. Caitlin was the first to come up to me. A fellow freshman, she soon became my activist sidekick. Mark, president of the gay student group, told me about all the things the LGBA (Lesbian, Gay, Bisexual Alliance) offered and invited me to come to the men's group meetings.

While I appreciated everybody's support, all I wanted was to flee to my dorm and tell Jeff what had happened. After a few more good-byes, I stepped into the cold fall night, lit a cigarette, and finally breathed out.

Jeff was stunned when I told him, and he was disappointed he had missed it. "I can't believe you didn't invite me to watch!"

I assured him I hadn't planned it. As I told him in painstaking detail what had happened, I couldn't stop smiling and laughing. I'd never felt so free, so liberated. When I finished Jeff looked me in the eye. "Are you ready to tell your roommates?" That brought me back to reality.

"Tonight?"

"Why not? It's as good a night as any."

So with Jeff as my bodyguard (I was, after all, living with three varsity athletes), I went to my room. Marc, Steve, and Derek were sitting in our living room playing a video game when we walked in. Jeff quickly took control. "Hey, guys, turn that off." They obliged, and I took a seat in a chair facing them. I figured the best place to start was the debate.

"I was at the ROTC debate tonight, and I need to tell you about something that happened. Since other people are already finding out, I wanted to make sure you heard it from me." My voice was trembling, and I looked to Jeff for support. He smiled and nodded in encouragement.

I told them about the debate, about my struggles the past few months, and about how important it was to me that they know. Leaning back in my chair, I waited for the fallout. There was none.

"I figured you were gay when we had that big argument," Marc said.

I laughed when he said that no one could be that tolerant and still be straight. I think he said it jokingly.

The other two were silent at first. Jeff looked at them. "Anything to say?"

"What do you want us to do if you bring a guy home?" Derek asked. Since the thought had never occurred to me, I could only stutter and laugh.

Steve remained fairly quiet, though he did say he appreciated my telling them. While I don't know how they'd have handled things if I'd been out when we first moved in together, they were supportive now, and I was deeply touched.

Never one to do things halfway, I threw myself into the joy of my new-found liberation. It didn't take long for me to tell the rest of my friends. I grew active in the gay student group, becoming president early my sophomore year. I relished being out, even if it did mean I had to bear my share of homophobia and intolerance. Hardly a month went by in which one conservative campus journal or another wasn't publishing a piece about how I was an intolerant radical gay activist. I mostly shrugged them off and kept up my work.

I never did lose my taste for public coming-out scenes. My junior year, the university asked me to give the "Reflections on Diversity" speech Jason had given my class. While I wanted to be for others what Jason had been to me, I was also a bit apprehensive. I had become a minority affairs adviser to first-year students and had struggled for a long time with how I was going to come out to them. The welcome letter I'd sent them during the summer would have been one way, but that seemed inappropriate. Of course, since I was trying to forge one-on-one relationships with them, coming out in front of 1,300 people didn't seem exactly cozy either.

I knew there would be no time to tell them before I gave my speech, and I was determined that if I had to come out to so many people at once, it had to be personal and honest. That night before I was introduced, I asked the dean not to mention in her opening words that I was president of the gay student group. And while I had told my freshmen I would be speaking, they all assumed my "diversity" was embodied in my ethnicity and nationality. I let them think that but struggled with how I would cover all parts of my identity in a short speech.

Outing myself as a gay man was only the first step in reconciling myself as an out person of color. I was still struggling with my Indian ethnic identity, with all its definitions of what a "real man" should be and with the realities of my life as a gay man. Sometimes I felt I had to choose which minority mask to wear depending on who I was with or what I was doing. There never seemed to be a meeting ground for these two parts of my identity. But I wanted the assembled freshmen to know that I experienced my life at Princeton through the filter of all my identities. I wasn't a gay man or an Indian man. I was a gay Indian. Nothing could disconnect that.

"Welcome. Thanks for coming tonight. We're all pleased you're here," I began. "I'm especially glad you came, because for me, this talk two years ago changed my Princeton experience. That night one of the speakers who stood before my class was gay, and I remember sitting in my chair, in complete surprise, thinking to myself, *Oh, my God, there are out gay people at Princeton*. I don't remember much of what he said that night; I was just stunned.

"It sometimes feels as if tradition is the most important thing at Princeton, that there are certain things a Princeton student has to be or has to do to fit in. When I first came here, I was in the midst of the 'everybody syndrome.' That's when you come to Princeton and think everybody's white, everybody's rich, everybody's an A+ student, everybody's a varsity athlete, and everybody's straight. I wanted to be like everyone else, but I knew I was different. And though I could deal with many of these differences, I didn't want to be gay, I didn't want to be isolated one more way. But somewhere inside I knew I was."

I put my emotions out for the entire room to see, and it went better than I could have imagined. Many of my freshmen came up to me afterward to give me hugs, as did many gay and lesbian first-year students. Only then did I truly start to understand the power of being out and the power of speaking out. It wasn't so much what I said or how I said it but that I *could* say it. Not since the debate had I felt so empowered, so free, so liberated from the confines of the closet. It was like coming out all over again.

Late my senior year one of the private high schools in the area asked me to speak at their Chapel Talk. It was a weekly event where either a faculty member or a guest speaker addressed the entire student body and where the gay-straight alliance had fought for a talk on homosexuality.

For some reason, the prospect of addressing high school students scared me more than any of the speeches I'd made before. With my best friend Derrick in tow for moral support, I walked onto the campus with flashes of my own high school days running through my mind.

Sure, it wasn't my high school, and these weren't the people from whom I'd desperately hid my emotions, but it might as well have been. For those few moments, I let myself become a scared ninth-grader again. Though I had my Princeton experience to give me confidence, I wanted these students to know who I'd been in high school. Lips dry, voice trembling, and hands shaking, I finally closed a chapter in my life. And while the memories of the fear, the anxiety, and the mystery boy I longed for are still with me, the locker room walls no longer surround any part of my mind or heart.

Four years and a college degree later, I finally came out in high school. And I have college to thank for it.

Resources

It is nearly impossible for any one publication to summarize all the resources available to lesbian, gay, bisexual, transgender, and questioning college students; their student allies; and the administrators, faculty, and staff who work with them. As a result this section reflects specific resources (books, films, Internet Web sites, newsgroups, and listservs) that the contributors to this book indicated they have found particularly helpful. We hope that if their stories resonated with you, you may also find their resources of interest. We have also listed additional resources relevant to LGBTQ college student issues under "Editors' Recommendations" as well as a separate section on regional conferences.

Books

Richard Joseph Andreoli

Books by Pat Califia.

Kramer, L. (1985). *The Normal Heart*. New York: New American Library.

Monette, P. (1988). *On Borrowed Time*. San Diego: Harcourt Brace Jovanovich.

Obejas, A. (1994). *We Came All the Way From Cuba So You Could Dress Like This?* Pittsburgh, Pa.: Cleis Press.

Obejas, A. (1996). *Memory Mambo: A Novel*. Pittsburgh, Pa.: Cleis Press.

Shilts, R. (1982). *Mayor of Castro Street*. New York: St. Martin's Press.

Shilts, R. (1987). *And the Band Played On: Politics, People, and the AIDS Epidemic*. New York: St. Martin's Press.

christopher m. bell

Boykin, K. (1996). *One More River to Cross: Black and Gay in America*. New York: Anchor Books.

Canfield, J. & Hansen, M.V. (Eds.). (1993). *Chicken Soup for the Soul: 101 Stories to Open the Heart and Rekindle the Spirit*. Deer Field Beach, Fla.: Health Communications.

Lorde, A. (1982). *Zami: A New Spelling of My Name*. Trumansburg, N.Y.: Crossing Press.

Monette, P. (1988). *On Borrowed Time: An AIDS Memoir*. New York: Harcourt Brace Jovanovich.

Monette, P. (1992). *Becoming a Man: Half a Life Story*. New York: Harcourt Brace Jovanovich.

Monette, P. (1994). *Last Watch of the Night*. New York: Harcourt Brace Jovanovich.

Shilts, R. (1987). *And the Band Played On: Politics, People, and the AIDS Epidemic*. New York: St. Martin's Press.

Whitman, W. (1959). *Leaves of Grass*. New York: Penguin Books.

Susie Bullington

Barrington, J. (Ed.). (1991). *An Intimate Wilderness: Lesbian Writers on Sexuality*. Portland, Ore.: Eighth Mountain Press.

Johnson, S. (1987). *Going Out of Our Minds: The Metaphysics of Liberation*. Freedom, Calif.: Crossing Press.

Kaufman, K. (1987). *Free Your Mind*. Freedom, Calif: Crossing Press.

Lorde, A. (1984). *Sister Outsider*. Trumansburg, N.Y.: Crossing Press.

Loulan, J. A. and Nelson, M.B. (1987). *Lesbian Passion: Loving Ourselves and Each Other*. San Francisco, Calif: Spinsters/Aunt Lute.

Moore, L. (Ed.). (1997). *Does Your Mama Know? An Anthology of Black Lesbian Coming-Out Stories*. Decatur, Ga.: Red Bone Press.

Only Women Press & Leeds Revolutionary Feminist Group. (1981). *Love Your Enemy? The Debate Between Heterosexual Feminism and Political Lesbianism*. London: Only Women Press.

Penelope, J. and Valentine, S. (Eds.). (1990). *Finding the Lesbians: Personal Accounts From Around the World*. Freedom, Calif.: Crossing Press.

Rich, A. (1979). *On Lies, Secrets, and Silence: Selected Prose, 1966-1978*. New York: W.W. Norton and Co. Inc.

Suman Chakraborty

Bram, C. (1989). *In Memory of Angel Clare*. New York: D.I. Fine.

Hemphill, E. (1991). *Brother to Brother*. Boston, Mass.: Alyson Books.

Monette, P. (1992). *Becoming a Man: Half a Life Story*. New York: Harcourt Brace Jovanovich.

Olshan, J. (1994). *Nightswimmer*. New York: Simon and Schuster.

Rodi, R. (1993). *Honor Bound: A Gay American Fights for the Right to Serve His Country*. New York: Villard Books.

John Preston has edited several anthologies dealing with family, hometowns, religion, and AIDS.

Terry Dublinski

Abelove, H., Barale, M.A., and Halperin, D.M.(Eds.). (1993). *The Lesbian and Gay Studies Reader*. New York: Routledge.

Beemyn, B. and Eliason, M. (Eds.). (1996). *Queer Studies*. New York: New York University Press.

Duberman, M., Vicinus, M. and Chauncey, G. (Eds.). (1990). *Hidden From History: Reclaiming the Gay and Lesbian Past*. New York: Meridian.

Seidman, S. (Ed.). (1996). *Queer Theory/Sociology*. Cambridge, Mass.: Blackwell.

Ian Fried

Allen, M.P. (1989). *Transformations: Crossdressers and Those Who Love Them*. New York: Dutton.

Bornstein, K. (1994). *Gender Outlaw: On Men, Women and the Rest of Us*. New York: Routledge.

Feinberg, L. (1993). *Stone Butch Blues*. Ithaca, N.Y.: Firebrand Books.

Feinberg, L. (1996). *Transgender Warriors*. Boston: Beacon Press.

Owen Garcia

Boswell, J. (1980). *Christianity, Social Tolerance and Homosexuality*. Chicago: University of Chicago Press.

Gomes, P.J. (1996). *The Good Book*. New York: W. Morrow.

Helminiak, D. (1994). *What the Bible Really Says About Homosexuality*. San Francisco, Calif.: Alamo Square Press.

Schow, R., Schow, W. and Raynes, M. (Eds.) (1991). *Peculiar People: Mormons and Same Sex Orientation*. Salt Lake City, Utah: Signature Books.

Quinn, M.D. (1996). *Same Sex Dynamics in 19th-Century Americans: A Mormon Example*. Urbana, Ill.: University of Illinois Press.

Jerome J. Graber

Shear, C. (1995). *Blown Sideways Through Life*. New York: Dial Press.

Books by Andre Dubus, Edmund White, and Felice Picano.

Andrew T. Gray

Bornstein, K. (1994). *Gender Outlaw: On Men, Women, and the Rest of Us*. New York: Routledge.

Burke, P. (1996). *Gender Shock: Exploding the Myths of Male and Female*. New York: Anchor Books.

Califia, P. (1994). *Public Sex: The Culture of Radical Sex*. Pittsburgh, Pa.: Cleis Press.

Feinberg, L. (1993). *Stone Butch Blues*. Ithaca, N.Y.: Firebrand Books.

Feinberg, D.B. (1994). *Queer and Loathing: Rants and Raves of a Raging AIDS Clone*. New York: Viking Press.

Lorde, A. (1982). *Zami: A New Spelling of My Name*. Trumansburg, N.Y.: Crossing Press.

Spry, J. (1997). *Orlando's Sleep: An Autobiography of Gender*. Norwich, Vt.: New Victoria Publishers.

Wilchins, R.A. (1997). *Read My Lips: Sexual Subversion and the End of Gender*. Ithaca, N.Y.: Firebrand Books.

Ruth Hackford-Peer

Brown, R.M. (1973). *Rubyfruit Jungle*. Plainfield, Vt.: Daughters Inc.

Clyde, L. and Lobban, M. (1992). *Out of the Closet and Into the Classroom: Homosexuality in Books for Young People*. Deakin, ACT, Australia: ALIA; Melbourne, Vic., Australia: Thorpe.

Garden, N. (1992). *Annie On My Mind*. New York: Farrar, Straus, Giroux.

Julie A. Holland

Bannon, A. (1975). *Odd Girl Out*. New York: Arno Press.

Winterson, J. (1987). *Oranges Are Not the Only Fruit*. New York: Atlantic Monthly Press.

Winterson, J. (1993). *Written on the Body*. New York: Knopf.

Cory Liebmann

Boswell, J. (1980). *Christianity, Social Tolerance, and Homosexuality*. Chicago: University of Chicago Press.

Gomes, P. (1996). *The Good*. New York: William Morrow.

Helminiak, D.A. (1994). *What the Bible Really Says About Homosexuality*. San Francisco: Alamo Square Press.

Perry, T. (1972). *The Lord Is My Shepherd and He Knows That I'm Gay; The Autobiography of the Rev. Troy D. Perry, as Told to Charles L. Lucas*. Los Angeles: Nash Publishers.

White, M. (1994). *Stranger at the Gate*. New York: Simon and Schuster.

Carlos Manuel

Humm, A. (1989). *Growing Up Gay*. Boston: Alyson Books.

Powell, J.J. (1969). *Why Am I Afraid to Tell You Who I Am?* Chicago: Argus Communications.

White, E. (1982). *Boy's Own Story*. New York: Dutton.

Jennifer R. Mayer

Brown, R.M. (1973). *Rubyfruit Jungle*. Plainfield, Vt.: Daughters Inc.

Cruikshank, M. (Ed.). (1985). *The Lesbian Path*. San Francisco: Grey Fox Press.

Hochman, A. (1994). *Everyday Acts and Small Subversions: Women Reinventing Family, Community, and Home*. Portland, Ore.: Eight Mountain Press.

Penelope, J. and Wolfe, S.J. (Eds.). (1989). *The Original Coming-Out Stories*. Freedom, Calif.: Crossing Press.

Frankie M. Morris

Lorde, A. (1982). *Zami: A New Spelling of My Name*. Trumansburg, N.Y.: Crossing Press.

Taran Rabideau

Feinberg, L. (1993). *Stone Butch Blues*. Ithaca, N.Y.: Firebrand Books.

Pratt, M.B. (1995). *S/He*. Ithaca, N.Y.: Firebrand Books.

Johnny Rogers

Brown, M.L. (1996). *True Selves: Understanding Transsexualism*. San Francisco: Jossey-Bass.

Cameron, L. (1996). *Body Alchemy: Transsexual Portraits*. Pittsburgh, Pa.: Cleiss Press.

Sapphrodykie

Lorde, A. (1982). *Zami: A New Spelling of My Name*. Trumansburg, N.Y.: Crossing Press.

Moore, L. (Ed.). (1997). *Does Your Mama Know: An Anthology of Black Lesbian Coming-Out Stories*. Decatur, Ga.: Red Bone Press.

Sinclair, A. (1996). *Ain't Gonna Be the Same Fool Twice*. New York: Hyperion.

Sinclair, A. (1994). *Coffee Will Make You Black*. New York: Hyperion.

Wyatt, G. (1997). *Stolen Women: Reclaiming Our Sexuality, Taking Back Our Lives*. New York: J. Wiley.

Jared S. Scherer

Bawer, B. (1993). *A Place at the Table: The Gay Individual in American Society*. New York: Poseidon Press.

Rhoads, R. (1994). *Coming Out in College: The Struggle for a Queer Identity*. Westport, Conn.: Bergin & Garvey.

Shyer, M.F., Shyer, C. (1995). *Not Like Other Boys, Growing Up Gay: A Mother and Son Look Back*. Wilmington, Mass.: Houghton Mifflin.

Daniel A. Sloane

Signorile, M. (1995). *Outing Yourself: How to Come Out as Lesbian or Gay to Your Family, Friends, and Coworkers*. New York: Random House.

Warren, P.N. (1974). *The Front Runner*. New York: Morrow.

Stephanie J. Stillman

Bawer, B. (1993). *A Place at the Table: The Gay Individual in American Society*. New York: Poseiden Press.

Blumenfeld, W. J. (1992). *Homophobia, How We All Pay the Price*. Boston: Beacon Press.

Vaid, U. (1995). *Virtual Equality*. New York: Anchor Books.

Weston, K. (1991). *Families We Choose*. New York: Columbia University Press.

White, M. (1994). *Stranger at the Gate*. New York: Simon and Schuster.

AJ Tschupp

Eichberg, R. (1990). *Coming Out: An Act of Love*. New York: Dutton.

David P. Vintinner

Bartlett, N. (1990). *Ready to Catch Him Should He Fall*. New York: Dutton.

White, E. (Ed.). (1991). *The Faber Book of Gay Short Fiction*. Boston: Faber and Faber.

Lisa Walter

Brown, R.M. (1973). *Rubyfruit Jungle*. Plainfield, Vt.: Daughters Inc.

Stephen Paul Whitaker

Ablelove, H, Barale, M.A., and Halperin, D.M. (Eds.). (1993). *The Lesbian and Gay Studies Reader*. New York: Routledge.

Allison, D. (1995). *Two or Three Things I Know for Sure*. New York: Dutton.

Collins, P. H. (1990). *Black Feminist Thought: Knowledge, Consciousness, and the Politics of Empowerment*. Boston: Unwin Hyman.

D'Emilio, J. (1992). *Making Trouble: Essays on Gay History, Politics, and the University*. New York: Routledge.

Ruth Wielgosz

Bechdel, A. (1986). *Dykes to Watch Out For: The Sequel and Spawn of Dykes to Watch Out For*. Ithaca, N.Y.: Firebrand Books.

Bright, S. (1997). *The Sexual State of the Union*. New York: Simon and Schuster.

Horowitz, H.L. (1984). *Alma Mater: Design and Experience in the Women's Colleges From Their 19th-Century Beginnings to the 1930s*. New York: Knopf.

Hutchins, L. and Kaahumanu, L. (Eds.). (1991). *Bi Any Other Name: Bisexual People Speak Out*. Los Angeles: Alyson Books.

Plaskow, J. (1990). *Standing Again at Sinai: Judaism From a Feminist Perspective*. San Francisco: Harper & Row.

Rust, P.C. (1995). *Bisexuality and the Challenge to Lesbian Politics: Sex, Loyalty and Revolution*. New York: New York University Press.

Weise, E.R. (Ed.). (1992). *Closer to Home: Bisexuality and Feminism*. Seattle, Wash.: Seal Press.

Editors' Recommendations

Evans, N.J. and Wall, V.A. (Eds.). (1991). *Beyond Tolerance: Gays, Lesbians, and Bisexuals on Campus*. Alexandria, Va.: American College Personnel Association.

Garber, L. (Ed.). (1994). *Tilting the Ivory Tower: Lesbians Teaching Queer Subjects*. New York: Routledge.

Herek, G.M. and Berrill, K.T. (Eds.). (1992). *Hate Crimes: Confronting Violence Against Lesbians and Gay Men*. Newbury Park, Calif.: Sage.

Rhoads, R.A. (1994). *Coming Out in College: The Struggle for a Queer Identity*. Westport, Conn.: Bergin & Garvey.

National Gay and Lesbian Task Force. (1995). *Lesbian, Gay, Bisexual, and Transgender Campus Organizing: A Comprehensive Manual*. Washington, D.C.

Sanlo, R.L. (Ed.). (1998). *Working With Lesbian, Gay, Bisexual, and Transgender College Students: A Handbook for Faculty and Administrators*. Westport, Conn.: Greenwood Press.

Windmeyer, S.L. & Freeman, P.W. (Eds.). (1998). *Out on Fraternity Row*. Los Angeles: Alyson Books.

Films

Richard Joseph Andreoli

Long-Time Companion. Samuel Goldwyn Co., (made for TV), 1990.
Without You I'm Nothing (Sandra Bernhard). VHS, HBO Video, 1990.
Jeffrey. Metromedia Home Video, VHS, 1996.
Tales of the City. Polygrane Video, VHS, 1994.
Stonewall. BMG Video, VHS, 1997.

christopher m. bell

The Crying Game. Avid Home Video, VHS, 1993.

Andrew T. Gray

Ma Vie En Rose. Sony Pictures Classics, VHS, 1997.

Ruth Hackford-Peer

The Incredibly True Adventure of Two Girls in Love. New Line Home Video, VHS, 1995.
The Celluloid Closet. Columbia Tristar Home Video, VHS, 1996.

Brandi Lyons

Go Fish. Hallmark Hall Entertainment, VHS, 1995.

Carlos Manuel

Torch Song Trilogy. New Line Home Video, VHS, 1988.
Maurice. Cinecom, Laserdisc, 1987.
Beautiful Thing. Columbia Tristar, VHS, 1997.

Jennifer R. Mayer

I've Heard the Mermaids Singing. Charter Entertainment, VHS, 1987.
Desert Hearts. Samuel Goldwyn Co., VHS, 1986.
When Night Is Falling. Hallmark Home Entertainment, VHS, 1995.

Frankie M. Morris

Oranges Are Not the Only Fruit. 20th Century Fox Home Entertainment, VHS, 1997.

Johnny Rogers

You Don't Know Dick: The Courageous Hearts of Transsexual Men. UC, Berkeley Extension Center for Media and Independent Learning, 1996.

Sapphrodykie

The Incredibly True Adventure of Two Girls in Love. New Line Home Video, VHS, 1995.

Jared S. Scherer

Beautiful Thing. Columbia Tristar, VHS, 1997.
The Adventure of Priscilla, Queen of the Desert. Polygram Video, VHS, 1995.

Daniel A. Sloane

Torch Song Trilogy. New Line Home Video, VHS, 1988.
Beautiful Thing. Columbia Tristar, VHS, 1997.

Stephanie J. Stillman

It's in the Water. Herd Film Co./Water Island Films, 1997.

Lisa Walter

Chasing Amy. Miramax/View Askew, VHS, 1997.

Editors' Recommendations

Because the number of films that may be useful on college campuses are too many to name, we recommend the following guide to assess which might best meet your campus needs: Olson, J. (Ed.). (1996). *The Ultimate Guide to Lesbian & Gay Film and Video*. New York: Serpent's Tail.

Internet Web sites, Newsgroups, and Listservs

Suman Chakraborty

Youth Organization
  http://www.youth.org/loco/PERSONProject
Queer Resources Directory
  http://www.qrd.org/QRD
Oasis Youth Magazine
  http://www.oasismag.com
Newsgroup
  Soc.support.youth.gay.lesbian.bi

Terry Dublinski

Gay/Lesbian/Bisexual TV Characters
  http://home.cc.umanitoba.ca/~wyatt/tv-characters.html

Ian Fried

Newsgroups
  alt.transgendered
  soc.support.transgendered
  transgender community forum on America Online
A Primer by Transgender Nation
  http://www.critpath.org/pflag-talk/tgprimer.htm
FTM International
  http://www.ftm-intl.org
Free Gender Zone
  http://www.geocities.com/WestHollywood/Stonewall/4418/

Owen Garcia

Affirmation Gay and Lesbian Mormons
  http://www.affirmation.org
BYU Student Poll
  http://www.california.com/~rpcman/byu_gay.htm
Youth Organization
  http://www.youth.org/loco/PERSONProject

Elight: Youth Ezine
  http://www.elight.org
Youth Guardian Services
  http://www.youth-guard.org
Gay, Lesbian, and Straight Education Network
  http://www.glsen.org

Parents, Families, and Friends of Lesbians and Gays
  http://www.pflag.org

Cory Liebmann
Whosoever: An online magazine for Gay, Lesbian, and Transgender
  Christians
  http://www.whosoever.org
Steps to Recovery From Bible Abuse
  http://www.truluck.com
Chapel of Hope
  http://www.chapelofhope.org

Taran Rabideau
Dub's FTM Page for Trans Guys
  http://web.ukonline.co.uk/agitor/ftm
MTM Information
  http://www.demona.com/damon/MTM.html
Angel Fire Free Pages
  http://www.angelfire.com/
FTM International
  http://www.ftm-intl.org/
Ingersoll Gender Center
  http://www.ingersollcenter.org/
Significant Other E-mail list, contact: FTMSO@aol.com (support for people in a relationship with an FTM)

Johnny Rogers
FTM International
  http://www.ftm-intl.org

Sapphrodykie

National Black Lesbian and Gay Leadership Forum
   http://www.nblglf.org
Sistahnet
   http://demeter.hampshire.edu/~sistah/
Womyn of Zami
   http://www.geocities.com/WestHollywood/9005/
A Dykes' World
   http://dykesworld.de/
Gay Universe
   http://www.gayuniverse.com/
Pride Links
   http://www.pridelinks.com/
Planet Out
   http://www.planetout.com/
Lesbian Avengers
   Search keywords *Lesbian Avengers* for groups across the country

Daniel A. Sloane

University of Pennsylvania Lesbian, Gay, Bisexual Alliance
   http://dolphin.upenn.edu/~lgba
The Lesbian Gay Bisexual Center for the Penn Community
   http://dolphin.upenn.edu/~center
The William Way Lesbian, Gay, Bisexual, and Transgender Community
   Center
   http://www.waygay.org

Stephanie J. Stillman

Cathedral of Hope: World's Largest Gay and Lesbian Church (Dallas,
   Texas)
   http://www.cathedralofhope.com
Parents, Families and Friends of Lesbians and Gays
   http://www.pflag.org

Stephen Paul Whitaker

E-mailing other campus activist organizations was helpful for me.

Ruth Wielgosz
Youth Resource: A Project of Advocates for Youth
  http://www.youthresource.com

Editors' Recommendations

For an excellent overview of E-mail listservs, newsgroups, and Web sites, please see "The Lavender Web: LGBT Resources on the Internet," an article written by David C. Barnett and Ronni L. Sanlo in *Working with Lesbian, Gay, Bisexual, and Transgender College Students* (Greenwood Press, 1998), edited by Ronni L. Sanlo. This article, with Web site links, is available at http://www.uic.edu/orgs/lgbt/internet_chapter.html. Also useful is Jeff Dawson's book *Gay & Lesbian Online* (Alyson Books, 1999), which includes encyclopedic listings from "Activism" to "'Zines."

The following are sites particularly relevant to higher education:
American College Personnel Association (ACPA) Standing Committee
  for LGBT Awareness
  http://www.acpa.nche.edu/comms/scomma/sclgbta.htm
Lambda 10 Project: National Clearinghouse for GLB Greek Issues
  http://www.lambda10.org/
National Association of Student Personnel Administrators (NASPA)
  Network on GLBT Issues
  http://www.naspa.org/networks/gayle/htm
National Consortium of Directors of LGBT Resources in Higher
  Education
  http://www.uic.edu/orgs/lgbt/index.html

LGBTQA Conferences

Each year conferences across the country are attended by thousands of lesbian, gay, bisexual, transgender, questioning, and ally college students. Some conferences are specifically for college students, and most take place in the spring. Among these are:

• Eastern United States Lesbian, Gay, Bisexual, and Transgender Conference
• Midwest Bisexual, Lesbian, Gay, and Transgender College Conference
  http://www.uic.edu/depts/quic/mblgtcc/index.html

- Northeast Regional Gay, Lesbian, Bisexual, and Transgender Student Leadership Conference
- Northwest Regional Queer Conference
- Southeastern Lesbian, Gay, Bisexual, and Transgender College Conference
- University of California Lesbian, Gay, Bisexual, and Transgender Association Annual Conference
- Upper Midwest Bisexual, Gay, Lesbian, and Ally Development Conference

Because each of these conferences is hosted by a different institution each year, central Web sites for each conference are generally unavailable. For an up-to-date listing of upcoming conferences, including registration information, please check the resource section on the National Consortium of Directors of LGBT Resources in Higher Education Web page at http://www.uic.edu/orgs/lgbt/resources.html.

The Young, Loud, and Proud Conference, though not college-specific, may also be of interest to traditional-aged college students. More information is available on the conference's Web site at http://www.incite.org/YLP.

Contributors

Richard Joseph Andreoli is a GWM, 5'7", 170 lbs., enjoys long walks on the beach after intense workouts, deep philosophical conversations, and romantic evenings involving not-so-deep philosophical conversations. He graduated from UCLA in 1995, majoring in English literature with an emphasis in creative writing. He writes constantly, hoping his hard work will get him someplace and, at the moment, more than survives by running development for a film and television production company in Hollywood.

christopher m. bell left the University of Missouri in February 1998. He returned a month later to accept the University's Human Rights Achievement Award for his candor and willingness to address HIV/AIDS issues. He continues to speak about HIV/AIDS to high school and college audiences across the Midwest. He lives in Chicago, where you might spot him strolling with a book in hand and a carefree smile on his face.

Susie Bullington is a graduate student in anthropology and feminist studies at the University of Minnesota. Her research focuses on gays and lesbians in South Africa and the new constitution there, the first in the world to protect individuals on the basis of sexual orientation. She lives in Minneapolis with her wonderful partner, Amanda, and their two cats, Ari and Zami. She prefers now to express her spirituality through yoga, dance, and her sexuality.

Suman Chakraborty graduated from Princeton University in 1997. At Princeton he was a resident adviser, a minority affairs adviser, and president of the Lesbian, Gay, Bisexual Alliance. Also while at college, he founded Operation PLAY, a creative-arts program for gay and lesbian youth in Oakland, Calif. Suman resides in Washington, D.C., where he attends Georgetown Law School.

Terry Dublinski, a recent college graduate, is now deciding what to do for the rest of his life. A Midwest native, he recently moved to Portland, Ore., to expand his cultural horizons and take a break before graduate school. Terry hopes to find a job using his research skills and spend his free time exploring the vast wilderness of the Pacific Northwest.

Ian Fried wandered back to the West Coast after college and is a writer living in San Francisco. He welcomes questions, thoughts on the meaning of life, stories, recipes, and anything else at Tomgirlca@geocities.com.

Owen Garcia is a Ph.D. student in philosophy at Teachers College, Columbia University. He is also coordinator of Columbia's Queer Cooperative and a peer counselor at Columbia's Gay Health Advocacy Project. In addition, Owen is the New York City chapter director of Affirmation: Gay and Lesbian Mormons.

Jerome J. Graber is a junior at Loyola College in Baltimore, majoring in biology. He was born in Muncie, Ind., and grew up in Hunterdon County, New Jersey. Upon graduation he hopes to continue to medical school.

Andrew T. Gray graduated with a B.A. in English from the University of Texas-Austin. He lives in Los Angeles, seeking adventures and continuing to explore gender dysphoria.

Ruth Hackford-Peer was born and raised in Roosevelt, Utah. She graduated from Utah State University with a B.S. in English and a minor in psychology and now attends graduate school in Massachusetts. She recently celebrated a commitment ceremony with her partner, Kim.

Julie A. Holland received her bachelor's and master's of science in aeronautical and astronautical engineering from Purdue University in 1991 and 1993, respectively. She grew up near Chicago and now lives in Lafayette, Ind., with her dog, Sam-I-Am, and two cats, Corky and

Kepler. She enjoys reading, traveling, and playing sports and is an avid Bulls fan.

Cory Liebmann graduated in 1995 from a fundamentalist Bible college. He served as a youth pastor in the Assemblies of God for a short time before turning in his pastoral credentials. Cory is working on a graduate degree in theology and plans to teach on the college level.

Brandi Lyons, a 24-year-old aspiring author, lives in Boston and is working on a mystery novel. This is her first published work.

Carlos Manuel, originally from Mexico City, graduated from Santa Clara University in 1995 and obtained a master's in playwriting and directing from the University of New Mexico in 1997. Carlos also writes for *QV Magazine*, a gay Latino publication, and directs, acts, and writes for Theatre Rhinoceros in San Francisco. He lives in the San Francisco Bay area.

Jennifer R. Mayer is a Jill-of-all-trades with a head for numbers and a mind for mischief. She barnstorms across the Western United States for an unnamed government agency, finding fun and creative ways to explain Byzantine fiscal regulations and complex financing schemes. A native of Arlington, Va., she lives in the Mission District of San Francisco.

Frankie M. Morris lives in Oakland, Calif., with her partner, Leatha Jones, and their cats. She obtained her master's of social work from San Francisco State University in 1999 and plans to begin a career in public child welfare.

Taran Rabideau has identified as transgendered since his freshman year at the University of Washington. He is now a sophomore and a pre-engineering major. He hasn't yet had surgery or started hormone treatments but plans to have completed his physical transition by the time he graduates.

Gabriela Rodriguez is a recent graduate of Stanford University with a B.A. in English, creative writing. She is also cochair of the second annual Queer Latino/a Youth Conference.

Johnny Rogers is a student of English literature, focusing on African-American and queer voices. While at Iowa State University, he has served as a member of the LGBT Student Services Advisory Committee, acted as a resource for people with questions about transgender issues, participated in diversity teach-ins and training, and served on the board of directors for an ecumenical campus ministry.

Sapphrodykie graduated with honors from Howard University in 1998 with a B.A. in Afro-American studies, a minor in political science, a B.S. in psychology, and a minor in business management. She is a Houston, Texas, native pursuing an M.A. in organizational psychology and an Ed.M. in psychological counseling at Columbia University. She plans to obtain a Ph.D. in public policy, concentrating on gender studies and social policy and spend her life loving Love.

Jared S. Scherer graduated from Brandeis University in 1996 with a B.A. in psychology. He went on to get his master's in higher education and student affairs administration from the University of Vermont. He loves life and lives it zestfully. He also enjoys working with people and has found his niche advising college students at the University of California, Berkeley. Jared enjoys the Bay Area but still longs for the East Coast. He is quick to admit he wishes he could write more but secretly yearns for time to pursue acting.

Daniel A. Sloane, after transferring from the University of Pennsylvania in 1997, now studies theater at the University of the Arts. He has co-edited the *University of Pennsylvania Bisexual, Gay, Lesbian, Transgender Awareness Days (B-GLAD) Magazine* for three years. He also participates in and volunteers with numerous LGB organizations and activities. Daniel has his own Web design company, Lion's Den Enterprises, and resides with his dog, Casey, in Philadelphia.

Stephanie J. Stillman, originally from Littleton, Colo., is a senior at Colgate University in Hamilton, N.Y. She is involved in a variety of activities including Residential Life, her sorority, and Konosoni, a peer-selected honor society. Steph is committed to working with other students to promote dialogue about diversity issues, including race, class, gender, and sexuality. After graduating with a double major in religion and sociology, she hopes to attend graduate school to study religious studies and public values. In her free time she enjoys being with her girlfriend, Heather, talking over good food or coffee or simply holding her hand.

AJ Tschupp graduated Summa Cum Laude from Trenton State College in 1996 with a bachelor's degree in psychology and a double minor in women's studies and sociology. After spending a year in the University of Pennsylvania's Master of Social Work program, she relocated to the San Francisco Bay area to pursue her academic and professional goals in a more liberal environment. Besides research, her interests in social work include sensitivity training for educators and employers, health education for the LGBT community, and counseling for female survivors of sexual assault and abuse.

David P. Vintinner was born in Philadelphia to a Navy family but has lived in Guam, Iceland, Scotland, and all along America's East Coast. Attending Duke University as a beneficiary of the North Carolina Writing Award, he graduated with a double major in applied mathematics and religion. He is a writer, actor, astronomy teacher, and computer systems consultant. Now in Durham, N.C., he is working on his second attempt at a novel.

Lisa Walter is from San Jose, Calif., and is a physics major. After graduation she plans to join the Peace Corps, then attend graduate school for neurobiology.

Stephen Paul Whitaker is a native of rural southeastern Kentucky. A former radio, television, and newspaper journalist, he continues to do broadcast freelance work while pursuing a Ph.D. in sociology.

Ruth Wielgosz was born in London and has lived in Bethesda, Md., since age 11. Her disdain for limiting her choices has led to dual nationality, bisexuality, an overloaded calendar, and sometimes eating three desserts. She went to Bryn Mawr so she wouldn't have to take any crap for being outspoken, intelligent, and a feminist.